The EVERYTHING. Divorce Book

Dear Reader,

A divorce is an unpleasant event at best. Often, it's a terrible experience, and it's costly—in dollars, emotions, and time. Why, then, do so many people want one? I've pondered this question over my thirty plus years working with divorcing families as an attorney in private practice and as a trial court judge. Every time I thought I'd seen it all, a new twist on the old story presented itself.

I have a lot of expertise when it comes to divorce. Apparently I'm less expert at marriage—I've been divorced twice and have four children from my first marriage. Consequently I have both book learning and actual experience with divorce.

I retired from the bench in July 2000. During my last eight years as a judge, I administered a program called Divorce with Dignity. This was a negotiations-based program that turned the decision-making back to the people involved. I found that people with good information could make good decisions and make them work.

I believe people who divorce should take responsibility for their divorces and for the divorce decrees that end their marriages. Couples who are able to do this lose much less than those who battle to the end.

Mary L. Davidson

The EVERYTHING® Series

Editorial

Publishing Director	Gary M. Krebs
Managing Editor	Kate McBride
Copy Chief	Laura MacLaughlin
Acquisitions Editor	Eric Hall
Development Editors	Lesley Bolton
	Micha.el Paydos
Production Editor	Khrysti Nazzaro

Production

Production Director	Susan Beale
Production Manager	Michelle Roy Kelly
Series Designers	Daria Perreault
	Colleen Cunningham
Cover Design	Paul Beatrice
	Frank Rivera
Layout and Graphics	Colleen Cunningham
	Rachael Eiben
	Michelle Roy Kelly
	Daria Perreault
	Erin Ring
Series Cover Artist	Barry Littmann

Visit the entire Everything® Series at everything.com

THE
EVERYTHING®
DIVORCE
BOOK

Know your rights, understand the law,
and regain control of your life

Mary L. Davidson

Adams Media Corporation
Avon, Massachusetts

To my kids: Anne, Catherine, Bill, and Peter. If you hadn't pitched in when the going was tough, we never would have made it. Sorry I'm not better at practicing what I preach. I love you.

An Everything® Series Book.
Everything® is a registered trademark of Adams Media Corporation.

Published by Adams Media Corporation
57 Littlefield Street, Avon, MA 02322 U.S.A.
www.adamsmedia.com

ISBN: 1-58062-669-6
Printed in the United States of America.

J I H G F E D C B A

Library of Congress Cataloging-in-Publication Data
Davidson, Mary L.
The everything divorce book / Mary L. Davidson.
p.   cm.   -- (An everything series book)
ISBN 1-58062-669-6
1.   Divorce–United States–Handbooks, manuals, etc. I. Title.
II. Everything series.

HQ834 .D38 2003
306.89'0973–dc21

2002014295

Many of the designations used by manufacturers and sellers to distinguish their products are claimed as trademarks. Where those designations appear in this book and Adams Media was aware of a trademark claim, the designations have been printed with initial capital letters.

This book is available at quantity discounts for bulk purchases.
For information, call 1-800-872-5627.

Contents

Acknowledgments

Many thanks to editor Gwen Ruff, who shaped up this book, so you'll enjoy reading it. Thanks, Gwen, for all your excellent, hard work.

Thank you to Jeanne Hanson who asked me to write this book.

Thank you to Eric Hall, my editor from Adams who shaped the book's format and kept me focused.

Thanks to Steve Farrand, who dared me to take the Law School Aptitude Test, lo those many years ago. Without your goading and support, I might not have become a lawyer.

And thanks to Paul Casperson who introduced me to the right people at the right time, including Justice Don King. You have been my idea guy. It's time you got some of the credit.

Thanks to my psychologist friends, especially Karen Irvin, Mindy Mitnick, and Ellie Poor, who have sensitized me to the needs of both parents and children and taught me what I know about the emotional side of divorce.

Thanks to my dad, who is always there for me. Remember when you cried at my swearing-in, and the crowd cried with you?

Top Ten Things You'll Learn
after Reading This Book

1. What to consider before deciding to divorce.

2. Who needs a lawyer, and how to choose the right lawyer to represent you.

3. How to avoid a lengthy legal battle and ensure a fair settlement.

4. How to handle the emotions that accompany the breakup of a marriage.

5. How to manage your finances and protect your assets before and during a divorce.

6. The ways to tell children about a divorce and how to get what's best for them.

7. How courts decide custody issues.

8. What legal paperwork you will need and how to prepare it.

9. How to develop a parenting plan after you've split up.

10. What issues are involved with child support or alimony expenses that you may be faced with.

Introduction

▶EVERYONE HAS HEARD THE STATISTICS: Half of first marriages in the United States end in divorce. The success rate for second marriages is even lower. When people marry for the first time, they rarely think about the possibility of divorce. They make a commitment "'til death do us part," and they intend to honor that commitment. Why, then, do so many marriages end in divorce? There's no simple answer.

Some marriages end because the parties married when they were very young. Many of these young people were probably expecting a baby and weren't ready for the hard work and commitment marriage demands. Other marriages end because one of the parties becomes emotionally involved with someone new. Long-term marriages end when children grow up and move away, and the parents realize they've grown too far apart to have a marriage.

Some people think the U.S. divorce rate is so high because the laws of divorce make it too easy to get divorced. These folks must never have gone through a divorce themselves because the only thing easy about divorce is the part where the law says a marriage can end if an "irretrievable breakdown" occurs.

Other people think the high divorce rate results from changes in how people view making a commitment to marriage. Instead of gritting their teeth and hanging in there for the sake of the children, people put themselves first and think more in terms of what they should be getting from marriage. If their expectations aren't met, they choose divorce.

Some marriages end when an abuse victim gathers the courage to escape. Domestic abuse is now recognized as a serious issue, and victims are no longer re-victimized by the system.

Whatever the reasons for the breakup, people do choose divorce. Often they make this choice with little or no knowledge of what lies ahead. However, it's hard to get information to couples contemplating divorce. Courts don't know about these divorcing couples until they file their papers with the court. Community divorce education programs provide helpful information, but divorcing couples don't always know about these programs.

You, too, may have precious little information about divorce. This book will take you through the entire process, from contemplation to implementation, with a lot of side trips into the little issues that may rear their heads along the way.

This book will be helpful if you're trying to decide whether to get a divorce, if you've made the decision and are about to begin, if you're in the middle of a divorce, or if the legal part of the divorce is over. It will help you handle being the person on the receiving end of divorce papers. It will also be useful if you're looking at a second (or third, or . . .) divorce.

Many judges and lawyers have a bias when it comes to the divorce process. They feel very strongly that litigation is rarely the right way to get divorced. It is usually contrary to your best interests to take your divorce to court and let a judge decide your disputes. It's extraordinarily expensive and seldom produces the results you were seeking. These judges and lawyers believe a negotiated settlement is the way to go. So, although this book will explain everything you need to know about the litigation process, the book will emphasize staying in charge and making the decisions you'll have to live with once the divorce is done. It is much better to make those decisions yourselves, than to have them imposed on you by a stranger, the judge.

Divorce is a painful and scary process. You can make it less scary by reading this book. If you can learn what's ahead and how to take care of yourself, you will reduce the pain. Knowledge is a powerful tool.

Read this book. Gain knowledge. Then move on to your new life.

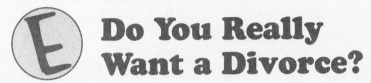

Chapter 1

Do You Really Want a Divorce?

Making a marriage work is hard. Many factors contribute to marital stress and dissatisfaction, but before you shout "divorce," you need to decide whether the marriage needs serious help or whether it's truly over. This chapter will help you find ways to reach and cope with this important decision.

Identify the Problem(s)

A successful marriage requires work and effort. Sometimes the problems of the marriage make divorce look like a good choice. But, surviving a divorce is difficult as well. Be sure that you've given your marriage every possible chance before deciding to end it. You should first pinpoint the reasons you're unhappy or dissatisfied with the marriage. Sometimes these problems can be fixed, and sometimes they can't. But you'll never know unless you first identify the problem.

The Thrill Is Gone

People have expectations about marriage. They believe marriage will be like courtship except that no one has to go home at the end of the evening. There's no way to appreciate the work that goes into making a marriage work until you actually get married and live with the day-to-day reality of sharing life with another person.

FACT

Even couples who live together before they marry are often unprepared for the long-term commitment the formal union requires. Couples who live together but aren't married may keep more of the elements of courtship in their relationship than couples who marry. This may be because their partners aren't yet a sure thing, and the couple needs to put some energy into keeping romance in their relationship.

When partners in a relationship do nice things for each other and say nice things to each other, they can more easily ignore the little things about the other person that they don't like very much. When the nice things and the nice words become few and far between, the little annoyances get much bigger. When you surprise each other with little presents, go out dancing on Saturday nights, and often say, "I love you," the work of taking care of your home and each other is more fun than drudgery.

Home and family responsibilities can feel quite different when you're awakened by a sick child at 3 A.M. for the third night in a row, and your spouse rolls over and tells you to deal with it. Or when you've gone out of your way to do something special for your spouse, and your efforts go unnoticed. Over time, the day-to-day responsibilities of home, spouse, and children become heavier and heavier. The happy moments become rarer and rarer. It becomes easier and easier to keep a score sheet on the times your spouse has disappointed you, and to create a mental list of your spouse's shortcomings. You feel overwhelmed by what's wrong with your marriage and find it harder and harder to find anything that's right.

Money Troubles Can Sabotage Marriages

Maybe you and your spouse have different ideas about finances. Maybe you both like more of the good life than you can afford. Or, one of you is controlling and penny-pinching while the other has a casual attitude toward spending. Is chronic unemployment an issue? Is there tension because she makes more than he does?

Financial issues can add a lot of stress to a marriage. If your money issues are attitudinal—that is, how you feel about spending and saving—you may be able to resolve them in counseling. If your money issues have led you into significant debt, you will need to do more than talk. You will probably need to meet with a financial counselor and develop a plan to pay off the debts.

Children Can Be the Breaking Point

Do you have children? It's not unusual for the imminent arrival of a baby to be the basis for a wedding. Many people really want to have children, so they do so early in the marriage. Kids are wonderful, but they can also increase the stress on a marriage. Do you and your spouse agree on how to raise children? Do you have similar goals and objectives for your kids? Do you agree on safety needs and appropriate supervision? Do you share the responsibility of caring for the children? Parenting disagreements can be incredible land mines in a marriage. If things are shaky for starters, fights over children can bring the marriage down.

FACT

The most frightening thing that can happen in a marriage is domestic abuse or violence. When one of you uses physical force, threats, or constant demeaning to control the other, the marriage is troubled. Sadly, it can be lethal to the victim.

Can the Marriage Be Saved?

Does anything you've read so far strike a chord for you? Probably, or you wouldn't be reading this book. When you're feeling low, it's easy to make a list of what's wrong in your marriage. So, what should you do?

First, make a list of what's right in your marriage. What about the good times? What about the qualities that attracted you to your spouse in the first place? On a good day, are they still there? If good moments still happen in your marriage, and especially if you have children, you might consider giving the marriage one more try. If the list doesn't help, don't lose heart, there are other options out there.

Marriage Counseling

Your spouse probably is aware the marriage is in trouble, too. Or not. If you tell your spouse you're unhappy, your spouse may or may not be surprised. But, you need to have a talk at a time when neither of you is angry or upset. Send the children off to Grandma or to the neighbors, fix his or her favorite dinner, and afterward raise some of your concerns. Take your spouse out for dinner at a favorite restaurant or cook up a storm if that's your thing. When it feels like the appropriate time, tell your spouse what's troubling you.

With any luck, your spouse will agree to go to marriage counseling. If you choose counseling, you both should make a commitment to give it a real try. Don't use marriage counseling as a way to tell your spouse the marriage is over. You'll need to put your energies into learning new ways to deal with each other and unlearning old ways that have been destructive. This is hard work. It's too easy to give up when you aren't really committed to saving the marriage.

Finding a Marriage Counselor

Many communities have marriage counselors. How can you find the right one? The good news is that most marriage counselors are good at what they do and can help you. Ask your friends, your pastor, priest, or rabbi, or a friend who is also a divorce lawyer. Check out the Yellow Pages. If cost is a concern, you may need to talk to your health insurance provider to see whether your insurance covers such counseling. If it does, you'll probably have to select a counselor from the provider's list.

Remember that you can pursue marriage counseling even after you begin a divorce, as long as both of you want to do so. By agreement, you can always put the divorce proceedings on hold while you try to save the marriage.

Meet two or three times with the counselor you select. Do you feel comfortable with this person? Are you getting helpful feedback? Are you able to discuss issues with your spouse with the counselor's help? Does the counselor give you homework? Are you seeing any changes in how things are going at home? If you can answer "yes" to these questions, you're on the right track. If not, you may need to look for a different counselor.

Getting into Therapy

If your spouse refuses to go to marriage counseling, what can you do? You can go to counseling by yourself. You may find it very helpful to get a sense of what's going on with yourself before you tackle what's going on in your marriage. If your spouse won't go to marriage counseling, at least you can take care of yourself. Find a therapist.

The same rules apply here as for finding a marriage counselor. Get referrals. Meet with the therapist a few times. Make sure you're comfortable, and see whether you're making progress.

Your therapist may suggest participating in a group. It's often comforting to know you aren't the only one experiencing marriage problems. Sometimes hearing how others see you and your marriage provides useful information . . . and it can be a bit of a shock. You may hear that some of the problems are yours. This kind of feedback from people outside the marriage is often better received than when it comes from your spouse.

What a Therapist Can Do

A therapist can help you see the big picture. A divorce may sound like a way out, but maybe it's too drastic a remedy right now—like having major surgery when a little physical therapy would do the trick.

Sometimes a therapist will suggest making a list of your mate's good points. When was the last time you thought about what you like about your spouse? What have you been doing to encourage these good features? A therapist can also teach you how to talk to your spouse in a nonblaming way. Instead of saying, "You make me so mad when you come home late," you can try to use what the therapists call "I" statements. You can say "I feel really sad (disappointed, worried, whatever) when I don't get to spend the evening with you."

ALERT!

Don't use your own therapist as a marriage counselor. Your spouse may be reluctant to do marriage counseling in the first place and is likely to see your therapist as someone who is biased in your favor. Besides, you don't want to compromise your relationship with your therapist by asking him or her to wear two hats. So, get the names of some neutral, new people for marriage counseling.

If you and the therapist work well together, chances are good you'll start to feel better about yourself. This may lead to feeling better about your marriage. Or not. Therapy may make it clearer that something in the marriage needs to change, or you'll have to end the relationship. For example. addiction to alcohol, drugs, or gambling may be a major problem in the marriage. Or use and abuse of money may be a major problem. You can try to address these issues before taking the divorce plunge.

Treating Addictions

Your counselor may be able to help you or your spouse get into treatment for whatever addiction is affecting your family. Sometimes it works better to have this recommendation come from an outsider—a nonfamily member—than from a spouse. However, sometimes it takes an intervention of family and friends to get the dependent spouse into treatment.

QUESTION?

What is an intervention?
Typically it's three sessions with someone trained in this type of work. The first two meetings prepare concerned family and friends for the third meeting with the addicted person. At the third meeting, family and friends tell the addict their concerns about his or her behavior, hoping to persuade him or her to get help. Usually the abuser does agree to treatment.

Managing Finances

Are finances your big problem? How about consulting a financial adviser? Here again, outside advice often produces better results than arguing with your spouse about money. A financial adviser can help you set a budget, reorganize or consolidate debt, and stick to the plan. It's kind of like going to Weight Watchers; you need to check in regularly to review your spending habits until you're sure you can live within your incomes on your own.

Rarely is too much money the problem, although it has been known to happen. Usually the money available to your household doesn't meet your needs and desires, and debts keep growing. Sometimes bankruptcy is the only option, but be careful because bankruptcy laws are tightening up in favor of the guys who issue the credit cards. It's so easy to get those pieces of plastic, but so hard to pay off all the debt.

FACT

Debt management and financial planning are two different things. Debt managers help you consolidate your debt and pay it off in affordable monthly payments. Financial planners help you develop an investment program. They charge a commission on the investments you make through them.

Helpful Resources Abound

If there's hope for the marriage, by all means first put your energies into trying to save it. All kinds of help are out there in your community. Check out local United Way agencies, Catholic Charities, Lutheran Brotherhood, Jewish Family and Children's Services, and your local county's social services. Resources abound. Use them to save your marriage.

If you can't save your marriage, then you may want to utilize the resources available to you to help you through the hard times. Psychologists who work with families going through divorce say most people need three years to complete the emotional divorce. To go through the process and emerge ready to begin anew means experiencing some enormous mental ups and downs. This is a bit easier when you ask for and accept outside help. A divorce isn't so different from a death in terms of adjustment stages people go through. Divorce is not to be entered into casually.

Moving Toward Divorce

Maybe you've been in counseling for several months, and your spouse has refused to work with you in any way—no individual or marriage counseling, no financial planning. Indeed, your spouse may refuse to see anything amiss in the marriage. The only thing that has changed is that you're feeling better about yourself and feeling clearer about what happens next.

Maybe at this point you decide you need to live separately from your spouse. Before discussing a separation, you would be wise to consult a financial adviser or debt manager to develop a budget for you and the children. You need to know what it will cost to live on your own, either in the place you now share with your spouse or somewhere new. If you have children and want them to live with you, you will need to figure their expenses into your budget.

The Summer 2001 edition of *The Family Advocate*, a publication of the American Bar Association (ABA) Family Law Section, has some useful divorce forms, including income and budget forms, to help figure out your financial needs and the funds available to meet them. Single copies of the publication can be ordered for about $17 from the ABA by calling ☎ 1-800-285-2221. Ask for publication number PC 513-1100-2401.

When you work out a budget, you may find you don't have enough income to support yourself and your children. If your spouse has no income or doesn't make much, you can't expect much help there. You may have to support your spouse, too. If you have no income and will have to look to your spouse, can he or she support two households? What if there isn't enough money?

Because you haven't dropped the separation bomb yet, you have the option of staying in the marriage, and the marital home, until there is more money. You or your spouse can get jobs. You both could do a better job of managing the income of the family—whatever it takes to get into financial position to live apart.

FACT

If you have children, consider their developmental levels before making that final decision to divorce, to avoid harming their mental health. For example, infants need to see their parents every day. They have no sense of time and become very anxious when separated from a caregiver. (In fact, infants react to their parents' moods, and an upset parent often will result in a fussy baby.)

Everyone Needs Legal Advice

Whether or not the money is there, maybe you have decided you need to separate. Before you burn the bridge, get some legal advice. The best place to get legal advice is from a divorce lawyer. This seems pretty obvious, but many people get their information from friends, family, clergy, and even their local librarian!

Do not seek legal advice from your friends and family. Do not ask your hairdresser for help. In fact, do not ask your friends and family for advice about your divorce, period. Some of your friends may have gone through a divorce. Their information will be based on their experiences, and their situations were different from yours.

ALERT!

Hiring a lawyer isn't going to be cheap. To protect your interests and your wallet, read the chapters on finding and using a lawyer before looking for one to talk to about separating. Definitely read them before hiring a lawyer.

Use Friends and Family for Support

Friends and family mean well, but they just can't give you the advice you need. They are biased in your favor. They are not divorce lawyers, and they don't—or shouldn't—have all the facts of your marriage. Besides, you haven't discussed separation or divorce with your spouse yet. You sure don't want someone else to break the news.

You should use friends and family as your support system to be there for you when you're feeling low, to help with the kids, and maybe to help financially. You may alienate the people you need the most if you talk constantly about your situation. Keep your focus on maintaining their friendship and support, try not to force your friends to take sides. The side they choose may disappoint you. You may want to work with your therapist on managing your need to vent appropriately.

Arm Yourself with Knowledge

You need to know if it's safe to move out with the kids if your spouse won't budge, or will you be in jeopardy of losing everything because, in the eyes of the law, you've abandoned your spouse? You need to know what kind of support you are entitled to. You need to know how you will meet your financial needs during the separation. You need to know how to protect the assets of the marriage.

You and your lawyer need to talk about these matters as they apply to you. You need to hear about the laws of divorce and separation in your state. This knowledge will give you a better sense of the many issues you need to address.

Protective Steps

Make sure you make copies of important household financial documents before you leave. Remove the originals to make your copies, then replace them. Put your copies in a safe place, such as a safety deposit box in your name alone. If you and your spouse each have a set of these documents, you won't have to spend time and money fighting over getting this information.

If you decide divorce is the only option, make sure you learn ahead of time what's involved. Talk to a lawyer. Work with a therapist. Be sure you have information about your finances. Take any steps necessary to protect yourself, your children, and your assets. Do not begin a divorce casually.

If you have financial accounts together, do what you can to protect your share. If you have joint checking and savings accounts, you can take part of each account and open new accounts in your name alone. If your spouse uses the checking account, you will need to notify your spouse soon after that you removed the funds and why, so the account doesn't get overdrawn, creating a problem you don't need. Also be sure to make copies of investment account and credit card statements, showing the balances at about the time you're planning to separate.

If you've had little to do with the finances of your household, now is the time to learn about them as fast as you can, so you can protect your interests. If your spouse has managed the finances from a joint account you rarely use, you'll need to borrow the ledger for a few days, make copies of the entries, then figure out what it costs to run your household. Even today, it's not unusual for one spouse to be totally ignorant of what it costs to keep the family going for a month.

Chapter 2

You've Decided to Divorce

At this point you're convinced you've taken all possible steps to save the marriage, and they didn't work. You want to separate and probably divorce. Now, you need to tell your spouse. Your spouse may be taken by surprise, especially if there's been denial about marital problems.

Breaking the News to Your Spouse

If you have children, it's very important to tell your spouse you want a separation when the children are somewhere else. You don't know how your spouse will react, so you want to give your spouse time to calm down and digest the information. A big scene can be frightening and harmful to your children. If you pick a fight with your spouse and one of you leaves the house (and the marriage), you will leave each other frozen in rage. It's very hard to negotiate when you're both so angry.

Don't announce your decision to divorce when you're angry. Don't pack a bag and leave in anger, because you're inviting retaliation. If you leave, your spouse is in control of the house, the children, and the marital assets. Besides, you're likely to say things you'll regret. Things said in anger may come back to haunt you during the divorce.

Involving a Counselor

Your spouse may now suggest counseling. You'll have to decide whether this is too little too late, or whether you're willing to do some counseling. You may be convinced the marriage is over, but the opportunity to actually communicate with your spouse with a counselor can help both of you deal better with whatever lies ahead.

If you do agree to counseling, be clear to your spouse that either you're participating in marriage counseling to save the marriage, or you're going to divorce (or exit) counseling to help your spouse accept that the marriage is over. Some marriage counselors do both marriage counseling and exit counseling. Exit counseling assists a couple in dealing with the death of their marriage and helps them develop tools to cope in the least harmful way. When people use divorce counseling to get a handle on the emotional issues, they're better able to focus on the legal and practical issues of their divorce and make good decisions. Emotional baggage creates most of the problems in the divorce for everyone—you, your spouse, your kids. Get rid of it if you can.

Taking Steps to Protect Yourself

If your spouse has been abusive to you or the children during the marriage, and you have reason to expect a violent reaction to your announcement, you must take precautionary steps for your protection. Discuss the nature of the violence and abuse that you've experienced with the lawyer you've selected, and find out what rights and protections you have under the law.

Most states have civil, as opposed to criminal, laws that make it possible for you to get a restraining order to get the abuser out of the house. A judge can order your spouse to stay away from you, your home, and even the children. Telling an abusive spouse that you want a separation may be very dangerous, even life threatening. You may need to get that restraining order to get the separation you want. Violation of a restraining order is a criminal offense.

Statistics collected since domestic abuse was recognized as a problem show that the most dangerous time for abuse victims is when they leave the abuser. Be careful. Protect yourself and your children. We'll discuss domestic violence in greater detail in a later chapter. Be sure to read it.

Breaking the News to Your Children

You've told your spouse. There have been tears, shouts, pleas, and promises, but now your spouse has calmed down. Maybe your spouse is even willing to move out. Now it's time to bring the children into the loop, because they already know that something is going on. Even little kids are quick to pick up on tensions in the household.

Stick to the Rules

It's very helpful if both of you sit down with them and tell them your decision to separate. Use language they can understand. Give your children an explanation that is not blaming and reassure them that, whatever happens, you'll still be their mom and dad and will still take care of them. This is not the time to take shots at each other. It's very important that you both decide the rules for this meeting ahead of time, perhaps with the help of a counselor, and stick to the rules.

Reassure Your Children

Your children may be very upset, even though they've been aware of problems between you and your spouse for some time. Kids will worry they've somehow caused this mess. "If only I'd been a better kid, my parents wouldn't have to get a divorce." And they'll worry a lot about being abandoned. If one parent is moving out, what's to say the other one won't suddenly disappear as well? Who will take care of me? That's why it's so important to tell them that the divorce is your decision, that the divorce is not their fault, and to reassure them that you'll be there to take care of them. This is a scary time for kids, so it's up to you, the grownups, to help your children deal with their sadness and fears. Your divorce will go better if you and the children make the adjustment together.

FACT

People experience many transitions in their lives. They move out of their parents' homes, get new jobs in new cities, get married, have children, and face empty nests as children grow up and move out. If you think of divorce as an unscheduled transition, it becomes more manageable and less crazy. However, it will still take time—up to several years for most people—to adjust.

Emotional Anatomy of a Divorce

Most divorcing couples experience something close to emotional breakdown at the outset of a divorce. Psychologists say that next to a spouse's or child's death, divorce is the second most stressful event for married people. It takes most people more than two years from deciding to divorce to regaining their equilibrium and moving on with their lives. For those who choose to litigate, maybe this is okay. It will probably take them two years to get to trial. By that time, they'll be eager to get the divorce over and may even be ready to negotiate a settlement.

Gender Differences

In divorces with children, it's usually the dad who leaves the home. Because money is tight, he moves to a smaller place and may resent this reduced living standard. In addition, he probably feels lonely and at loose ends when he comes home to his empty apartment. In most marriages, the women and children provide the social life of the family. Having the children for the entire weekend may be stressful because he rarely had sole responsibility for them for more than a few hours at a time.

Mom's primary problem is not loneliness. She has the children for company and the marital home to provide stability. However, she is faced with handling the family responsibilities alone. She may have to go back to work or to school to handle future financial needs. She may well be simply overwhelmed.

Emotional Honeymoon Period

Despite having to adjust to the new structure of the family, it's common to feel pretty good the first month or two following a separation. You don't have the daily stress of dealing with your spouse, and that absence of tension is energizing. You and your spouse may consider reconciling and may go to marriage counseling with the hope of putting the marriage back together. You may become SuperParent putting all your newfound energy into child-focused activities. Or you may become incredibly self-indulgent, focusing on yourself and ignoring your children. Whichever way you go, this sense of well-being will disappear all too soon.

Reality Returns

Marriage counseling isn't working. The relief of the first months becomes loneliness. This loneliness is not so much missing your spouse as having a sense of panic that you'll be alone forever, that you'll never share happy moments with a special someone again. With this loneliness, you also may experience depression that may affect your job performance. It can louse up your ability to concentrate. You may find yourself daydreaming on your job or simply unable to handle the daily routine at the office. Your health may suffer.

FACT

Statistics from a study done some years ago in Washington State show that people going through a divorce had 82 percent more automobile crashes than the average driver. This may be related in part to their reduced ability to concentrate.

Acknowledge Your Anger

Some people mask their depression with anger. While depression can be paralyzing, anger tends to be energizing. However, using anger to avoid mourning the end of a marriage can be dangerous. It's normal to be angry; it's not normal to obsess about getting even with your spouse for causing you this pain. Some people get stuck in the hostility and anger phase and spend years blaming their ex-spouses for everything that goes wrong in their lives. Excessive anger can cause stress that leads to system overload and results in domestic violence.

Acknowledge your anger. Express it safely—in counseling, in conversation with a good friend. Never express anger without restraint. If you can recognize anger and accept it, you can control it, rather than letting it control you.

Six to Twelve Months after Separation

Your life still feels chaotic. Family routines are nonexistent or minimal. The financial reality of maintaining two households creates more stress. Custodial parents, especially mothers, can become rigid, restrictive, and overprotective. They sometimes try to limit children's contact with the other parent whose behavior they believe is too cavalier about the safety and well-being of the kids. Visiting parents want to have happy children during their limited time together, so they become overindulgent. Overindulgence can translate into having no rules. If the custodial parent learns that the other parent has no rules, visitation may be denied.

If you are a custodial mother, you've probably gone to work, even if you stayed at home with the children during the marriage. Even with child support from your soon-to-be ex, your financial situation could be tenuous. You might find more often than not that you have to tell the children there's no extra money for a field trip at school or a new baseball glove. You might no longer be able to pay for child care, so your children come home to an empty house after school and are on their own until you get home from work. You might be exhausted when you get home and have little time and energy left for the kids. That lack of energy can translate into an inability to maintain any kind of consistency in the home. Meals can become erratic. Discipline can become inconsistent. Conflicts with the children might increase.

Depending on the level of difficulty your children have in coping with the divorce, you may want to consider taking your children to a counselor. You're undoubtedly going through a tough time and may not be able to give your very all to your children. A counselor can help.

Into the Second Year

It is common to experience regret and ambivalence about the wisdom of getting divorced. An especially lovely sunset may remind you of the times your family spent at the lake. It's likely that you'll see less and less of the friends you shared during the marriage. If you're a woman, you're likely to put your energies into projects. Typically, women take classes, garden, or join groups. Men are more likely to socialize frenetically. Sociologists who have studied the behavior of men and women after separation say that this is the time when lust runs high and commitment low. It's a year when both men and women search for ways to avoid being at home alone. You're seeking confirmation that you're attractive and competent, and social relationships can help bolster your recovering self-esteem.

Many relationships that led to the breakup of the marriage may now break up as well. Maybe the person who was there for you and gave you the courage to announce that you wanted a divorce no longer looks like the person with whom you want to spend the rest of your life.

The Third Year Approaches

Household routines, often much different from those of the marriage, have evolved and stabilized. You've figured out how to manage with less money. You have a closer relationship with your children than you had during the marriage. If you're the visiting parent, you have blocks of uninterrupted time to talk more and do things together. If you're the custodial parent, you find yourself talking more, in part, because your children are the only other people at home with you. As you settle down, so do they, and a new equilibrium is established. If you've been able to work through your anger and recognize your role in the death of your marriage, you're probably ready to work with the other parent to develop a workable, affordable arrangement for you and your children's future. It's about time.

ALERT!

By the end of the third year after separation, most divorced people are ready to consider a new relationship. Before that time, they're working their way through the stages of adjustment needed to move on with their lives. Entering into a relationship with someone who is still struggling with the fallout from a divorce is probably not in your best interest.

If Your Spouse Wants the Divorce

So far, we've assumed that you're in the driver's seat in this divorce. What if, instead, your spouse surprises you with the announcement that he or she wants the divorce? You'll probably feel as if you've been punched in the stomach. You may react by denying what you've just heard. You may get very angry. You may well spend the night of the announcement sleepless, going over and over your marriage and wondering where it went wrong. In the days and weeks that follow, you'll be on an emotional roller coaster. Your world is in chaos. Even so, you need to pull yourself together enough to take action to protect yourself. How quickly you need to move depends on your relationship with your spouse. If you don't trust your spouse, you need to move sooner rather than later.

If You Don't Want to Divorce

What can you do? You can ask your spouse to go to counseling. If your spouse is willing to go to counseling, you may be able to save the marriage. If counseling can't save the marriage, it can give you some insight into your spouse's issues. It can also give you some time to adjust to the likelihood that there will be a divorce.

It is not uncommon for one spouse to decide the marriage is over long before the other has any idea that the marriage is in trouble. Lack of communication is a major factor in many divorces. When the spouse who wants the divorce pushes to move forward, the other spouse may use all kinds of tactics to delay the process. The spouse who is being left may plead and bargain with the other spouse to reconsider. Counseling can be very useful in helping the reluctant spouse accept the fact that a divorce will occur.

If you don't want to get a divorce, don't simply ignore the matter and assume your lack of cooperation will stop the proceedings. Your spouse can get a divorce without your consent and may be able to get whatever he or she wants unless you take steps to protect yourself and your interests.

Allowing Time for Acceptance

If the spouse who wants the divorce pushes too hard, the spouse being left may use desperate tactics to try to prevent it from happening. The left spouse may become irrational or threatening. This spouse may try to hide important papers, bring unnecessary motions in court, or try to convince the children that the other parent is immoral or otherwise unfit. It is wise to give the left spouse time to accept the fact of the divorce. While this may take some time and patience, it will pay off if the spouse being left stops trying to keep the divorce from happening and cooperates in resolving the issues.

If your spouse has made the decision to divorce, in the eyes of the law there will be a divorce. Some states retain vestiges of fault in their divorce laws, but those states apply fault in specific ways. Today, "fault" applies more to how the property is divided, whether there will be spousal maintenance, and the length of time the parties are required to live apart before they can be divorced. For instance, in some states, a spouse who has been unfaithful can't get alimony. In some states, claims of mental cruelty or desertion may have an impact on the final property division.

FACT

All U.S. states now have no-fault divorce. Each state has its own requirements but will grant a divorce based on "irretrievable breakdown" or "irreconcilable differences." Under no-fault law, if your spouse says it's over, it's over. When one spouse says the marriage can't be saved, the marriage is irretrievably broken. When one spouse says the parties have grown so far apart that their differences can't be resolved, there are irreconcilable differences.

Steps to Protect Your Assets

If your spouse wants a divorce, consider the worst-case scenario. Suppose the marriage has been stormy, and you and your spouse have had many arguments. One consequence is that you've hidden things from each other. You have some credit cards your spouse doesn't know about. Your spouse hides extra spending in the grocery budget. The bottom line is that you trust each other very little. Now your spouse is very angry and threatening to leave or to make you leave the house. You need to act quickly. At a minimum, you need to do the following things if you and your spouse have accumulated assets during the marriage:

• See a lawyer. Take every financial document you can find with you so the lawyer's staff can make copies before these papers disappear.

• Take your share of funds out of all joint accounts and open new accounts in your name alone. You will need to do this before any restraining orders (on assets or behavior) are in place.

- Begin a divorce proceeding, so a court order prohibiting transfer of assets gets served on your spouse immediately.

- Get the balances on every account you know about—savings, checking, retirement, credit cards—right away and keep track of what goes on in the accounts in case you need to show that your spouse wrongfully withdrew funds or improperly ran up charges on the credit cards.

- If your spouse has ever struck you or you were afraid your spouse would, you may need a restraining order on behavior as well as a restraining order on assets. Discuss this with your lawyer.

Your spouse may already have transferred assets into new bank accounts and may have tried to put various pieces of marital property out of your reach before telling you the divorce is imminent. While your spouse probably can't get away with this, you will have a long, costly legal battle to get what is rightfully yours.

ALERT!

When people behave badly, nobody can do much about it, and that includes the judge. Fortunately, few divorces involve such high levels of acrimony and bad behavior. They are the ones that make the headlines and color the public's perception of divorce and divorce lawyers.

Taking Care of Yourself

If your spouse is still intent on leaving, and you've done as much as you can to protect your assets, you'll need to go through all the steps discussed in the preceding chapter. You may feel you have less time to get ready for the divorce, but you should take the time needed to adjust to the idea. If you didn't need to get a restraining order and neither of you has filed any court papers, you're still in charge. You have time to take care of your psyche, get personal counseling, and maybe even get marriage or divorce counseling.

Catching Up Emotionally

Getting divorced is never easy. It is harder when you're the one being left, although both parties need time to adjust to the idea of divorce. The spouse who initiates the divorce has probably thought about it a lot before making the move. The other spouse may be totally surprised. This spouse needs time to catch up emotionally. The spouse who is pushed too hard and too fast may react badly and cause the divorce to take longer and be more painful. While it may take awhile for the spouse who gets left to catch up, it's probably worth it in the long run to give that spouse the time he or she needs.

Don't try to play the hero and resist the urge to ask for help. This is a very trying time. If you need professional help to make it through, then by all means seek it out.

Riding the Emotional Roller Coaster

Both parties probably will experience an emotional roller coaster after the separation. Typically there's an initial euphoria, followed by a sense of loss and failure, followed by loneliness, followed by lots of activity to fill the void and avoid the loneliness. This activity may lead to new friends and a better sense of self, which in turn leads to more reasonable activity levels and, finally, settling in to your new life as a divorced person.

The bad news is that this period of adjustment is very hard on the parties and their children. The good news is that most people do work through all the emotions of divorce and get on with their lives, and most of their children come through this turmoil without too many permanent scars.

Is Divorce Harder Than Saving the Marriage?

When you look at the problems of your marriage, take a hard look at possible solutions. If your complaints are many but relatively minor, they can be addressed in counseling. If your issues are major—say, chemical addiction or domestic abuse—they may still be resolvable without a divorce, but with a lot of hard work. The work it takes to solve problems within a marriage may be far less than the work needed to make a new life after divorce. Make sure you've exhausted all possible alternatives before choosing divorce.

If you're convinced that divorce is the only solution, again make sure you know what's involved before you begin. Take appropriate steps to take care of yourself and your children, if you have children. Make sure you have copies of all the important papers of your marriage. If possible, be civil to your spouse. The more reasonable and rational you and your spouse can be, the less everyone will lose.

Chapter 3

What About the Children?

Children will both enrich and complicate your divorce. Enrich because they'll be there to hug you when the going gets tough, to make you laugh when you most need it, and to give continued meaning to your life. Complicate because they will need your care, support, and reassurance at a time when you have little energy left after taking care of yourself.

Telling Your Children

As your world is turning upside down, you're probably spending most of the time thinking about yourself. What will happen to you? How will you cope with your new status as a divorced person? Your emotions will run the gamut from relief to despair. Just think: If you are having a hard time dealing with the changes, what must be going on in the minds of your children? Fortunately, you have some control over what happens to you. But your children have no control; they depend on you and your spouse. On top of all your other worries, you need to be worried about your children, too.

Both Parents Should Participate

It's important to tell the children what's going on. Think how devastating it is for a child to wake up one morning and find one of his parents gone. When this happens, children immediately start to worry that another morning they'll wake up to find you both gone. Ideally you and your spouse should tell children about the impending divorce together. If possible, you need to plan together how this will happen. Decide in advance what you will say. Pick a time when the family normally is together, say, Sunday dinner. If you don't have such a time, call a family conference when no one has to run off to an activity.

If you've made specific plans for your separation, tell the children what they are. If you're the parent who is moving out, be sure to tell the children they will always be welcome at your new place. And tell them you will spend as much time with them as you possibly can.

Both of you should participate. Tell the children you've decided to separate. Tell them the fact you're getting divorced doesn't change the fact you love them very much. Reassure the children that you will continue to spend lots of time with them and that you will always be their parents.

Use Simple Language

When you tell your children about the divorce, you need to use language they understand. All children old enough to understand language should be included in this process. While two-year-olds may not know the word *divorce*, they'll be able to understand, "Mommy and Daddy aren't going to live together anymore." Little kids don't have a good grasp of time, so it's better to say "I'll see you a lot," rather than "I'll see you in two weeks."

All children involved in a divorce wonder if they were so bad they drove their parents to it, so you need to be clear that the divorce is an adult decision for reasons having nothing to do with them. If children are old enough to understand, it's helpful to give them a concrete plan for the future. Kids don't do well with ambiguity. Most adults don't, either; but kids especially need specifics. They need to know where you're going, when you're going, and when they'll see you. They need to know whether they'll move and whom they'll live with.

If you tell the children you're sad, you give them permission to be sad, too. They need to be able to express their emotions about the divorce. And they need to know you'll continue to be their parents.

ALERT!

Even though your children may not drastically change their behavior or even act as though the news of divorce affects them, this doesn't mean that they're not suffering. Some children live in a state of shock or denial following the news.

Give an Explanation

Give your children an explanation. You might say, "You kids have probably noticed Mom and I have been arguing a lot recently. We haven't had many fun times, like we used to. We just can't seem to get along." It's probably not a good idea to tell children you're getting divorced because one of you has found someone else. Children will have enough on their plates without dealing with the idea that their beloved dad has dumped their beloved mom for someone else, or vice versa. This is not the time to place blame on the other parent. The idea here is to give the children a reasonable explanation to help them understand and to make it clear the divorce is not their fault.

Develop Your Parenting Plan Quickly

Once you've told the children about the divorce and reassured them you have a plan for taking care of them, you'd better develop that plan. If you're one of the lucky ones, you've been able to sit down and work out how you'll take care of the children after you separate. Unfortunately, many divorcing parents are too caught up in their own issues to give much thought to a plan for their children until the separation is imminent or has already happened.

It's common for a dad who has taken his role as a father for granted to suddenly realize how important his children are. He may want to spend every evening with them, either at the marital home or at his new place. He may want them to live with him, even though historically he has been mostly a Sunday afternoon parent.

Mom may be feeling overwhelmed and resentful of the responsibilities about to fall in her lap. She's probably facing taking care of the house, the kids, and her job—by herself. She's probably worrying about money, too. She may be feeling more protective toward the children and may not want the children to be out of her control. As a result she may not want Dad to have so much time with the children.

These are normal responses to a divorce, but they make it harder to negotiate a parenting plan, especially if you've never done it before. You need to know your options, and you need to know your children's needs, depending on their ages and developmental levels.

The Legal Perspective

Before you separated, perhaps you made many decisions together. You chose an obstetrician for yourself or your spouse when a pregnancy was confirmed. After children were born, you selected a pediatrician. You decided whether to rear your children in a religion. If you were both working, you selected child care. As the children grew older, you decided whether to send them to nursery school. When it came time for kindergarten, you decided when to start your children and picked their schools. Then you chose grade schools. You decided to put braces on your children's teeth. You probably planned to decide on high schools together and to help your children make college choices.

Legal Custody

The law calls making decisions about your children's health care, education, and religious upbringing, legal custody. As part of your divorce you'll choose, or the court will decide, whether you'll have joint legal custody or whether one of you will have sole legal custody. Joint legal custody means that you make these decisions together. Sole legal custody means one of you will have total authority over these decisions.

FACT

There are several divorce education programs available in the United States today. If you're having difficulty helping your children understand certain aspects of divorce, such as custody issues, you may want to consider attending one of these programs to help both you and your children through these trying times.

Physical Custody

Before you separated, maybe you divided responsibility for taking care of the children. One or both of you got the children up, fed them breakfast, and got them to school or to the school bus. One of you took them to soccer practice. One of you volunteered in your children's classrooms. Maybe Dad took the kids to the park on Saturday mornings and was a volunteer coach. Perhaps Mom took the kids to the movies one afternoon on the weekend. On Sunday evenings you all cooked and ate dinner together. Each of you spent time with your children. The law calls the actual time you spend with your children physical custody.

If both of you continue to share the actual hands-on care of the children, this is called joint or shared physical custody. If the children spend most of their time with one parent, that parent is said to have "sole physical custody." Sometimes parents divide responsibility by actually dividing the children. One parent takes the older children and one the younger. Or, one takes the boys and one takes the girls. This arrangement is called split custody. Courts and psychologists agree this usually isn't good for children. Most take the position that children should stay together whenever possible.

A Responsibility to Your Children

You chose to take on the responsibility of children, and as you already know, parenting is a big job in the best of circumstances. Divorce is not the best of circumstances. All the same, you want your children to make it through the divorce with as little damage as possible. Psychologists tell us over and over that parental conflict causes the most harm to children of divorce.

> While there are certainly levels of psychological development that you need to be aware of as a parent, you must also remember that your children are all individuals and will handle the divorce in their own ways.

If you want to minimize parental conflict, you will need to develop a workable parenting plan. To develop such a plan, you need to know something about the developmental needs of your children. Children at different ages and levels of psychological development have different needs. The kids who do the best when their parents divorce are the kids whose parents take those needs into account.

The Psychological Perspective

You'll want your parenting plan to fit the psychological needs of your children as well as meet the legal definitions. Experts tell us children have very specific needs, depending on their ages and levels of development. Even in the womb, your children respond to what is going on. A pregnant woman's physical and emotional health has a huge impact on a baby's development. When a woman is pregnant, she shares her circulatory system with the fetus. If she is upset, her system sends out extra hormones and chemicals. These may circulate into the fetus, making it more agitated and active. Stress during pregnancy can result in premature birth. It can result in a cranky baby who has a troubled digestive system. Add these stresses to the other stresses of divorce, and a baby's arrival can be more a nightmare than a dream come true.

Boys and Girls React Differently

Psychologists who have studied the children of divorce report that boys at all ages are more likely to react with increased aggression and stubborn opposition to household rules. Experts don't really know why this is true but report that boys just seem to have a harder time dealing with their parents' divorce. Boys generally—in intact families as well—are resistant to authority, more demanding than girls of their parents, and more likely to get into trouble. These behaviors are intensified by divorce, perhaps because it is usually the father who leaves the household.

Girls tend to turn their hurt inward. They try to be very, very good, to make sure their remaining parent doesn't leave, too. They create a fantasy world where their parents are still together. They may be bossy and crabby at school and whiny and petulant at home for a while, but they tend to get over this behavior quickly.

Society responds differently to boys and girls of divorce, as well. When a little girl expresses her sadness, she is likely to be comforted. A little boy, on the other hand, is more likely to be told to act more like a man when he gets teary. And peers are more likely to forgive the bossy behavior of girls than the aggressive, angry behavior of boys. It is harder to be a boy child when your parents divorce.

If you and your spouse are able to communicate well (at least in matters of the children) and live relatively close, try to be flexible with the children's visitation schedules.

Infancy to Age Two

Infants may not be able to understand words or recognize all the people in their world, but they're very aware of emotions. They soon respond to familiar faces. One of the first things they learn is trust When they are wet or hungry, they cry and someone comes to care for them. Divorcing parents may be less responsive, and the infant may suffer. The interaction between infant and caregiver is critical to the baby's development. Infants and children up to about two years of age need a consistent caregiver. Their sense of security comes from the quality and consistency of care they get during this time.

At about a year old, children develop a fear of strangers. They also develop a deep fear of losing the parent who is their primary caretaker. This may make putting them in day care traumatic for child and parent.

Two-year-olds are just beginning to develop a little independence. If parents separate, children this age are likely to redevelop fears they had seemed to outgrow. They may resist going to bed, both because they're afraid of losing their primary caretaker and because their nightmares may have intensified. Having a parent move out may make these fears worse.

Little kids need to see their parents frequently. The absent parent should spend time with these little ones at least every third day. The visits should be frequent but short. Ideally, they should take place at the child's home, because small children aren't ready for overnights with the visiting parent. Children under two need consistent caregivers. This is the time when children bond, or develop human attachments.

One piece of good news: Very young children, except for two-year-old boys, often are less affected by a divorce because they have a much shorter history of living with both parents and less exposure to fighting and stress in the home.

Ages Three to Five

Children from three to five may react to a divorce with regression, going back to a happier time when Mom and Dad lived together. They may deny their parents are divorced because it's too scary to admit they've lost one parent. They're afraid they may well lose the other.

Children this age may believe they caused the breakup, and if they're just good enough their parents will get back together.

This also is a time when children begin to develop sexual identity. During this Oedipal period, a little boy may be thinking "If only I could get rid of Dad, I would have Mom all to myself." Then Dad leaves. This is really scary because the child wasn't supposed to "win." He feels really guilty and frightened and may have difficulty moving through and out of this stage.

ALERT!

Regardless of their ages, never assume that your children don't have at least some understanding of what's going on. Though you may believe they're too young to understand what you're saying, they'll often get the gist of the conversation, or at the very least pick up on the tension.

Boys of this age are more affected than girls by their parents' divorce. This is the time when boys are moving from identification with Mother to a positive identification with Father. They need frequent contact with their fathers or another male to help them develop this sense of maleness. If Dad—and the example he provides—moves away, it is harder for a young boy to understand who he is and how he should behave. When Dad is gone, there's no safe place to direct the aggressive behavior typical of boys this age. A boy may fear his maleness, reasoning that being male got his father removed from the household. Boys and girls from three to five see Dad as the strong figure in the household, but little girls seem to move past this more easily than their brothers.

You need to give both boys and girls this age a specific, concrete plan in language and concepts they can understand. They need frequent contact with both parents, and boys need to spend as much time as possible with their dads. They need predictability and consistency. It's extremely important that parents handle exchanges with a minimum of stress. By this age children can handle overnights and weekends with the visiting parent.

Ages Six to Eight

Children from six to eight experience enormous sadness when their parents divorce. They feel torn between their parents. When they're with Mom, they miss Dad. When they're with Dad, they miss Mom. They often cry when moving from one parent to the other. Despite these strong emotions at exchanges, they need to spend time with each parent. They often worry the other parent will forget about them. Frequent time with both parents helps them get past their feelings of loss and abandonment.

Divorced or separated parents often misread this behavior. The fact that your child misses his other parent when he's with you doesn't mean he loves you less. The fact that he cries when he leaves you doesn't mean he loves you more.

Encourage your children to voice their feelings. Your children could be suffering silently, allowing the unspoken feelings to fester until they become too much for the children to handle. The buried emotions could then be released in unhealthy ways.

Children this age have strong and elaborate fantasies about their parents getting back together. At the same time, they welcome their parents' new partners, as long as they are included in the "new family." A danger here is that children will attach to the new partner. If this new relationship ends, the children will be devastated all over again.

While children this age will benefit from spending frequent time with each parent, they may not be ready for a shared arrangement that has them spending part of each week with each parent. They have a lot of sorting out to do, so managing such a schedule may be more than they can comfortably handle. The ideal arrangement is for parents to live near each other, so the children can easily spend time with each parent without actually moving from one house to the other for prolonged stays.

Children of this age are particularly troubled when their parents remain hostile. Fear of losing both parents may force a child to avoid mentioning one parent in the other's presence for fear of triggering an angry reaction. This can even result in a child's refusing to see one parent to appease the other parent.

Ages Nine to Twelve

Kids from ages nine to twelve have rigid moral rules, and when they believe one parent has violated these rules, they get very angry. They may refuse to see or talk to that parent, or may act hostile and revengeful when they're together. Sometimes they may take the side of the parent with whom they live, out of a sense of self-preservation, and never mention the other parent and act badly toward that parent.

The custodial parent needs to stress the absent parent's good points and try to defuse the child's anger, even if that parent secretly agrees the other parent has behaved badly. The parent who feeds into a child's anger may become the object of the child's anger in later years. The older child may blame that parent for depriving him of a relationship with the other parent.

While children this age have a better understanding of what led to the divorce and are less likely to blame themselves, they still want their parents to be figures worthy of veneration. When parents try to put children in the middle, the youngsters are resentful, and rightfully so. Boys at this age may become defiant toward their mothers.

Kids this age may be well aware of the financial differences between their household and that of their other parent. This may make them even more protective of the parent with whom they live. In addition, adult responsibilities are too often imposed on children this age. If the custodial parent works, one child might need to pick up a little sister from day care and care for her until the parent gets home. A son living with his mother may be told he's now "the man of the house," and may worry unnaturally about keeping his household safe.

It's important to remember children perceive themselves as "part-Mom" and "part-Dad." When Mom criticizes Dad, or vice versa, children hear it as criticism of themselves. Boys at this age need their fathers, and a firm hand. It's important for children this age to make peace with both parents, so they can get on with their development.

The Teen Years

As children get older, their activities at school and with friends become very important to them. Parents need to accommodate their children's activities, but these activities shouldn't be used to limit their time with the visiting parent.

Teenagers are on the cusp of wanting to be adults, so they are constantly testing family limits and values. At the same time, they want a secure home base from which to operate. The teenage years are turbulent in any family. One moment teens want to be treated as adults, and the next they want to have their parents' advice and guidance.

ALERT!

Teenagers without rules tend to get into trouble or drop out of school. Even though they pretend otherwise, they want their parents to provide a structure within which they can operate, resentfully sometimes, but safely.

While these older children may understand the reasons for a divorce—and may be better able to distance themselves from guilt—they still seek a family history that says their parents wanted them. They want happy memories of their childhoods. Their sense of self can be badly damaged by a parent's offhand comment such as, "We had to get married because I was pregnant with you." Not exactly a teenager's dream of love and romance.

Even teenagers may have a hard time with a shared parenting arrangement. With so many demands on their lives—activities, friends, dating—they seek a secure home base. They need rules. Some parents go through a second adolescence after divorce, trying to experience things they think they missed the first time around. They may eliminate rules for themselves and their children, too.

Parents need to respect the many activities that compete for time with their teenagers. They need to work very hard at saying good things about the other parent. Teens are very aware that they are part-Mom and part-Dad. They need to believe this is a good thing.

Ten Tips for Divorcing Parents

Divorce is never easy on kids, but parents can help lessen the impact of their breakup on their children. Consider these tips compiled by the American Academy of Matrimonial Lawyers. Make a copy. Put it on the refrigerator. Read it every day. And do your best to follow this advice:

1. **Never disparage your former spouse in front of your children.** Because children know they are part-Mom and part-Dad the criticism can batter youngsters' self-esteem.

2. **Do not use your children as messengers between you and your former spouse.** The less the children feel a part of the battle between you, the better.

3. **Reassure your children they are loved and the divorce is not their fault.** Many children assume they are to blame for their parents' hostility.

4. **Encourage your children to see their other parent frequently.** Do everything within your power to accommodate the visitation.

5. **At every step of your divorce, remind yourself that the children's interests—not yours—are paramount, and act accordingly.** Lavish them with love at every opportunity.

6. **Resist the temptation to let your children act as your caretaker.** Let your peers, adult family members, and mental health professionals be your counselors and sounding boards. Let your children be children.

7. **If you have a drinking or drug problem, get counseling right away.** An impairment inhibits your ability to reassure your children and give them the attention they need at this difficult time.

8. **If you are the noncustodial parent, pay your child support.** Loss of income facing many children after divorce puts them at a financial disadvantage that has a pervasive effect on the rest of their lives.

9. **If you are the custodial parent and you are not receiving child support, do not tell your children.** It feeds into the child's sense of abandonment and further erodes his or her stability.

10. **If at all possible, do not uproot your children.** Stability in their home and school life helps buffer children from the trauma of their parents' divorce.

Children at different ages and different levels of development have different needs. You must consider these needs as you move toward divorce. You may even consider delaying your divorce until your children are less fragile.

While the divorce is your decision, your children will have no choice but to deal with the consequences. For many children, their whole world is turned upside down with the discovery that their parents don't love each other anymore and are not going to stay together. This means that they really need you during this time. This also means that you need to listen to them carefully, to try to discover the things they're too afraid to say out loud.

Now that you know how children of different ages respond to divorce, you can deal with their behaviors in helpful, supportive ways. Of course, this means you need to be able to focus on your children's needs as well as your own. Not an easy task during this time of emotional upheaval for the whole family. (E)

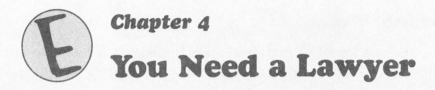

Chapter 4

You Need a Lawyer

Getting a divorce is a complex stew of laws and emotions. Few people go into a divorce with no possessions or children. A divorce lawyer is trained to help you navigate a path through important issues tied to your rights, actions, and hopes for the future.

Why You Need a Lawyer

You may wonder if you really need a lawyer to get divorced. Divorce is a creation of law, which is why only courts can grant a legal divorce. Clergy can perform marriages but not divorces. Some religious institutions have divorce ceremonies, but these are personal and have no legal bearing.

In English, Please

Go to a local law library and ask a librarian for a copy of your state's divorce laws. Start reading. Do you notice anything? You should notice pretty quickly that laws are written in legalese, a form of archaic language that many nonlawyers find confusing.

If that weren't enough to make you nervous, you should know that laws may differ from what's in the statute book because appellate courts have issued decisions changing them. The legislature writes the laws, and the courts interpret them. After a case is tried, one or both of the parties may challenge the trial court's decision by appealing it. The appellate court reviews the trial and the trial judge's decision, and then issues a decision that may agree or disagree with the trial court. In the process of agreeing and disagreeing, the appellate court will decide what the law really means. Their decision becomes what is known as case law. Good lawyers understand the statutes and the case law, or judicial decisions, modifying those statutes. They will read the weekly decisions of the appellate courts and stay up-to-date on all aspects of the law.

You can get legal services without paying a fortune. Call or visit your local bar association and ask for their attorney referral list; the lawyers listed will give a thirty-minute consultation at a reduced cost. You may also be eligible for pro bono services; check with Legal Aid to see if you meet the minimum income requirements. If you do qualify, be ready to be placed on a very long waiting list.

A good divorce lawyer will know the divorce law of your state as it applies to you and translate the law into language you can understand.

A good divorce lawyer will listen to you carefully and ask focused questions. The lawyer will read a history of the marriage that you have written and quickly pull out the most legally important facts. He or she will explain why some facts are legally important and some are not. The lawyer will explain your rights and responsibilities and tell you how the law will affect your divorce.

The Divorce Process

You need to know about the divorce process. A good divorce lawyer will explain the divorce process in language you can understand. The lawyer will tell you about preparing and serving the summons and petition and probably ask you how you think your spouse will react. The lawyer will want to know whether papers should be served on your spouse at work or whether your spouse will come to the office to pick up the papers.

A good divorce lawyer will know whether the papers need to be served right away to protect you, the children, and your assets. The lawyer then will explain the process from preparing these initial papers to preparing for a first court appearance if it's necessary for collecting information from your spouse and others. The lawyer will explain how and where settlement negotiations fit into the picture and under what circumstances you may consider going to trial before a judge.

You'll probably need to go over these steps a number of times. Although your lawyer is totally familiar and comfortable with the process, you'll probably feel as if you're visiting a foreign country where you don't speak the language. It's important that you feel comfortable asking your lawyer to explain things to you and that you understand the explanations.

A lawyer may tell you that you need other professionals to help you through the divorce. Good divorce lawyers know the top psychologists, custody evaluators, accountants, and financial advisers in your community who work with families going through divorce. They work with them all the time. Your lawyer can refer you to good people to help you with specific issues in your case.

Divorce Behavior

You need to know the rules of divorce behavior. A good divorce lawyer will explain how certain behaviors can help or hurt you during the divorce. The lawyer can give you advice about the wisdom of getting involved with a new person, about losing your temper with your spouse or your children, and about how to behave during a custody evaluation. The lawyer will tell you how judges expect you to act in a courtroom or in a judge's office.

Not Any Lawyer Will Do

Have you noticed the words *good divorce lawyer* in this discussion? It's essential that you find a lawyer who really knows divorce law. Most of us wouldn't ask our dermatologist to pull a tooth. Likewise, you don't want a personal injury attorney to handle your divorce. Some lawyers think divorce law is a no-brainer and anyone can do it. Not so. Beware the lawyer who does only one or two divorces a year, because divorce law changes, and you want a specialist who keeps up with the changes. Specialists also know the judges and other lawyers who practice divorce law. The kindly general law practitioner who's a long-time family friend may be someone who's comfortable to talk to and may be able to refer you to a good divorce lawyer. However, don't hire the general law practitioner as your divorce lawyer.

ALERT!

Divorce law is complex and difficult. It requires a lawyer who does this kind of work all the time. Do not hire a lawyer whose practice is less than 50 percent divorce law.

The Exception

If your marriage is short-term (five years or less) and you have no children, earn similar incomes or are at least able to support yourselves, own no real estate, have inherited nothing of value during the marriage, have no valuable stuff, and have minimal debt, you can probably do your own divorce. Most states offer blank forms of the papers you need to get divorced, and usually sell these for a modest sum. Forms also are available from a local law library. Some counties even have self-help centers where staff members will help you fill out these forms.

You'll need to fill out the required papers, sign them before a notary public, pay your filing fee, and file your papers. In some states, this is all you need to do. Your divorce will be made final through an administrative process. When the decree has been signed, you'll be notified by mail that your divorce is final, or that it will be final a specific number of days after the decree was entered into the court system.

In other states, you'll need to go to court for a final hearing. You bring your judgment and decree, which you have prepared ahead of time, for the judge to approve and sign. If you have to go to court and have no idea what to do when you get there, call the judge's clerk and ask. Some judges get pretty testy when an unrepresented person shows up without the right papers or not knowing what happens next.

Finding a Good Divorce Lawyer

This is one area in which you can ask friends and family for advice. If they've gone through a divorce, ask friends or family for names of lawyers they believe did a good job. Don't be surprised if they give you the name of their spouse's lawyer. Is there higher praise? If you have a friend who's a lawyer, ask your friend who he or she would hire for a divorce lawyer, and why.

Ask other professionals who work with families. Do you know any therapists or social workers? Anyone who works at the courthouse? Sometimes the deputy sheriffs who work in the divorce courtrooms have a pretty good idea of which lawyers are effective. Again, ask them who they would hire if they needed a divorce lawyer, and why.

Check with your local bar association. It often has a lawyer referral service. Check the credentials of these lawyers carefully, because they are often lawyers who just got out of law school and are trying to build their practices. This doesn't mean they aren't capable; but it may mean that they don't have a lot of experience.

Look in the Yellow Pages under "Attorneys—Divorce and Family."

Check the listings for the lawyers who belong to the American Academy of Matrimonial Lawyers. These lawyers are usually the best divorce lawyers in the area.

To belong to the American Academy of Matrimonial Lawyers, lawyers must be in practice a minimum of five years, specialize in divorce law, have a number of trials under their belts, and be recognized by the other members as skilled and ethical in what they do.

Family Law Practitioners Differ

Within the specialty practice of family law, some lawyers see themselves as trial specialists and some as settlement specialists. Trial specialists are very good at presenting a case in court. They know how to use the rules of trial practice and how to best present a case to the judge. Settlement specialists focus on helping you reach agreement on the issues of your divorce. They try to give you options from which you can choose in resolving your issues. Once you reach agreement, they prepare the papers needed to complete the divorce. Both trial specialists and settlement specialists know the law of divorce well. They will use their expertise to tell you how they think the law applies to your case and how they will use the law to try the case or to settle it.

You may notice that some lawyers describe themselves as collaborative lawyers. These divorce lawyers are settlement oriented. They believe you will get a better result if you and your spouse negotiate an agreement on all the issues of your marriage. In fact, they want to work with another collaborative lawyer representing your spouse to help you reach a settlement. If both lawyers belong to this group, all four of you will sign a contract agreeing you will focus on settlement. If you don't reach an agreement and need to use the court, and, if court is needed, the lawyers will withdraw from the case. While this is true commitment to settlement, it may also mean you will have to essentially start over with a new lawyer if you are unable to agree.

What You Want Steers Your Choice

What do you want your lawyer to do for you? What are your objectives? The answers to these questions have an important effect on whom you select to represent you.

For example, suppose you and your spouse get along reasonably well. You've been married more than ten years and have two children. You own a house, two cars, retirement assets, and a time-share. You need a divorce attorney because you need to protect your children and your property, but you're confident you can work out a settlement. You don't want to fight with your spouse. You just don't want to be married any longer. You may want to try to use the collaborative approach. Of course, this will work only if your spouse is willing to hire a collaborative lawyer, too.

QUESTION?

What is a collaborative lawyer?
One who uses problem-solving and cooperative strategies to resolve divorce issues. The vast majority of collaborative lawyers are former divorce litigators who believe trying your case in court is contrary to your best interests. They know the law, and they know the advantages of settlement.

Maybe you're pretty emotionally charged. You surprised your spouse in bed with someone else, and now you want to tell the judge and anyone else who will listen how you've been done wrong. You want the toughest, meanest divorce litigator in your community. The first lawyer you talk to says judges aren't that interested in hearing your sob story. You ignore that lawyer's advice and continue looking until you find a divorce lawyer who agrees to your wishes. You've now selected a lawyer using your emotions instead of your intelligence.

Maybe you're a dad who's worried about your ongoing role with your children. You may want to look for a lawyer who specializes in fathers' rights. Maybe some parents' rights organizations in your area can give you some referrals. You want to be sure that your lawyer supports ongoing parental involvement of fathers.

Like Your Lawyer

Choosing a divorce lawyer is a lot like choosing a spouse. You want someone you can trust, someone who's smart. You want someone who really listens to you and is honest about what will happen. You want someone who answers your calls, keeps you informed, and is on your side. Sounds like a marriage partner, doesn't it? Indeed, you do want to like—but not love—your lawyer.

You'll probably end up spending a fair amount of time with this person, so listen to your gut as well as your brain. It's extremely important that you trust your lawyer and feel comfortable asking questions. You're under no obligation to hire a lawyer just because you met with that person. If you're intimidated or uncomfortable with the lawyer, look for someone else. You'll have to ask your lawyer a lot of questions and work closely with him or her during the divorce. Make sure you're compatible.

Interviewing Lawyers

You've gotten a list of names from friends, family, the Yellow Pages, and your therapist. Now you're ready to interview some lawyers. How do you start? First of all, call the office for an appointment. Ask whether the lawyer you want to interview charges for an initial consultation. If there's a charge, find out how much. Is it a flat fee? Is it an hourly rate? If the fee is by the clock, you may hurry through the interview to keep the cost down, so that's probably not the best way to get the information you need.

Conflict of Interest

A lawyer can't represent you in your divorce if he or she had previous dealings with your family or your spouse. However, it's okay for the lawyer to represent you if previous contact was with you alone and if that contact did not involve the issues of your marriage.

Some divorcing people meet with certain lawyers in the community just to try to prevent these lawyers from representing their spouses. Ethically, once a lawyer has discussed a divorce with one spouse, he or she is disqualified from representing the other spouse. Here's how it works.

There's a local divorce lawyer known for tough tactics and making divorce cases long and painful. You don't want to hire that lawyer, but you don't want your spouse to hire that lawyer, either. So, you meet with the lawyer and give him or her some information about your marriage. You don't hire the lawyer. Now that lawyer may be disqualified from representing your spouse unless he or she can show that you and the lawyer didn't discuss the substance of your case. While this tactic doesn't always prevent the "barracuda" lawyer from representing your spouse, it may work.

Sometimes a lawyer can't represent you because you and your spouse have worked with another lawyer in the firm. For example, you and your spouse had one of the divorce lawyer's partners draft your wills. This lawyer has obtained information about your assets; therefore, he or she can't represent you unless your spouse says it's okay. Maybe a lawyer in the firm handled a personal injury case for your spouse. That means that none of the lawyers from the firm can represent you without your spouse's agreement.

Be sure to ask how you will be billed. Most lawyers provide a detailed bill every month. Compare the bill against your own records so you can settle any discrepancies as soon as possible.

Busy Lawyers

When you call the lawyer's office to schedule an initial consultation, ask to speak with the lawyer directly. If the lawyer is too busy to talk with you, this probably is a bad sign. It may be a warning the lawyer will be too busy to talk with you after you've hired him or her.

You want to speak directly with the lawyer, so you can briefly outline your case before scheduling a meeting, and confirm that the lawyer handles your kind of case. For example, if you have a custody issue, you need to know whether the lawyer handles custody cases, and whether the lawyer has the time to take one on at this time. You save yourself time and money by finding this out by telephone.

If the lawyer can't take your case, ask for a referral. If the lawyer asks whether you're considering other lawyers, give their names and see if the lawyer recommends others not on your list. Lawyers rarely say bad things about other lawyers. They're more subtle, so try to pick up on the message. If the lawyer suggests names other than the ones you have, the lawyer is telling you that he or she doesn't think too highly of the people on your list.

When lawyers give you referrals, they will give you names of other lawyers they believe are competent and possibly right for you. They won't steer you to someone they believe isn't qualified. They want you to remember they gave you good advice. Follow their suggestions.

Prepare Questions

Review your objectives again as you prepare to interview prospective lawyers. You should plan to interview at least two or three lawyers. Prepare a list of questions to include the following:

What is your lawyering style? You want to know how a lawyer sees him- or herself. You want to know if the lawyer is proud of his or her trial work, the ability to help negotiate a settlement, or perhaps a combination of these skills.

What are your credentials? You want to know how long this lawyer has practiced family law and what is his or her range of experience. In particular, you want to know how much experience the lawyer has with cases like yours.

How busy are you? You want to know whether the lawyer will be available to answer your telephone calls. You want to be sure the lawyer will be the person you talk to, and the person who comes to court with you for all matters, not just the trial.

Will you take the initiative to seek a settlement? It's important that your lawyer stay current with your case and take positive steps to get your issues resolved.

How much do you charge? You need to know how the lawyer charges for his or her work. You want the lawyer to explain the fee agreement in language you can understand. You want the lawyer to be very clear about fees.

Who makes final decisions as to tactics and objectives? It's important to know that you will have the final say on tactics and objectives.

Custody Issues

If you anticipate you'll be dealing with a custody disagreement, you need to find out what experience the lawyer has in this area. When your children's future is at stake, you want a lawyer who has significant experience working with the courts and the experts who work with families. You need a lawyer who can evaluate your chances of obtaining the result you want and who will tell you when you aren't being realistic.

FACT

An important indication that the lawyer knows his or her stuff is the lawyer's willingness to tell it like it is. The knowledgeable, experienced lawyer doesn't shrink from bad news. The lawyer will help you develop reasonable expectations about the future parenting of your children.

Big Money Cases

If you have significant assets, you need to find out whether the lawyer has handled "big money" cases. Is yours the biggest to ever walk into this lawyer's office? Maybe the lawyer doesn't have enough experience in handling complex asset issues to handle your marital estate. You don't want the lawyer to develop expertise at your expense. Rather, you want someone who knows the money experts in town and how to work with them to get an understanding of your situation.

Should You Hire the Hotshot?

Should you select a hotshot big-city lawyer? Your case is in another county, but you're attracted by this lawyer's reputation. Consider using an attorney who lives in your county. A local lawyer knows the judges and the other lawyers, and any quirks of the local practice. Big-city hotshots often aren't well received in the country. Mr. Local Lawyer probably will enjoy beating up on Ms. Big-City Hotshot. If you're paying your fancy lawyer's travel costs at a significant hourly rate, your spouse may take advantage of this by setting lots of hearings that eventually will wear you down financially and lead you to settle for less just to be done.

Should You Hire a Gladiator?

If you want to trash your spouse in court, you'll need to know whether the lawyer supports such courtroom tactics. Most good divorce lawyers don't. Chances are you'll calm down after a bit and become more interested in getting the divorce over than in getting your spouse. Then you may not want to take every little issue to court. At that point, you'll have to figure out a way to shed the shark. You may find that other lawyers are reluctant to take your case when they learn the name of your current lawyer. Other lawyers will figure that if you hired Ms. Gladiator and can't get along with her, you're really bad news. Who you hire usually says something about you.

If you want to try to stay out of court, you should find a lawyer who knows about alternative dispute resolution, and how the lawyer feels about it. This is a relatively new approach to divorce.

Some lawyers are uncomfortable bringing in a third party to help resolve issues. They believe adding a third party undermines their control of the case. Others are knowledgeable and very supportive of this approach, knowing it has the potential to keep costs down and dignity intact. They may do mediation and collaborative law as well as litigate when necessary. Ask them.

Does Gender Matter?

In a metropolitan area, gender isn't an issue because as many good men as good women practice family law. In that locale the real issues for you are competence and personality of your lawyer. However, in some rural jurisdictions, a "good old boy" mentality that believes women should be at home with the kids still may exist, so check this out if your case will be heard in a rural court. By the same token, hiring a woman probably won't give you an edge in a custody case, nor will it make you look better, if you're male, if your spouse has accused you of domestic abuse. Good lawyers are good lawyers, regardless of gender.

Legal Insurance

If you believe you need a lawyer or some legal advice but are worried about the cost, you may want to consider purchasing a prepaid legal plan. For a manageable sum, you can purchase a year's worth of legal help, including phone consultations, drafting of legal documents, and preparation of a will. Prepaid legal insurance will get you a discount on attorney's fees for your divorce. You can find several options for legal insurance in your local Yellow Pages or on the Internet.

ALERT!

Divorce invalidates your will, so you will need a new one after the divorce. Prepaid legal insurance will cover the creation of this important document.

If you choose such a plan, you can use only the lawyers who belong to the plan. If you only need some advice over the telephone or someone to review your agreement, this might be an affordable way to get legal advice.

It's a Small (Divorce Court) World

Good divorce lawyers in a community know each another. They're a tightly knit group: They see each another often in court; they belong to the local family law section of the Bar Association; they attend continuing education courses together; and they may have a drink together after court to talk about cases and the stresses of their profession. Not only do the lawyers know each other, they also know the family court judges.

This is good. You want your lawyer to know the judge who will decide your divorce. This doesn't mean the judge will be biased in your favor. It means your lawyer will be able to tell you what to expect and how to present issues in the way most likely to get the results you want. So don't be alarmed if the lawyers greet each other or the judge by first names. The fact these folks are friends doesn't mean collusion or bias will occur. It simply reflects the practice of this specialized area of the law.

Lawyer Teamwork

Hope that your spouse hires a good attorney, too. Nothing louses up your divorce more than incompetence—on either side. If both lawyers are good at their jobs, they can do a better job for you and at less cost.

You and your spouse may consider hiring one lawyer to act as scrivener for your divorce. Be aware that this lawyer can only represent one of you (the petitioner or the plaintiff). It is unethical for one lawyer to represent both parties in a divorce. And probably not a good idea, to boot.

Suppose you hire a highly competent attorney, and you and your lawyer develop an action plan that makes good sense. On the other hand, your spouse hires Mr. Wet-Behind-the-Ears, who is full of good intentions but has no clear sense of the case or how to proceed. So he brings motions, makes all kinds of burdensome demands for documents, and, in general, escalates the animosity and cost of the divorce. A good lawyer on your spouse's side will see the wisdom in your plan and probably add some wisdom of his or her own. Everyone can work as a team in reaching a resolution appropriate for you and your spouse.

Let the Buyer Beware

A few words of caution: Beware of the lawyer who promises you all the things you ask for, because it's unlikely you'll get everything. You want a lawyer who helps you develop realistic expectations. The lawyer who promises more than he or she can deliver often will end up being evasive and difficult to reach by telephone when the day of reckoning arrives.

Beware the lawyer who is "very, very busy," but who "has an associate" who will work on your case. Chances are good you'll never see the lawyer you thought you hired until the day of trial, despite your best efforts to do so.

ALERT!

While you do want the lawyer to explain your options, you should be the one who decides which ones to pursue. You want to stay in charge. Remember, you hired the lawyer, and that lawyer works for you. Don't let your lawyer lead you away from your own carefully thought-out choices.

Beware the lawyer who tries to talk you out of a well-reasoned position, saying things like, "I can get you way more than that" or "You're entitled to permanent alimony" when you don't even want alimony. This is your divorce, after all.

Unless your marriage has been brief, you have no children, and you own minimal property, you need a lawyer to explain the divorce process, the law, and what result you can reasonably expect based on the specific facts of your situation. You need to use great care in selecting a lawyer who is an expert in divorce, one you trust and with whom you can talk. You need to feel that your lawyer listens to you and has your best interests in mind. You'll be working closely with your lawyer over the course of your divorce, so you need to feel comfortable and protected by the lawyer you choose.

Chapter 5

Hiring and Working with Your Lawyer

You've interviewed several lawyers and decided to hire one. Now get ready to talk money, facts, and strategy. This chapter gives you the lowdown on working with your lawyer. By knowing what to expect and how to work together, you can have a positive and productive experience.

Money Talk

It's time to talk money. Lawyers charge by the hour, and no doubt fees will vary among the lawyers you interview. Cheaper isn't necessarily less good, and expensive isn't necessarily better. You should hire the expertise you need for your case, so if your case is simple and straightforward, you don't need the local custody expert or the big-estate guy. An experienced family law lawyer whose practice is primarily the uncomplicated divorce will serve you ably. If you do have a tough case, then by all means hire the expertise you need, and be ready to pay for it.

Lawyers usually ask for a retainer—a down payment—to be applied to the hours put in on your case. Many divorce lawyers ask you to sign a retainer agreement, which is a document that outlines the rules you and your attorney will follow in handling your divorce. The agreement should clearly state the lawyer's hourly rate and the rates of paralegals and secretarial staff. Most lawyers charge in quarter-hour increments. This means that a five-minute task or telephone call will be billed as fifteen minutes. Some lawyers also charge double for telephone calls taken at their homes. The agreement should be clear about how the lawyer bills for telephone calls, travel to court, copies, and faxes. A provision stating the lawyer will fire you as a client if you don't keep your bill current probably will be included.

ALERT!

If your attorney asks you to sign a retainer agreement, be sure to read it carefully. If you don't understand something, ask for an explanation. During your divorce, it's important that you never sign something you don't understand.

Sample Fee/Retainer Agreement

Here is what a fee/retainer agreement looks like. Obviously, the dollar amounts will correspond with what the lawyer you're hiring charges.

Fee Agreement

1. <u>Purpose</u>

By this agreement I hire <u>Excellent Law Firm</u> to represent me and to be my lawyers in my marriage dissolution proceeding. I understand that <u>Lawyer's Name</u> will be my primary attorney and that she may use other attorneys in the firm to assist her.

2. <u>Fees</u>

(A) Hourly and per-occurrence fees

Legal work done on my file by <u>Lawyer's Name</u> will be billed at <u>$300</u> per hour. Other lawyers who work on my case will bill at their normal hourly rate. Legal assistants who work on my case will bill at <u>$75</u> per hour. Law clerks will bill at <u>$75</u> per hour. Secretarial work will be billed at <u>$20</u> an hour or will not be billed. Fees will be updated annually, and I will be notified of any rate changes. Billing is done in quarter-hour segments.

I also will be billed for any copying and faxing done for my case.

The hourly fees include the time my attorney and staff spend traveling to and from court, depositions, meeting with experts, etc.

I will be responsible for all filing fees.

I will be billed for all telephone calls generated by my case.

I have ten (10) days to object to items on my monthly bill. If I do not object, I will waive any subsequent objection to the fees on the statement. [This means you need to review your bill as soon as you get it and raise any objections right away. Otherwise, you'll be deemed to have agreed to all charges.]

(B) Retainer [The following are three variations of the retainer. Your lawyer may use one or more of these, so read the retainer provisions carefully.]

Variation 1: I will pay you a retainer of <u>$5,000</u> when I sign this contract. You will use these funds as an advance to be applied to the time spent on my case.

When the retainer is exhausted, you will bill me monthly, and I will pay the monthly statement in full within thirty (30) days of receiving it.

If there is money remaining from the retainer when our attorney/client relationship ends, you will refund any balance to me. [This retainer is the least beneficial to the lawyer because once the money is used up, the lawyer has no recourse but to bill for his or her time.]

Variation 2: I agree to pay <u>Excellent Law Firm $5,000</u> in advance, which will be held by the law firm in its trust account to secure my payments.

<u>Excellent</u> will send me an itemized bill each month. I will pay the bill in full each month within thirty (30) days of receipt. If I do not pay in full and on time, <u>Excellent</u> has the right to refuse to provide future legal services on my case and to withdraw as my lawyer.

Should <u>Excellent</u> withdraw, it may pay itself any outstanding amounts I owe for services up to the date of withdrawal. If the <u>$5,000</u> advance payment exceeds what I owe, <u>Excellent</u> will return any surplus. [The fact that the law firm has $5,000 of your money in its account may encourage you to use your lawyer's time well and to pay your bills. Your lawyer can withdraw if you don't pay, and take what you owe from the money in the lawyer's account, so you're not ahead if you don't pay. You lose your lawyer and your money.]

ALERT!

Do not lie to your lawyer, ever. Do not "forget" important information. Do not try to blame your spouse for something you did.

Variation 3: In addition to the hourly fees, I will pay a nonrefundable retainer fee of <u>$5,000</u> that, when paid, immediately becomes a fee that has been earned by my attorney. This is a minimum fee. It is paid in consideration of my attorney reserving and committing time to be available in representing me, thereby precluding my attorney from accepting other clients and employment, including potentially conflicting interests. If more time is spent on this case than this fee would cover at the stated hourly rates, <u>Excellent</u> will bill me monthly, and I will pay in full within thirty (30) days of receipt. [Even if your case settles after your lawyer has put in three hours of time, or $900 in his hour fees, your lawyer keeps your $5,000. This may not be as bad as it looks. Maybe this lawyer is an expert in an area in which you had issues. Maybe hiring this expert lawyer helped get the case settled faster. Your lawyer still will have to participate in drafting the final documents, so maybe it was a good idea to hire the expert attorney after all.]

(C) Premium fee

The final fee may include such an additional fee as justified by the complexity, difficulty, and results of the case. [It's unethical for divorce lawyers to charge a contingency fee; that is, a fee based on a percentage of whatever money is awarded to you. To get around this, some lawyers charge a performance bonus—extra money to them if they get you an outstanding result. This premium fee appears to pass muster with the ethics people.]

3. Decisions

I reserve the right to make all important decisions regarding my case. Excellent Law Firm cannot settle the case without my permission. [And the law firm is obligated to disclose any settlement offers to you.]

4. Communications

Excellent will keep me informed about what is happening in my case and will send me copies of papers it sends out or receives. When I have to make an important decision, Excellent will explain my choices and offer me advice.

I will inform Excellent Law Firm of any change in my address, telephone number, e-mail address, employment, and circumstances. I will not withhold information from my attorneys.

5. Problems

If I am unhappy with the manner in which Excellent Law Firm is handling my case, I will first explain the problem to Excellent. If we cannot resolve our differences, I can terminate this agreement and (a) hire another lawyer, (b) represent myself, or (c) choose not to pursue the case. [In a divorce, you can't stop the case unilaterally unless you're the petitioner—the instigator—and no answer has been filed by your spouse. So, in reality, you're limited to hiring another lawyer or representing yourself.]

If we terminate our relationship for any reason, I owe the fees generated to that point.

6. Responsibility for and Collection of Fees

I am ultimately responsible for my fees. The court may order the other side to pay all or part of my fees, and, if they do so, I will receive credit for same. If they don't pay, I can either pay my attorney to try to collect them, or pay them myself. [You are responsible for paying your lawyer, no matter that the court ordered your spouse to pay.]

I grant to my attorney a lien on all property, money, assets, spousal maintenance, or things of value that are recovered, obtained, preserved, or protected for me in the lawsuit. Any amounts I owe shall be payable from them. [If your lawyer places a lien on your homestead real estate (the marital residence), the lawyer can't foreclose the lien and force you to sell your house. However, when the house is sold, you must pay the lawyer from the sale proceeds.]

7. Capacity

I am of sound mind and body. I am not under the influence of alcohol or mind-altering drugs. I have read this agreement and understand it. I have had any parts that I did not initially understand explained to me. [Make sure you do this. Don't worry about looking dumb. Better a little dumb now than a lot poorer later.]

I approve and accept this contract. I agree to be bound by its terms.

Dated   Client Signature

[If a nonrefundable retainer is used, a second signature like the one following probably will be required.]

I understand that the retainer fee paid herein will not be held in a trust account, and I will not receive a refund if I terminate the services of Excellent Law Firm.

Date   Client Signature

After you've drawn a huge breath and signed the retainer agreement, you're officially your lawyer's client. And now that you've agreed to pay your lawyer huge sums of money, you need to do everything possible to use his or her time well.

Tell the Truth

It's of utmost importance that you tell your lawyer the truth, the whole truth, and nothing but the truth—no matter how ugly it may be. This often is hard to do, but it's the only way your lawyer can competently represent you. Your lawyer has to have all the facts. Nothing hurts your case more than for your lawyer to be surprised by information the other side produces. If your attorney is caught off guard and unprepared, your credibility with your lawyer will be permanently damaged. If you have skeletons in your closet, it's better to tell your lawyer before you have dealings with the other side. Your lawyer also can give you better advice with all the facts.

Write a complete history of the relationship with your spouse, including any relevant time before marriage. Today many people live together or begin to commingle their assets before they marry. For example, it's not uncommon for an unmarried couple to buy a house together, which may affect the characterization of their marriage assets. Give a complete history to your lawyer and review it with him or her, leaving nothing out. Have your lawyer explain which are the legally important pieces of the relationship, as compared to the emotional highlights.

Limit Your Calls

Limit telephone calls to your lawyer. Try not to call when you're angry or upset because you'll have a hard time focusing on issues. Make a written list of the things you want to discuss before you call, so you remember to ask all your questions. Write down your lawyer's answer, so you don't have to ask the same questions again. When your lawyer tells you how the law will affect a certain issue, you may respond, "but that's not fair." Remember, your lawyer is the messenger. Don't shoot the messenger who brings bad news.

It's best to keep a record of your phone calls to and from your lawyer. Compare your records to the monthly bills you receive. Though it's not likely that your lawyer will intentionally double-bill you, mistakes are made.

Keep Your Lawyer Informed

Be cordial to your lawyer's staff. They're the ones who put your calls through, so you want them on your side. Lawyers talk to their staff members and they'll hear about it if you're nasty to someone. The next time, that staff person may put your phone message on the bottom of the pile. This advice applies when you go to court, too. You and your lawyer should always be courteous to the judge's staff because they'll be quick to tell the judge who has been nasty or arrogant.

Do as much of the legwork as possible, because it costs a lot of money for your lawyer and legal staff to collect data that you can easily get yourself. Even though you may be operating at less than full efficiency, you can call your tax preparer for tax returns. You can get your credit card records. You can pull all your investment account statements. It will keep you busy with some nonintellectual tasks. Pay your lawyer to interpret documents, not merely collect them.

Keep your lawyer up-to-date. Notify your lawyer if you move, change telephone or fax numbers, or e-mail addresses. Your lawyer needs to stay in touch with you, so don't make the lawyer take extra time (that you'll end up paying for) to hunt you down.

Keep the lawyer up to speed about important developments in your life such as a change in your employment or a change in where your child lives. Keeping your lawyer up-to-date will help the lawyer represent you well.

Can't Get No Satisfaction?

If you're dissatisfied with the way your lawyer is handling your case, first take a look at the problems. Not returning telephone calls? Maybe you're calling too often and for the wrong reasons. (Your lawyer's not a therapist.) You don't like the answers to your questions? Your lawyer has no plan of action? This is indeed worrisome. If you and your lawyer can't agree on a plan and begin to implement it, perhaps you need to look elsewhere.

Getting a Second (or Third) Opinion

Perhaps this would be a good time to get a second opinion. You always can talk to another lawyer about your case. It may be that your lawyer is giving you legally correct answers to your questions, and you don't like the content of those answers. It may be the plan you want to adopt is impossible or unrealistic. If two lawyers tell you so, you may actually hear them!

FACT

You should be treated with respect. If you're uncomfortable with the way your lawyer talks to or treats you, you ought to consider looking elsewhere. A divorce can be a long and trying process, so you should have someone on your side you are comfortable with and can trust.

Firing Your Lawyer

You can, of course, fire your lawyer at any time. You probably won't have too much trouble finding a second lawyer. However, if you've run through three lawyers, a fourth is going to think long and hard before agreeing to represent you. Either you or the facts are troubling. And, timing is a consideration. For example, it's not a good idea to fire your lawyer the week before you're scheduled to go to trial. Your new lawyer may or may not be able to get a continuance (an adjournment to a future date) from the court for time to prepare.

Reporting Unethical Behavior

If your lawyer proposes a course of action you believe is unethical, you can report him or her to the Lawyers Board of Professional Responsibility. This board is made up of lawyers who oversee the behavior of practicing lawyers in your state. They review complaints from clients, other lawyers, judges, and citizens about the behavior of licensed attorneys, and they have the authority to discipline lawyers. They can also recommend that a lawyer lose his or her license—be disbarred—for unethical behavior.

More ethics complaints come out of family law cases than from any others—probably because divorce cases are highly emotional. Most complaints are probably made because lawyers have a hard time telling clients bad news, so clients' expectations are not met. Some lawyers do behave unethically. Fortunately, it's only very few, and you'll be doing everyone a favor by reporting them.

ALERT!

Be sure the behavior you complain about warrants discipline. Just because you didn't get the results your lawyer promised isn't enough to file a complaint. Unless your lawyer came to court unprepared or under the influence of drugs or alcohol, you probably don't have a case. Reviewing complaints and writing the responses are very time consuming. Make sure your complaint is real.

Disputing Fees

You can challenge your lawyer's bill. Most states have a fee arbitration program where you and your lawyer present your arguments about the bill. If you use fee arbitration, you both agree to abide by the arbitrators' decision.

You can also challenge the fees in court. If your attorney has kept good records and you signed a fee agreement, especially one in which you have to object within a few days or deem that you approve the bill, the court probably will award the lawyer fees that he or she can document. Especially in divorce cases, fees aren't adjusted by results obtained. This means you can't get a reduced fee if your lawyer didn't get you custody of your children.

If you chose your lawyer well, you probably won't have problems with communication or strategy. And if you do your share of the work, you'll keep your lawyer's fees manageable and won't have to fight over them. If you listen to your lawyer and accept his or her advice, you'll have reasonable expectations and be able to negotiate with the other side. Working with your lawyer can be a good experience. (E)

Chapter 6

What Courts Can and Can't Do

Many divorcing couples are mistaken about what courts can do for them. They expect a judge to right the wrongs of the marriage. However, the court process deals only with the legal part of a divorce. Judges and attorneys work with the law— they don't do therapy.

What Is a Divorce, Anyway?

A secular divorce—as opposed to a religious divorce—is a legal restructuring of a family. Many states now call divorce a marriage "dissolution," and some attorneys refer to divorce as a "disillusionment," which is probably even more accurate.

For the couple who has been married but a short time and has no children, divorce usually means cutting the ties that bind and moving on. The couple has some regrets, some sadness and, perhaps, some anger. Mostly, the couple decides the marriage isn't working and isn't healthy for either of them, so they divide their possessions, draft their papers, and begin a new life. Their restructuring is basically an ending of the relationship. If these people meet again in later months or years, it's usually by chance and usually feels okay.

Children Complicate Divorce

For people with children, divorce is more complex. The role of parent is for a lifetime, and for that reason, restructuring a family with children can't simply be an ending of the adult relationship and moving on, because the family will need to have contact for years to come.

Children see divorce as redesigning their relationship with their parents: "On Tuesdays I'm with Mom; on Wednesdays I'm with Dad." Regardless, they expect to continue relationships with their parents because, for the children, the concept of "family" doesn't change, only the structure does. Even so, children worry a lot about losing a parent through divorce. Entire books have been written on the anxieties of children of divorce. Sometimes one parent tries to punish the other by undermining the ex-spouse's relationship with the children, perhaps by putting up roadblocks to communication by refusing to let the children spend time with the other parent or by saying ugly things about him or her to the children. Some children lose years of knowing a parent, and vice versa. Sometimes a relationship is lost forever, a devastating loss to both parent and child.

Family Restructuring

An ideal family restructuring contains a plan for rearing the children in a cooperative, supportive way. This includes an ongoing financial arrangement for the new households that divides assets in a way that eases financial worries. If there aren't enough assets to overcome financial worries, the burden at least should be shared. That way, your energy can go to living your life and raising your children.

ALERT!

Courts can't make parents behave in a cooperative, supportive way. Only the parents themselves can choose to do this. When parents behave badly, the only option left to the court is to impose a structure on the parents for sharing the responsibility for the children. How the parents behave within that structure is beyond the power of the court.

Ending a Long-Term Marriage

Couples ending a long-term marriage need to balance many competing considerations. They may have adult children who are outside the authority of a divorce court, but law does not mirror life here. Children are staying in the nest longer and coming home "for a while" more often than they did in the past. Courts usually consider children to be adults when they have completed high school, which means the court lacks the ability to require parents to support their children through college or trade school, even when this was clearly a part of the marital plan.

A long-term marriage will more likely have the traditional roles of breadwinner and homemaker. For the homemaker, the prospect of old age without money is very scary, especially because people are living longer. It's very difficult for a woman in her fifties to get a job that pays reasonably well. Even then, she'll have only a few years to generate retirement savings.

Couples with adult children still living at home are faced with providing support, even though these children are legally adults. They need to finance two homes. They need to make arrangements for retirement. They need to set up separate, coordinated estate plans that operate for the benefit of their children and grandchildren. Older divorcing couples have issues that are different than couples whose children are under eighteen.

Parents Should Behave Respectfully

All parents need to divorce in a respectful, dignified way because they still will have to deal with each other as parents and grandparents. Their children will experience milestones of their own when they graduate from college, marry, and have their own children. The family still will celebrate birthdays and holidays—events children will want to be festive, not clouded by their parents' anger or bitterness over the past. Your children will want both of you to participate.

Presumably, most parents don't really want to spoil their children's big moments or expend negative energy every time they have to deal with their ex-spouse. Families need to get through the divorce and get on with their lives.

FACT

The court is limited to setting a visitation schedule and ordering financial support, and has no jurisdiction over how well complainants conduct themselves. The judge can encourage the parents to behave respectfully but has no ability to force them to do so.

Reality Rear-Ends Expectations

People end up frustrated and upset with the divorce process because they have expectations about the process that bear little semblance to the reality of going to court. People going through a divorce often use words like *fair*, *win*, and *punish*. It wasn't fair that the marriage failed. Why should the divorce be fair? Perhaps the words *fair* and *just* get confused. What about winning or losing? Nobody wins in court.

A Closer Look

Let's take a closer look at these unmet expectations. First of all, what is a court, really? It's a place where an elected or appointed person, the judge, makes decisions when you can't make them for yourselves. A judge makes decisions by applying the laws governing the issues in each case. Legislatures and appellate courts devise these laws, and many of the laws put limits on the trial judge's decision-making power. Even so, the judge's decisions will have a tremendous impact on your lives.

See You in Court

Couples often decide their marriage is over in the context of significant conflict. For many people it's not easy to have a rational discussion about ending a relationship. The relationship has hit the rocks because of factors that generate bad feelings: unmanageable debt, addictions to substances, gambling, spending, extramarital affairs, and clashing philosophies. On top of these causes lies an agonizing sense of failure or a sense of worthlessness. People beginning a divorce are angry, upset, and often irrational. Often, the parting shot from one party to the other is something like "See you in court!" What expectations lie behind this challenge? Many people believe courts will fix what is broken, shape up the wrongdoer, understand the issues, and see fairness as they do. Not likely.

The reality you must come to accept is that you're better off staying out of court. Court can be draining, both emotionally and financially. If it's at all possible for you to negotiate with your spouse, do so instead of trying to punish him or her with a court battle.

Reality Check

First of all, the judge probably was appointed to a vacant position by the governor, as a political favor. The judge probably didn't get the job because he or she was a sensitive, understanding person with a strong psychology or social work background and a strong interest in helping people through a divorce. Although judges have to run for election in many states, they usually run after being appointed and have the advantage of being incumbents.

Second, laws governing divorce limit what judges can do. Divorce laws are specific in most states, and most now have "no-fault" divorce laws that cite "irretrievable breakdown" or "irreconcilable differences" as the basis for the divorce. State laws spell out what factors judges should use in deciding custody of children and visitation, in determining what is marital property and how it should be divided, and in awarding spousal maintenance—formerly called alimony—and child support. The judge has to follow your state's rules unless he or she can show a good reason not to. The laws are one size fits all even though each divorce has its own particular set of problems requiring its own set of solutions.

So, you have a judge who probably has no training in how to deal with people going through a divorce and laws that don't consider the emotions of these people. The trouble is, the divorcing couple doesn't know about these limitations when hurling that "See you in court" challenge. As a rule, divorcing couples expect a judge to right the wrongs of the marriage using laws and the legal system. The result? Expectations and reality that just don't fit.

It's important to know that the laws of divorce don't deal with the feelings of people who are getting divorced. There are no provisions in the divorce laws to help mend your sadness or anger that the marriage is ending.

A Judge Can't Fix Your Spouse

Let's take a look at how "fair," "win," and "punish" fit into a system of courts and law. Suppose you go to see a lawyer to begin the divorce process. You tell the lawyer you've been through hell in your marriage and now you want out. You want a fair result—and by "fair" you really mean you want to win, and you want to punish your spouse for all you have suffered. You want the lawyer to draft court papers that will make your spouse feel bad, look bad, get his or her just deserts from the judge, and then reform.

You may well be able to make your spouse feel bad. After all, you'll feel pretty bad yourself, remembering and reliving all the ugly pieces of the marriage. Plus, your spouse can respond to your papers with his or her version of the marriage, which, in turn, probably won't make you feel very good. It will probably make you darned mad, and you'll want to file more papers with the court in response to your spouse's papers. Then your spouse will respond. Then you'll respond. On and on you go, generating more legal fees with each exchange.

Paper Merry-Go-Round

The papers you and your lawyer prepare and file with the court may well make your spouse look bad, but a judge doesn't care much. The judge's job is to implement the law, and the law has little to say about good and bad. So what you've gained, after expending a significant amount of energy—all negative—taking paper potshots at your spouse, is amassing a pile of papers for the judge, running up large legal fees, and making yourself good and mad.

Remember, you're hoping this paper mountain will lead to a judge shaping up your spouse. The judge has your papers, but the judge has your spouse's papers, too, denying he or she's a louse and pointing out that you're no angel, either. The judge doesn't know you two from Adam. And if the judge did, the judge couldn't ethically hear the case. All the judge knows about you is what's in your papers. The law doesn't empower the judge to shape anybody up. And besides, if you weren't able to do it, why do you think anyone else will be successful?

The Judge from Another Planet

So, the judge issues an order based upon the papers in the file, setting the rules to be followed while the divorce is in process. When you read it, you wonder what planet the judge lives on. The order bears absolutely no relationship to the reality of your life. Furthermore, no one is motivated to reform, and the possibility of reasonable negotiation between you and your spouse has become extremely unlikely.

"It's not fair," you cry.

Unrealistic Expectations

Think about the papers you and your spouse filed with the court. What was in those papers? They contained selective information about your lives and character designed to persuade the judge to make certain decisions. You compiled your list of complaints about your spouse, carefully editing out any information that might be construed in a positive light. Your spouse responded with another list of horrors.

Suppose you have children and one of the issues before the court is a temporary arrangement for caring for them. After you and your spouse have told the judge all the terrible things about each other you can remember (or create), the judge has precious little information to devise a workable parenting plan. The parents, who have all the information, give the judge, a stranger, only selected bits and pieces. The judge can't fill in the blanks that you left. The judge can't always determine who's lying and who's telling the truth. As a consequence, the judge's order often doesn't work and increases your frustration and misery. That means you've just spent a lot of money to obtain this unworkable order.

ALERT!

The judge can't make good decisions without accurate and complete information. Bad decisions are most often the result of too little good information.

Again, why does this happen? Because you, the divorcing couple, have inaccurate expectations about the court process.

Just the Facts, Ma'am

Fairness and winning are two of the most abused words in divorce court. Most of the time when someone says, "It's not fair," that person really means "I didn't win," because most people define fairness as getting the results they want. However, courts deal with justice and with decisions. Justice means properly applying the law to the facts before the court; a court decision means resolving the issues you and your spouse presented in your papers. Nobody wins in divorce court. Beware those who tell you otherwise! There is no more fairness in court than there is in life.

Too often divorcing couples have mistaken expectations of what the court process is about. The court process deals only with the legal part of a divorce; that is, the part addressed in laws. But divorcing couples often are much more concerned with the emotional part of the divorce. The emotional part of the divorce is just as important as the legal part, to be sure. However, the legal system is the wrong place to address emotional issues. Judges and attorneys work with the laws enacted by the legislature. They don't have the skills and training to do therapy, and should not be entrusted with this important piece of the uncoupling process.

FACT

Most communities have skilled therapists who truly can help the parties address the emotional issues of the divorce. They, not the court, should deal with the psychological impact of getting divorced.

The Court's Perspective

Look at it from the court's perspective. Angry, divorcing people in significant conflict bring issues to court because they want judges to solve their problems. At the very least they want judges to be the tiebreaker on issues they can't seem to resolve.

Selective Information

Divorcing people spend a lot of money, time, and energy preparing court papers with their lawyers. They provide selective information about themselves and the other guy. Some of that information may be untrue. (It's hard to believe, but some people lie in court.) Sometimes when both parties tell the court about an incident, the only way a judge knows they're talking about the same thing is that they have the same date, time, and location! For sure, they can't remember anything good about the person they once thought enough of to marry, have children with, and live with for all those years.

The court—the stranger—reads the papers. Sometimes a judge is tempted to tell the parties, "I've read your papers. Based on what you've said about each other, I've decided neither of you should be entrusted with the care of your children. I'm calling child protection to place them in foster care."

Relying on a Stranger

The information provided to the judge simply confuses rather than enlightens. It's impossible for a stranger to make a useful decision about other people's lives using information provided in a litigation setting. The couple that litigates ends up angrier, poorer, and forced to live with an unworkable court order. Again, why does this happen? Because divorcing parties have unreasonable and inaccurate expectations about the court process.

This same kind of scenario can play at any stage of the divorce. While the divorce is pending, under that unworkable order, you may come back to the court to get the order changed or to enforce it. You may bring another matter before the court. You may seek a final resolution of all issues from the court. Every time you bring your issues to court, you're turning over the decision-making authority to a stranger who has to rely on your information to make the decisions.

Not only do you lose significant amounts of control when taking your divorce to court, but you also pay for that loss of control. If you absolutely must go to trial, you may want to collect data, or do spreadsheets for your case, to save a little money. Talk to your lawyer about the possibilities.

Taking a Different Route

There is light at the end of the tunnel, however. Now that you know a judge can't fix what's broken and doesn't care what a louse your spouse is, you need to take a different approach. After all, you're an intelligent, if a bit angry, person who knows more than you think about this divorce thing. For sure, you know lots more about your family than the judge does. Why can't you, your spouse, and the lawyers negotiate a resolution of the issues at hand?

The advantages of negotiating a settlement of your divorce are significant: You don't run up huge bills drafting papers the judge doesn't want to read. You don't get your blood pressure up to dangerous levels. You do stay in control. You do end up with a document based on the reality of your situation. You do end up with a plan that works. (E)

Chapter 7

Alternative Dispute Resolution

You and your spouse can resolve your issues outside of court, because you're the ones who have the information needed to make the decisions. If you make the decisions, you'll put your energies into making those decisions work. Plus, you'll stay out of court.

You Have Alternatives

It's very important to know what you want from a divorce. You need to decide two things: the result (parenting, property, financial support) and the resolution process to get that result. After you've read this chapter, you'll be able to compare and contrast two dispute resolution processes—alternative dispute resolution and litigation. Think of dispute resolution as a range of possibilities, from you being totally in charge of decision-making to putting the decisions completely in the hands of a judge.

You've got three choices for how to resolve your disputes while still staying in control of the decision-making.

- **Negotiation.** If you and your spouse negotiate an agreement on how to divide your assets, parent your children, and support two households, you are totally in charge.
- **Negotiation with lawyers.** If you add lawyers to the process, you and your lawyers will try to resolve the issues, but you'll still be mostly in charge, although the lawyers may influence your decisions.
- **Mediation.** If your lawyers suggest mediation, you'll add another player—a mediator—who will meet with you and your spouse, and sometimes your lawyers, to try to resolve your issues.

In all three cases, you and your spouse will still be the decision-makers, but in two cases you'll be helped by professionals.

If you're unable to resolve your issues using negotiation or mediation, you'll have to give up your decision-making authority and look to someone else to do the job. Here you've got two choices:

- **Arbitration.** This means you, your spouse, and the lawyers select an arbitrator to resolve the issues you're unable to resolve yourselves. While you do choose the arbitrator, this person makes the decisions, so you don't have final say.
- **Court Trial.** If you don't want to use arbitration, your last choice is to turn the case over to a judge who will decide the issues. You don't get to choose the judge, so the decision-making is totally out of your hands.

When you're making the decision of how to proceed with the divorce, try to keep your emotions out of the decision-making process. If you're hurt or angry, you'll most likely want to punish your spouse by taking him or her to trial, but this may not be in your best interests.

Negotiation

In dispute resolution by negotiation, you and your spouse sit down and work out your settlement together; then you take your agreement to your lawyers for their input. Each of you should have a lawyer unless your marriage has been very short, you have minimal assets, and you have no kids. The lawyers may tell you that some of your agreements are not in your long-term best interests and that the law would provide a different result. They also may point out that you're missing some important information such as the value of certain assets.

Armed with new information, you and your spouse meet again, determine just what additional information you need, set a schedule to get it, and set a date to meet again. You meet again with your documents and negotiate some more. Finally, you reach an agreement that you and your lawyers agree is acceptable. Your lawyers put the deal into a written agreement, which ultimately becomes the final divorce decree. Sound impossible? Lots of divorcing couples really do this. Give it a try.

Keeping Control

By negotiating, you and your spouse stay totally in charge. Negotiation works best when you and your spouse still have some trust, you both know what your assets are, and when the power balance is pretty equal. Effective negotiations require the ability to communicate and a willingness to exchange relevant and reliable information, so you have to be able to talk with each other and stay focused on issues. You have to avoid blaming and attacking each other. If you can do these things, you can probably come up with creative solutions to various issues that enable both of you to get what you want.

The main advantages to negotiation are that you avoid stress, end up with an agreement that works, and lay the foundation for working together in the future if you have children.

Negotiations with Lawyers

If you and your spouse can't work it out at the kitchen table, each of you will need to hire a lawyer and detail what each of you wants from the divorce. The two of you and your lawyers will then meet to decide how to proceed and what information each of you needs to provide in order to discuss settlement. You set a date for another meeting, by which time everyone should have had a chance to review the information exchanged according to the plan developed. At this meeting, the four of you sit around the conference table in one of the lawyer's offices and negotiate a deal.

This process usually takes several meetings because you often don't have all the information you need by the second meeting, or a new issue comes up that requires additional information, and then you'll need some time to digest that information and the settlement proposals from the other side. If you have an emotional reaction to your spouse's settlement proposal, step away from your emotions and look at the proposal objectively—it's the bottom line that matters. This simple negotiation process is used successfully in many divorces.

Negotiations by Lawyers

If you and your spouse can't sit at the same table without taking cheap shots at each other, put your lawyers at the conference table to negotiate while you and your spouse are separated in other rooms. Again, these negotiations require the exchange of information about your assets and income before agreements can be made. Your lawyer will talk with you periodically as he or she and the other lawyer work out the issues, to make sure you're in agreement. Finally, a settlement will be reached, but as you can imagine, this process is somewhat cumbersome. The message has to travel from lawyer to client back to lawyer and back to the negotiating table. Sometimes the message gets lost or distorted moving from person to person, so sometimes it has to be done all over again.

Some lawyers really like the approach of keeping clients separated. It keeps the parties calm, and it keeps the lawyers in charge. While you have to give up most of the control, sometimes this is the only possible alternative to going to trial. This is especially true when one of the parties is very angry or very emotional. Although you have less control, you'll still decide the terms of the final agreement.

Levels of Control

As noted, you're definitely in charge when you negotiate face to face with your spouse. You have less control when you bring lawyers into the picture. In fact, your lawyers may straight out tell you to do certain things or to hold out for certain results that you may not even want. Be careful here. Remember this is your divorce.

Negotiation is probably the most common process used in getting divorced. The more complicated your assets, the more people will be involved in the negotiations. You may need to have your accountant (who should be certified), a business appraiser, a residential real estate appraiser, a vocational evaluator, and a child custody expert participate in negotiations. You can't reach agreements without information—information about your children's needs, your assets, and the law—but the greater the number of players in the negotiations, the higher the cost of the process. Even so, the negotiation process involving experts will still cost less than going to court.

Collaborative Law

Collaborative law is a form of negotiation with lawyers, but it differs from traditional forms. Collaborative lawyers are committed to assisting clients reach a settlement without going to court. In fact, they're so committed to this concept they require all players to sign a contract stating they will withdraw from representation if the case cannot be settled or if one of the parties doesn't play by the rules of collaborative practice. Collaborative lawyers describe the process as making a commitment to a principled, negotiated settlement without the threat or use of power.

FACT

The underlying tenet of collaborative law is that it takes away the threat of going to court—the ultimate hammer. If the parties agree to stay out of court, they will need to put all of their energies into the settlement process.

The Parties Agree

In collaborative law, parties agree that if an expert is needed, they will select a qualified neutral expert, and that any neutral expert used in collaboration can't be called as a witness if the case ultimately goes to trial. This means that you can use the expert to help you develop a settlement plan without fearing the expert might later be called to testify in a way that could be harmful to you, or to your spouse. There's a greater sense of informality and freedom in working with this expert.

The parties and the lawyers also agree that anything said in sessions is confidential and can't be used in a trial unless the parties agree to use it. This means that you can agree to values or a parenting plan for settlement purposes knowing that if you can't settle and have to go to trial the lawyers can't tell the court what went on during the negotiations.

The parties also agree to provide any relevant information and documents requested by the other side. Ordinarily, the parties also agree that the documents exchanged during this process won't be considered confidential and can be produced at a trial if the dispute can't be settled out of court. If you don't make this agreement, all the documents exchanged in negotiations will be shredded and you'll have to start all over with a formal discovery process. This would be unnecessarily time consuming and expensive.

A Variation on Collaboration

A variation of the collaborative approach requires the divorcing couple to hire a male-female coaching team of two licensed mental health professionals, a child specialist, and a financial specialist when the amount of assets of the marriage warrant. The coaching team helps the parties stay focused on interest-based negotiating, rather than posturing to try to gain a superior position or sniping at each other about the emotional stuff. The idea here is to promote a sense of everyone working together to resolve the issues.

QUESTION?

What is interest-based negotiating?
Interest-based negotiating focuses on the bottom line: for example, what ends up in your pocket when the dust settles or what kind of parenting plan works for you. The idea is to get what you want without worrying so much about what your spouse gets. Ideally, you both get what you want.

Collaborative Law Is Becoming Common

Collaborative law is growing in popularity. It arose because many family law practitioners believe the legal system is poorly adapted to the needs of people getting divorced. These lawyers have decided the legal system promotes hostilities rather than helps families develop new structures that let everyone get on with their lives. Collaborative law puts the parties in charge and gives them the responsibility for making decisions. Lawyers provide legal advice and explain potential legal consequences of the parties' decisions. Parties can focus on their children's needs instead of on their animosity toward each other. When the divorcing people reach a settlement using the collaborative process, they spend less money getting divorced and probably won't need to use the courts in the future. Sometimes they even like each other better!

You May Be a Groundbreaker

Collaborative law is a relatively new concept, so very few lawyers have much experience with it. This means you, your spouse, and your lawyers may have to do some learning about the best way to make the process work. This isn't a bad thing, but you should know you may be breaking new ground. If you'd like to try this approach to your divorce, you'll need to look for lawyers who advertise themselves as collaborative. Ask the lawyer at the initial interview about his or her experience with the process, and don't hire someone who says he or she has been doing this for years. It's being in use for only a few years, so no one has been doing it very long.

The Downside of Collaborative Law

When collaborative law works, it works very well. But when one side refuses to play by the rules, it does not work at all. Then, both of you have to hire new lawyers and basically start over (except you don't have to exchange documents a second time). This can be frustrating, time consuming, and expensive.

Collaborative lawyers have a number of Web sites where you can learn more about them. Search for "collaborative law" on your favorite Internet search engine (such as Google, Yahoo!, or AltaVista).

Mediation

Mediation, which is used for many kinds of disputes, not just for divorce, is a form of dispute resolution that uses a third person—a mediator—to help parties resolve issues. The basic idea is that the parties make the decisions, and the mediator is a facilitator. The mediator's job is to clarify positions and suggest possible alternative and creative ways to resolve the issues. It's possible to have two people serve as co-mediators; so, for example, if each of you wants a same-sex person to be the mediator, you can hire a man and a woman to work together.

You Still Need a Lawyer

Although it's important that the mediator understands divorce law, most mediators want spouses to have their own attorneys, because it's not the mediator's job to tell you about the law. When you and your spouse reach agreements in mediation, you will run them past your lawyers who will make sure you're making informed agreements. Sometimes lawyers and experts, such as certified public accountants or appraisers, attend the mediation sessions with you. They can bring to the mediation session useful information that you may need to resolve your issues.

The Mediation Process

When you make an appointment with a mediator, expect to receive a detailed questionnaire to be filled out and returned to the mediator prior to the session. At the first session, the mediator will explain the process and will probably ask you to sign a contract that includes rules and an agreement to pay for the mediation. You may want to review the contract with your lawyer before agreeing to mediate.

ALERT!

Remember, it's not the mediator's job to come up with the solution to the problem. That's your job. The mediator can give you helpful information, but ultimately, you make the decisions.

Once you agree to mediate, the real sessions begin. You, your spouse, and the mediator will decide what issue needs to be addressed first. Suppose the top item on your agenda is how to survive financially while the divorce is going on. You and your spouse can present your budgets and together take a look at the money available to support two households. Maybe there isn't enough money to support two households, in which case you may negotiate a way to continue to live in the same household. Or you may agree that one of you will pay the other temporary support, so each of you can live in separate locations during the divorce. You'll be better able to focus on all issues of the divorce if you aren't constantly worrying about financial survival. If you make the agreement, you'll make the effort to make it work.

When you reach an agreement acceptable to everyone, the mediator prepares a memorandum of agreement, and your lawyers can prepare the necessary legal documents to complete your divorce.

Finding a Mediator

Every community has excellent mediators—the trick is finding them. The first step is to hire your lawyer, and then have your lawyer help you find a competent mediator. Most states have a list of certified mediators, which means the mediator has completed state-approved mediation training. Successful completion of such a course means only that. Although mediators may or may not be lawyers themselves and licensed to practice law, mediators are not licensed in order to practice mediation. No state has a governing body that keeps mediators toeing the line.

Advantages of Mediation

Mediation has several advantages over going to court:

- Mediation is voluntary and nonbinding. If you don't reach agreement, you're free to try another avenue such as arbitration or going to trial.
- You're in charge of the process, and you make the decisions.
- Mediation is usually a quick way to resolve disputes.
- The process is private and mediation sessions are confidential.
- In most states, you can meet with a mediator much more quickly than you can get your case heard in court.
- You'll probably be able to talk to your ex-spouse after the divorce. This is good for your mental health, your kids' mental health, and your financial health.
- You're more likely to comply with an agreement of your own making.
- The techniques you learn in mediation can be used to resolve disputes in the future.

If you can make it work, you'll be satisfied with the mediation process and the results it gets you.

Some Cautionary Notes

Mediation doesn't work if one party goes into it with the wrong attitude—if one party is trying to prevent a divorce and undermines the effectiveness of the process by dragging out the negotiations for as long as possible; if one of the parties is too angry to focus on issues and wastes time arguing with the other party; or if one of the parties refuses to play by the rules of respectful communication.

Mediation also doesn't work when one of the parties is afraid of the other. If domestic violence has occurred in the marriage, the power imbalance often is too great to successfully mediate a settlement. Sometimes lawyer-based negotiations where the parties don't sit at the same table can be used when there has been a history of domestic violence. And finally, mediation doesn't work when one of the parties hides or transfers marital assets.

Of course, when any of these conditions are present, no process works very well. Then the only alternative is to go to court and give control over the decision-making to the judge.

If you're making no headway in trying to mediate a settlement, your best plan is to get on the court calendar, help your lawyer present your position well, and let the judge decide.

Arbitration

In arbitration, you and your lawyers meet with a neutral arbitrator you select, at a hearing that is less formal than a court proceeding. However, the hearing follows the rules of evidence used by courts, and the arbitrator's decision normally is binding and final. Arbitration has a number of advantages.

- It's voluntary; it happens only if you choose it.
- It's informal, simple, and less stressful than going to court.
- You can select your own arbitrator, usually an expert in divorce law, and often a retired family court judge.

- The focus is on cooperation and maintaining good relations in the future.
- Like mediation, it's a private process, and the information provided at the hearing is confidential.
- No lengthy and expensive appeals are needed.
- Arbitration is a lot less expensive than trial.

However, arbitration also has disadvantages:

- You may have your arbitration hearing without doing complete discovery (the gathering of information), because the arbitrator, unlike a judge, can make a decision based on incomplete evidence if he or she deems the evidence to date is conclusive.
- The arbitrator may not explain the reasoning in his or her opinion and order.
- You can't appeal. (This also may be an advantage depending on how you feel about the decision.)

As you can see, arbitration isn't a cure-all, but it can still outweigh the disadvantages of giving a judge the power to make all your decisions.

Mediation-Arbitration Hybrid

It's possible to combine forms of alternative dispute resolution. The most common hybrid is using mediation and arbitration in tandem, often referred to as "med-arb." For example, you and your spouse mediate and resolve all your issues, except spousal maintenance; you then agree to submit this issue to arbitration. The beauty of this concept is that you exercise control over all the decisions that you can agree on, then let a third person resolve issues the two of you can't resolve.

When you choose med-arb, you should have your lawyers prepare a written agreement stating that you'll mediate all issues that you can, and if you're unable to mediate an issue, you'll submit that issue to arbitration. It's critical to be clear about whether this arbitration is binding or nonbinding. If it's binding, the arbitrator's decision is final. No appeal is possible and your divorce is done. This is cheaper and faster than going to court, and you'll be happier with the product. If it's nonbinding, you can decide you don't like the decision and go to trial.

ALERT!

If you go to trial on top of having an arbitration hearing, you'll have duplicated your costs, and the amount of time you've invested. You'll also risk losing whatever you gained in the arbitrator's decision.

Alternatives Are Becoming Popular

Alternative dispute resolution is a recent development in divorce, but it's becoming more popular. Courts across the country are running behind, so getting a divorce through the court can take several years. As a result, judges and lawyers are looking for better ways to get divorcing families through the system.

Downsides to Going to Trial

You may not get what you want if you go to trial. Many a divorce lawyer has awakened one morning and realized he or she is the only person who benefited from the last trial. Perhaps the client expected a better result but now owes her spouse half of the marital estate. Now the children are in therapy trying to deal with their parents' anger. Or maybe the spouse declared he wouldn't pay his spouse anything until faced with going to jail. In any event, the lawyer at least got his fees.

You might have to wait for what seems like an eternity to get your case tried. Some court systems are so clogged with cases you have to wait more than a year, and even then, your case might be heard in bits and pieces—two hours here, an afternoon there. Because you're mentally ready to be done with your divorce a couple years after the whole thing started, you may be frustrated by the court's inability to hear your case now.

The Special Master

In most states, you and your spouse can agree to hire a private sector expert, called a special master, to be your judge. This is similar to binding arbitration, except that your agreement will state you have the right to appeal the decision of the special master. That is, you give this person the authority to decide your case as if he or she were a trial court judge, and, just as if you were in a trial court, you reserve the right to appeal. A special master will charge for his or her time, and it will be expensive, but you get your case heard by an expert in the field, and you get it heard now. Avoiding delay may save you money in the long run. For sure, it will mitigate the emotional stress of having the case drag on and on and on. Your divorce will be as legal and final as if a judge had heard it.

Chapter 8

Using (and Overusing) the Courts

Much of what happens in court seems unrelated to reality, partly because the laws that govern the legal system may or may not have much to do with your life and your divorce. This is why you should use the courts only when you have no alternative.

Picking Your Court Battles

Some divorces never use the courts, except to get the final judgment and decree signed. Some divorces have minimal involvement with the courts, maybe a temporary hearing, a pretrial hearing, or a settlement conference in which an agreement is reached and put on the record. Putting an agreement on the record is legalese for reciting the agreement in front of a judge and a court reporter, usually in a courtroom. Both parties agree under oath that this is, in fact, their agreement and that they will be bound by it.

Once the agreement is presented, agreed to by the parties, and approved by the court, one of the lawyers prepares the judgment and decree incorporating that agreement. Usually the lawyer representing the petitioner will do this, or maybe it will be the one who has the information in his or her computer. The other lawyer signs the document, showing that the lawyer and client both approve it. Then the judge signs it. Once you've made your agreement in front of the judge, you don't have to go back to court again, because the lawyers will take care of the paperwork. Your lawyer will let you know that the decree has been entered and when the divorce is final.

ALERT!

Some couples use the courts as a way to threaten or punish each other. Unfortunately, most learn too late that they have succeeded in hurting themselves as well—both financially and emotionally. If you're determined to take your issues to court, stop first to consider why.

Back and Forth to Court

Other divorce cases are in court almost monthly for years. She brings him to court for paying support a few days late. He takes her to court for claiming the children are sick on his visitation days. Her lawyer hauls him and his lawyer into court because he hasn't answered the interrogatories that were due two days ago. He sells his car and she brings a motion for half the money.

On and on and on it goes. These repeated trips to the courthouse often are symptoms of the parties' inability to let go of their relationship. These litigious folks really haven't finished the marriage. Their frequent court appearances are one way to guarantee seeing each other on a regular basis. What an expensive—and negative—way to continue a relationship.

The Courts as a Battering Ram

Some people use the courts as a battering ram. They want to repeatedly tell the judge, and anyone else who will listen, that their spouse is a louse. Maybe they want to exhaust their spouse emotionally and financially, so that the spouse finally caves in and accepts an unfavorable settlement. When one of the parties uses the courts in this way, he or she also uses financial resources that could be better used to take care of the family. The result is that everyone loses.

Think Before You Act

As you may have heard in other contexts, "Pick your battles." Some things are way more important than others. For example, protecting your kids is paramount, so going to court may be the only way to protect them. If you can't make the mortgage payment because your spouse is behind in his support payments, this is another reason you need to go to court. But if you want to try to get spousal maintenance reduced by $20 a month, you may be better off waiting until you have other issues to present to the court. A motion will probably cost you $500 in lawyer fees. You'd have to save that $20 a month for over two years just to pay your lawyer.

Divorce is a very traumatic experience, especially if you spend a lot of time in the courts. You will undoubtedly suffer several ups and downs throughout the process, so you may want to join a support group to help you cope. Others in your situation can offer advice, relay their own experiences, or just be there to listen.

Going to Court Is Stressful

You won't realize the stress of constant litigating until you do it. Going to court requires careful, time-consuming preparation. The time you have to spend preparing papers and documents for court is time away from your children and your job. Being in court is stressful because you're on unfamiliar ground, you don't know the rules, and you don't know what a judge will do. When you're in court, you can't do anything else but sit and wait. (No cell phones allowed.)

Waiting for a court order is stressful, because once again you're not in control. Getting that court order at long last can be stressful, too, because you may be very unhappy with it. Often it feels as if the judge didn't read your papers, didn't listen to your lawyer, or simply didn't believe you. The court's order can turn your whole world upside down.

Deciding how much to use the courts is a judgment call that's best made by your lawyer.

Judges Differ

You'll benefit by understanding the terminology used in court, what the jobs are of the people you'll come in contact with, and some of the procedures that you must follow when filing for divorce. Most of all you should know that different judges have different opinions and the resolution of your divorce can vary depending on who renders the final judgment.

FACT

While judicial officers are a step lower on the power ladder, they're usually the most capable and knowledgeable people working in the family court. Most of them have had lots of experience in family court and really know the law.

Judicial Officers

Judicial officers are judgelike people whom courts hire to help judges handle the caseload. They're called different names in different jurisdictions, although the most common names are "referee," "commissioner," and "magistrate." They hear cases and issue orders just like judges but usually their orders have to be countersigned by a "real" judge.

Notice to Remove

When a case is filed with the court, the court administrator working in family court will assign the case to a judge. Your lawyer may be unhappy about the assignment and recommend that you exercise your right to have the case assigned to a different judge. This is not a decision your lawyer makes lightly, because there are often repercussions to the lawyer if the judge is insulted by the request. Therefore, you should accept your lawyer's recommendation, knowing that your lawyer is willing to risk the downside of the judge's reaction in order to get a better result for your case.

You have one chance to say you want another judge to hear your case. You don't have to give any reasons, but you do have to exercise this right quickly, usually within ten days of getting notice of a judge's assignment. In most systems, this is called a Notice to Remove. The other side gets one free shot, too. Of course, when you remove the judge assigned to your case, you may get another who is just as worrisome, given the facts of your case.

ALERT!

If you want to contest a court order, you may not get the same judge and might have to start all over again. Whether you get the same judge varies from state to state and from county to county. Some courts have a special family court, and once your case is filed, it stays with the same judge or judicial officer.

If you don't use the Notice to Remove and at some later time you want a different judge—for instance, after you get your first order from the judge—you will have to exercise a Removal for Cause to show that the judge assigned to your case has shown actual bias toward you or your spouse. This is very hard to do, especially because the judge you're trying to get rid of usually is the one who will hear your motion to remove for cause.

Your lawyer will be reluctant to use either the Notice to Remove or the Removal for Cause, because judges have long memories and thin skins. The judge may hold such filing against your lawyer for a long time, and this is not good for your lawyer's practice. So, if your lawyer suggests removing the judge, you know your lawyer didn't reach this decision lightly. You would be wise to listen to your lawyer's advice.

The Judge's Reputation

Judges develop reputations for delivering certain kinds of opinions most of the time. Some seem to award high alimony. Some always give children to their mothers. Some are pretty wishy-washy about enforcing orders. Some are not good listeners. Some make decisions based on what happened to them in their divorces.

Lawyers talk to each other about judges, and they know the reputations of the judges in their courts. Your lawyer will advise you about a judge and whether it's worth trying to get a different one. While you should make the final decision, you probably will have to rely on your lawyer's advice pretty heavily here. A judge with a known bias who also has a reputation for fairness and for listening to the facts may be persuaded to abandon his or her bias in a specific case—maybe yours. Only your lawyer can tell you the risks and options here.

Using the Discovery Period

After a temporary order is issued, the court system will probably allow a specific period of time for your lawyer to conduct discovery before setting another court date, usually called the pretrial hearing. The discovery period is the time during which you and your lawyer collect all the information you will need at the trial.

Hiring Experts

This is the time to hire your experts. If you need a business valuation, get an expert on the job as soon as possible. If you need a custody evaluation, line up the person who will do it. The good experts are busy people, and they'll need adequate time and information to do their job well.

Let's assume you and your spouse are working collaboratively, and that you've selected an independent neutral expert to value the family business. With this cooperative approach, your side can simply ask the other side to give the documents and information it possesses to the expert, and the other side will get them to the expert in timely fashion. The expert does his or her work, and you use the information to resolve the issue.

If you bring in a big-city lawyer, you may be at a disadvantage. The local lawyers will know the ins and outs of the courts as well as pertinent information about the judges that an out-of-town lawyer couldn't possibly know. You should think twice before spending the big bucks.

Or, assume you and your spouse don't agree on experts, so each of you hires an expert. Your expert needs certain information to conduct the evaluation and complete the report. In a contested case, you can get the information from the other side only by asking for it using a legal process requiring you and your lawyer to serve a Request for Production of Documents.

Requesting Documents

The other side has thirty days to reply to your request for documents, but it's unusual for the other side to provide the documents in timely fashion. In addition, the other side often says it doesn't have some of the documents you've requested. As a result, if your expert doesn't get the documents he or she needs, the expert can't get the report completed in the time the court has set aside for discovery.

Do you see where this is going? Your pretrial date is looming, and you're nowhere near ready. If your judge is a stickler for the rules, he or she will require the lawyers to make a motion for a continuance, or an extension of time, to get the expert's reports done. This requires another court appearance, which means another dip into your pocket for attorney's fees, unless you can persuade the judge to make the other side pay all the fees because its failure to cooperate necessitated the motion. A more flexible judge may agree to address the continuance request by conference call.

Sometimes both sides show up unprepared at the pretrial hearing, which in most courts is a bad idea. The judge can assess fines and court costs to anyone who shows up unprepared. And, the judge has a long memory, so you don't want to annoy the judge who will ultimately decide your case.

Discovery Can Be Costly

Discovery, or preparing for trial, is a necessary part of the divorce process, but it's also costly. Look at the number of players involved: your lawyer, your spouse's lawyer, the experts for both sides, the court reporter. All of these folks expect to be paid for their time. How much help do you need and how much can you afford? Let's look at some of the discovery tools that are available to you.

1. **Interrogatories.** These are a series of questions your lawyer sends to the other side which must be answered under oath within thirty days. The questions ask for information about income, assets, parenting attributes, and other things you and your lawyer want to know. It takes time and effort to prepare interrogatories because they need to be carefully and thoughtfully prepared to be useful.

   Interrogatory questions rarely are answered in the thirty days allotted. Failure to answer interrogatories is a basis for bringing a motion before the court demanding the questions be answered or the violating side be fined or found in contempt. When lawyers bring such a motion, they are mostly posturing—at your expense—but it's sometimes the necessary push required to get the other side to act.

2. **Request for admissions.** This is a list of statements that, if not denied within thirty days, are taken to be true. Your lawyer can send a series of statements to your spouse, through your spouse's lawyer, along with a notice that says, "If you don't respond within thirty days, these statements will be deemed to be admitted to the court as fact." These statements can be something like: "I will be able to get a good job within three months, and I will be able to support myself" (meaning your spouse won't need financial support).

   In reality, it's unlikely a court will deem the statements admitted if a spouse fails to respond in thirty days, partly because this failure is very common. Most judges will extend the time to respond, rather than have statements become facts by default. On the other hand, some judges are tough and strictly follow the rules. You'll need to rely on your lawyer's information about your judge. To be safe, answer all discovery requests on time.

As silly as it may seem in the face of the seriousness of divorce, you should make time for play. Play with your children, play with your friends and family, play by yourself. However you choose to do it, have some fun. This will relieve some of the stress you're feeling as well as give you an emotional lift.

3. **Request for production of documents.** This is a legal demand for documents you want within thirty days. It means just what it says— your spouse must get you the documents you listed in your request. These documents can range from the checkbooks of your closely held corporation, to verification of Uncle Albert's cash gift in 1978, and to your children's medical records.

   As with the interrogatories, your spouse has thirty days to produce the documents. Failure to do so in a timely fashion is another basis for going back to court. Of course, it will take another thirty days to get a court hearing. The good news is that usually the threat of seeking a court order is enough to get the documents.

4. **Depositions.** These are sessions in which your lawyer asks questions of your spouse or your spouse's expert or any other person your lawyer thinks may have information useful to your case. The person answering the questions has been sworn to reply truthfully. A court reporter records everything and later provides a written transcript.

   An expert's deposition can be helpful in preparing for trial. This deposition usually takes place after the expert has completed and submitted a report, at which time your lawyer can ask questions about that report. Sometimes your lawyer will invite your expert to attend the deposition of your spouse's expert to help your lawyer ask the right questions.

5. **The witness list for trial.** This is a list of witnesses you intend to call. If you fail to submit your witness list to the court and the other lawyer by a certain day before the trial, you won't be able to call your witnesses at all. The other side is entitled to know whom you will call as witness.

6. **The exhibit list for trial.** This is the same deal. If you don't give the other side your list of exhibits by a certain date, you can't introduce the exhibits.

Circumstances Do Change

While you're collecting the data, or doing discovery, you may learn new information. You may find out your spouse has gotten a job—a good job, in fact. Now, your spouse earns as much as you do. This might be a reason to go back to court to get your support obligation reduced if you're paying your spouse support (called spousal maintenance) or if you have joint custody of children. If you're paying child support according to statutory guidelines, the fact that your spouse now has a job might mean only that more money is available to meet needs. But if your child support was determined by using both your income and that of your spouse, child support would be affected. Check this out with your lawyer.

In discovery, you might learn that your spouse has been involved in some worrisome activities, or hasn't been taking parental responsibilities very seriously. You may want to ask the judge to change a temporary custody order and give the children to you. Ask your lawyer.

FACT

Temporary orders can be modified as circumstances change or as new information is learned. To be sure the change warrants going back to court, consult your lawyer.

If a child moves from one parent's household to the other, this change will affect child support and custody. You may want to have this change reflected in a new court order. In fact, you may feel that you need a new court order to protect the child. Your lawyer can help you decide whether to take this matter back to court.

Use the courts effectively. Bring a motion when you have a real reason to do so. Provide the court with clear and helpful information, so that the court understands your position. Remember that every time you let the court decide something, you give up control. The court may make some decisions that seem unrelated to the reality of your life and the lives of your children, so try not to give the court too many opportunities to issue orders regulating your life.

Chapter 9

Courts Try New Approaches

Many family court judges are sensitive to the court system's inability to meet the needs of families going through divorce. New approaches are being tried in courts all over the country. These changes are making the divorce process better for all concerned: divorcing spouses, children, lawyers, and judges.

Case Management

Lawyers and judges have commiserated for years about the fact that divorces don't belong in court. Recently some courts have developed new approaches to divorce. The most common is called case management. When a case is filed with the court and assigned to a judge, the judge's clerk schedules a meeting as soon as possible with the parties and their lawyers to exchange information, hire experts, begin a custody study, and schedule depositions. The first objective is to get the parties into alternative dispute resolution (see Chapter 7). The second objective is to get all the preparation needed for trial completed as quickly as possible, so if the case does go to trial, it won't drag on forever.

While part of the delay in divorce court is because judges have too many cases, the other part is because many times lawyers aren't ready to try cases when the judge is ready. Case management tries to get the parties to settle and to get the lawyers ready for trial.

One County's Experiment

Hennepin County District Court in Minneapolis, Minnesota, prides itself on being innovative, with personnel who are able to think "outside the box." More than ten years ago, a group of lawyers, psychologists, and judges developed a program that would send restructured families back into the world with greater ability to work cooperatively and get on with their lives.

The program was called Divorce with Dignity, or Collaborative Judicial Case Management. The approach was based on the belief that early intervention with alternative dispute resolution is crucial for divorcing families to avoid crippling hostilities. The court system can get involved only after parties have filed papers. The court has no idea what's going on in people's lives until they bring their issues to it by filing their actions. Some divorces are begun months or even years before any papers are filed, so that the court gets involved late in the process.

A two-year study concluded the program did move cases through the system more quickly than the traditional model. Clients also indicated a higher degree of satisfaction than in the litigation approach. (Not too many people could actually compare the processes, however. Only people unfortunate enough to have gone through two or more divorces would be in that position, and those were few.)

Another significant result of the Divorce with Dignity approach was that cases didn't come back to court after the divorces were final. Apparently, people who learned to negotiate with one another during the divorce process, used those skills to adapt to changes that happened after the divorce. Rather than bring the case to court, the parties worked out their differences outside the courts. Often they used one of the alternative dispute resolution processes talked about in Chapter 7.

The pilot project has ended and some pieces of the program have been incorporated into the county court's current approach to divorce. Other courts around the country are using case management and early intervention to help divorcing families.

The Divorce with Dignity Approach

You may want to use this approach in your divorce. If your court doesn't practice case management, you may want to set up your own private "divorce court" using the following approach.

Hire a Judge

Schedule a four-way meeting of the lawyers and the parties. Do this as early in the process as possible, before any damaging affidavits have been exchanged. Select a person to act as your judge, someone with knowledge and authority, such as a retired judge with family law experience, or a highly respected divorce lawyer.

What are the advantages of hiring a private judge? You set the rules for your divorce. You select someone interested in and knowledgeable about family law. You do not have to wait months to be heard. You're likely to negotiate a settlement that works and unlikely to need to return to court after the divorce is completed. In fact, when this approach is used, the judge is rarely used as a decision-maker on the substantive issues. The parties settle.

Indeed, the success of case management, in or out of the courts, seems to depend on the presence of this ultimate decision-maker. This person can tell the parties the likely result of trying a particular issue. Input from the person the parties have chosen for his or her expertise can be a strong impetus toward settlement.

Once you've selected your judge, you'll need to decide on the rules for your divorce. The rules of the Divorce with Dignity program that follow can be a good starting point.

Hiring a judge provides an interesting and important psychological benefit. In areas where this approach has been used, almost none of the cases went to trial. It appears that knowing there is a person with final authority, and meeting with that person, motivates the parties to reach settlement.

The Divorce with Dignity Rules

Procedures are established at the initial meeting of the parties, the lawyers, and the judge. The parties who agreed to use the Divorce with Dignity program agreed to abide by the following rules, and you can, too.

Rule 1. All parties involved will use their combined energies to settle the issues.

Parties behave differently when they expect to settle. You can compare going to trial with going to war. Each side stockpiles weapons and tries not to let the other side know what it's doing, just like people going to trial stockpile evidence and don't talk to each other. Each side has a special theory of the case that he or she believes will enable him or her to prevail. Under discovery rules, if one side asks the other questions the party has to answer, but this information is rarely volunteered.

Divorce with Dignity is about drafting a peace treaty. Instead of putting energy into battle preparations, the energy goes into dispute resolution. The idea is for you to draft a peace treaty to enable you to get on with your lives.

Rule 2. The divorcing parties won't let their lawyers fight.

It's kind of a tongue-in-cheek rule but a real one, too. Suppose this is what you tell your lawyer: "I am so angry with my spouse. I want to punish him. I want him to hurt as much as I do. Sock it to 'em!" It will be hard for your lawyer to be courteous and cooperative with the other side. If, on the other hand, you say something like: "I'm really sad the marriage is ending. Sometimes I'm really mad, too, but, bottom line, I want you to help me settle this fairly," this encourages your lawyer to work with the other side.

FACT

Ninety percent of the papers filed in ugly divorce cases address emotional issues that can't be addressed in court. People get angry and poor when they try to get the court to do something it can't do— therapy. Use your head. Take your emotional issues to a therapist.

Lawyers are trained to be litigators, and sometimes they need to be reminded you are not at war. The divorcing parties and the judge may have to repeat a number of times that the lawyers need to help settle the case, not add to the friction. This rule is to help everyone remember that this is court, where the legal part of a divorce is done. The emotional part is equally important, but judges and lawyers are not trained to address that. Judges are lawyers, not therapists.

When you have a four-way meeting, bring a whistle. Have a "whistle-blower" for the day give a tweet when the emotional stuff starts to surface. This will help you all remember to stay on the legal stuff. If you feel silly using a whistle, clap your hands or call for a recess. You can't focus on settlement negotiations when your emotions are in charge. You also aren't making good use of your lawyers' time. You don't want to pay them to listen to you fight, nor do you want them to take up your emotional battle.

These first two rules are rules of social conduct; the next six are legal-procedure rules.

Rule 3. Your judge must approve all motions.

A motion is the way you get the court's attention. The court is essentially passive and it doesn't get involved in your lives unless you ask it to. A motion is how you ask. In family law, motions usually ask courts to address parenting, child support, spousal maintenance, who will live in the house, who will pay the bills, and so on.

ALERT!

Motion practice produces angry, frustrated, and poorer parties. They're angry because of the content of the affidavits. They're frustrated with the judge's decision. They're poorer because attorneys need to be paid for producing these papers, working with you, and appearing in court. Not a very appealing prospect, no pun intended.

Rules require every motion be accompanied by an affidavit, a written statement given under oath, from the person asking the court to act. Affidavits are where trouble starts. The party who starts the motion drafts, with the lawyer, an affidavit that may say ugly things about the other person. When that person gets the papers, he or she is hurt, angry, upset, and probably responds with a similarly ugly affidavit. Now, the first person is equally angry and upset and probably responds with at least one more affidavit. After all the papers have been exchanged, the parties come to court for a hearing on their motions. When judges come into court, many could say something like, "Well, good day. I've reviewed your file and based on what you've told me about each other, your children are coming home with me!"

Stunned silence. Does the judge really mean it? No, but the judge is trying to point out the problem with bringing issues to court by affidavit. All too often, parties use affidavits to vent their feelings rather than to inform a judge. One-time events are portrayed as daily happenings. An old charge of driving while under the influence of alcohol is reported to support a claim that a party has a serious alcohol problem. Reality is seriously distorted. It's from this misinformation that you ask the judge to make decisions that will have a lasting impact on your lives. Small wonder no one is pleased with the results.

Instead of using motions, parties involved in Divorcing with Dignity will negotiate to resolve issues. You and your attorneys will sit down and work out the terms of any orders you need. The judge will issue orders based on your agreements. This is far less costly in time, emotion, and dollars, and far more likely to result in an order that will work for you.

Rule 4. Lawyers will conduct informal discovery.

Discovery is the legal term for finding facts. The discovery process can be very expensive. If one party chooses to play hardball and refuses to disclose assets, the other will, somehow, know this and will direct his or her lawyer to find these assets. The lawyer will find them—at a great cost. Sometimes, the cost even equals or exceeds the value of the assets. Sometimes, the parties spend the marital estate just trying to figure out what it is!

Consider this scenario: The wife has always prepared tax returns, simply telling her husband, "Sign here." She has all copies of the tax documents. When the husband asks for them, she refuses. So, his lawyer brings a motion, with client affidavit, before the court.

In a Divorce with Dignity approach, each side will provide the other with the information, plus all supporting documentation, about assets and income. Each side will respond promptly to requests for information and will meet deadlines established by the attorneys. All parties involved will resolve any discovery disputes by a conference call among the attorneys and the judge.

At the hearing, the judge orders the spouse to give copies of the tax returns to her husband by such and such a date. That day comes and goes, and no tax returns.

The husband's lawyer brings a contempt motion and an "order to show cause," with an affidavit, before the court. At this hearing, the judge finds the spouse in contempt and has her taken into custody, to be released when the tax returns have been provided.

This little operetta has cost the parties a great deal of time, money, and emotion. For what purpose? Information about family finances and assets is relevant and must be provided. It makes much more sense for the parties to voluntarily provide all information about their assets and income.

Informal, voluntary discovery is cheaper and faster. The parties need to know the extent of the marital estate to divide it fairly. All involved need to know what income is available to support both households after the marriage is dissolved.

At some point, you will both tell the judge, under oath, that all information has been disclosed and that you need no more discovery work done by your attorneys.

Rule 5. If either side needs an expert, an independent, neutral third-party professional will be used.

You are most likely to need an expert's input when determining an optimum parenting plan, valuing a business or other asset such as your house or rental property, and doing a cash-flow analysis. Obviously, two experts cost more than one, but, more important, you get better, more useful data from an independent neutral. If you each hire an expert, that person will work to further your objectives. The information she will provide will be directed toward your objectives.

It's not unusual for the experts hired by each spouse to disagree widely, especially when valuing a business or professional practice. When two experts give the court widely differing values, the court will have a hard time coming up with a usable, acceptable value. It doesn't make sense to ask a nonexpert court to interpret expert data.

If, instead, you select one person whose job it is to give both parties and the court the best possible information, you can then use your attorneys' skills to figure out what to do with the information.

FACT

Sometimes, an informal meeting of the parties—lawyers, expert, and judge—will be scheduled to discuss an expert's report and resolve issues covered. This is often a very productive meeting.

Rule 6. Your judge will decide any issues about attorney's fees.

Attorney's fees are usually decided in a separate proceeding, but there are far fewer fee issues in this program. For one thing, fees stay much more manageable. For another, the parties still like their lawyers at the end of the process, so they pay them.

Rule 7. Your judge will be the final decision-maker when you can't agree.

If you can resolve all but one, maybe two, issues but are impossibly stuck on those remaining, you can submit them to the judge for resolution. You will need to explain how you have resolved the other issues because the judge will need to decide the contested issues in the context of what you already have worked out. You can submit the issues with testimony, written arguments, exhibits, or a combination of all three. The parties can submit a written statement to the judge.

If you decide to do this, you can't opt out of the program if you don't like the judge's decision. When the judge decides the contested issues, you have three choices: you can live with the decision, you can negotiate something different, or you can appeal.

Rule 8. Conference calls are an integral part of the program.

Conference calls are used a lot because they're quick, effective, and less expensive than any other form of communication with the court. If parties need an expert, the lawyers and the judge can review several names and make a choice without anyone having to draft expensive papers and without anyone having to incur the expense of coming to court.

You may or may not be a part of a conference call. A routine procedural matter may not require any input from you. But it is important that you be present when decisions affecting your lives are made. It's disrespectful to decide things without you, even if it's sometimes much easier. The conference call will be an important tool to both speed the process and cut the costs.

Next Steps

Once you have agreed upon your rules, you, your spouse, and your lawyers need to meet with your judge. At this meeting you can negotiate a temporary order if you need one. If you are unable to agree on the terms of this order, you can ask the judge to decide contested issues. This would be your first experience with letting a stranger tell you how to live.

This would be a good time to develop a scheduling order, the heart of the case management approach. This order says that certain tasks will be completed by specific dates. For instance, you will exchange all documents in three weeks. Or, you will retain an expert to value your business and have her report in two months. Part of the judge's job is to make sure you meet these deadlines, so your divorce moves along.

Once discovery is completed, you four again meet with the judge. You may ask for his thoughts on areas where you disagree. He may suggest some alternatives for resolving these issues and tell you what would probably happen if you tried the issue. Because he will be the one who tries the case, his input has great weight.

Make sure you do several "reality checks" throughout the divorce process. Sometimes you can get so caught up in the paperwork, the arguments, the emotional stress, etc., that you lose sight of your objectives.

At this meeting, or soon after, you will know whether you can reach an agreement. You and your spouse with the help of your lawyers can settle or schedule your trial. Sometimes just setting the trial date is such a tremendous reality check that the parties settle rather than face preparing for trial.

The Advantages for You

A Divorce with Dignity format encourages you to look forward, to think about where you hope to be one year, five years, ten years from now. You develop a plan and work toward achieving it.

Trial requires you to look backward, to rehash in excruciating detail the events that led you to divorce court. For most people, this is not a happy time and having to keep thinking about it does not produce good feelings. Educating a trial judge, so she can find the facts means you must provide her with historical information. This means taking a close look at your past relationship to pull out the details that may help the judge understand your present issues.

A Divorce with Dignity approach makes it possible for you to be creative, to resolve issues in a way that works for you. A judge can't be creative. She must follow the law—the statutes and the law as interpreted by the appellate courts. If a judge does get creative, and you don't agree with her creativity, you can appeal. An appeals court most likely will reverse the decision and send you back to the trial judge because the judge didn't follow the law.

Finally, a Divorce with Dignity approach encourages you to get on with your life. What has happened has happened. The rest of your life lies ahead. You can decide whether you are going to enjoy it or spend your energies on anger, bitterness, and distress.

Some people spend a lot of time, energy, and money hoping the court will do things it cannot do. Courts can't change people. The factors that led to the relationship's demise will exist after you leave the courthouse. Courts can't fix things. If there isn't enough money, courts can't print any. Courts are stuck with the same realities you are. And courts don't decide who is the good person or the bad person in a divorce.

The Advantages for Your Lawyer

Many divorce lawyers really do care about their clients. They know that it is seldom in their clients' best interests to litigate. Divorce lawyers like easy access to a judge. Input from a judge helps them help their clients develop reasonable objectives. It is easier to settle a case when the clients have reasonable expectations.

FACT

Trying divorce cases is stressful for lawyers, too. While some lawyers love the adrenaline rush of the courtroom, others find it hard on their health. These lawyers get their adrenaline rush from reaching a resolution of the issues that is in their client's best interests.

Divorce lawyers don't make their money trying cases. When a lawyer is in trial, his whole focus is on one case. All his other cases have to wait until that trial is over. And, he can't take new cases. Lawyers make more money when they can settle cases. A lawyer can handle many more cases when he can be in his office most of the day. The fees generated in negotiating a settlement are usually much lower than those generated in trial, and, thus, much more likely to be paid.

Stay Tuned

The professionals in the field of divorce continue to try to create a better system. While everyone seems to agree that dispute resolution is superior to litigation in divorce, not many court systems have developed dispute resolution programs. If the system you want doesn't exist, ask your lawyers to help you create it. Develop a program that meets your needs. Settle and move on with your life.

Chapter 10

The Emotions of Divorce and Domestic Violence

People experience many emotions in the divorce process. They run the gamut from justifiable sadness and a sense of profound loss to raging anger and a desire for revenge. The emotions of divorce can be dangerous in households where there is domestic violence.

A Roller Coaster of Emotions

Some experts compare the emotions of divorce to those experienced when a loved one dies. The death of a marriage often generates feelings of sadness and loss, and a similar mourning period occurs. However, there are some important differences. Divorce has no ritual form of mourning, no memorial service that brings you the support of friends and family. In divorce, your friends tend to back away, hoping to avoid taking sides or getting caught in the middle. In divorce, an added sense of failure occurs that is rarely part of mourning a death. Also, the formerly loved one is alive and kicking and may be making your life miserable.

FACT

Emotions run very high during a divorce. You may find it helpful to speak with a counselor or therapist or even join a support group. There's help out there—you only need ask for it.

When you separate from your spouse you may experience a sense of relief, even exhilaration. You feel a release from the stress of having to deal with that person daily. The knot in your gut goes away. Your energy level increases, and for a few weeks you feel really great. But then the euphoria collapses, like a balloon losing its air. You may feel a tremendous sense of disappointment because your dreams for the future have been destroyed. Total responsibility for the children feels like drudgery, or not seeing the children leads to a profound sense of loss. Maybe you try going on a date, with less than wonderful results. You want to talk about your situation with your friends, but they lose interest just as you're warming up to your topic. Your initial high becomes an unpleasant low.

You feel a sense of failure. You see your kids missing their other parent and showing signs of anxiety or anger. You wonder, "What could I have done to save the marriage? Is there something wrong with me? Who changed?" Such thoughts plague sleepless, soul-searching nights, which are followed by cheerless days. You may feel abandoned and frightened of an unknown future. You want to go back to the way it was.

Initiating the Divorce or Responding to It?

If you're the one who initiated the divorce, you probably gave this decision a lot of thought before telling your spouse. How you break the news may have a huge impact on how you go through the divorce itself, especially if your spouse is totally shocked and surprised. If you can tell your spouse your decision calmly and without placing blame, and if you then give your spouse time to catch up emotionally, you may be able to reach a point where the decision to end the marriage is mutual. When this happens, you have a much better chance of negotiating the terms of your divorce.

Sometimes one of the parties makes the decision to divorce, but doesn't tell the other. Instead, the initiator creates a crisis—a discovered affair, a contrived fight—to make the announcement. This is a cruel parting that may leave the other spouse filled with rage, as well as surprised and hurt. That spouse may have a very hard time letting go.

The hurt and angry spouse responding to a divorce may assume the role of victim and blame the initiator. When this happens, the victim may obsess on the initiator's fault and use this obsession to justify getting even. The victim may harass the initiator, may drag out the divorce proceedings—in short, may make the divorce as difficult as possible.

The person who begins the divorce discussion needs to realize it's too early to discuss long-term plans with the spouse who is just in the beginning stages of the emotional response to the idea of divorce.

Trying to Reconcile

If you're emotionally ready to divorce, you should say so. Hedging your position by saying that you want to separate for a little while because you need some space is deceitful. If you hold out false hope to your spouse, your spouse will have a hard time trusting you once that hope is destroyed. Separation rarely leads to reconciliation.

It makes sense that couples would choose one last try to save a difficult relationship rather than face the unknown. Most couples make a significant investment in their relationship, and a sense of attachment continues even when the love and excitement are gone. That's why many divorcing couples try to reconcile. However, successful reconciliation requires the help of a talented therapist, and even then, the prospects for success are dim. Too many past hurts, too much damaged trust, and too much focus on the shortcomings of the other interfere. The most positive results of reconciliation counseling are often a better understanding of why the marriage failed and acceptance that it is over.

ALERT!

Successful reconciliation works only if both parties want the marriage to work. If your spouse truly wants the divorce and you try to force him or her into therapy to save the marriage, you're only going to end up hurting yourself. You can't force your spouse to stay with you if the decision has been made.

Emotional Abuse

Some relationships have an emotional abuse component. Name calling and humiliation can do terrible things to the recipient, and so can emotional inconsistency and volatility. Power imbalances in a relationship can sometimes lead to psychological abuse. One spouse belittles the other, criticizing aspects of appearance like clothes, weight, cooking, housekeeping, driving, sexual performance, intelligence, you name it.

In addition, the abusive spouse may try to limit the victim's contact with others, so the victim gets feedback only from the abuser. As a result, the victim eventually begins to believe the criticism, and his or her sense of self begins to diminish. The victim may start to function poorly at work and get fired, or may look outside the marriage for praise or positive feedback. The victim may leave the marriage.

Reacting to News of Divorce

Typically, when the victim announces the decision to end the marriage, the abuser is enraged and often plays the role of victim, putting energy into blaming the spouse for causing the marriage to fail. The abuser rewrites the marital history to suit his or her needs, and then becomes the person who won't let go and move on.

The abuser may drag the children into the fray and threaten to abandon them if they don't take his or her side against the other spouse. The abuser may punish the children for spending time with the other spouse by withdrawing and accusing them of being unloving. Imagine how this must feel to a child. Dad left, now Mom is threatening to leave, too. Is it any wonder some children handle this behavior by refusing to have any relationship with Dad at all? They figure they can't afford to lose both parents, so they'll stick with the security of the house and their mom, doing whatever it takes to appease her.

Ugly? You bet, and it happens way too often.

Headed for Litigation

When one spouse refuses to let go and accept the reality of a divorce, it's unlikely that the parties will be able to negotiate a settlement. At some point, the initiator of the divorce will lose the ability to stay calm in the face of the spouse's behavior and fight back. When that happens, the divorce is headed for litigation, and lots of it.

Physical Abuse

Emotional abuse can lead to or be a part of physical abuse. All states have laws to protect the victims of domestic abuse. However, these laws are surprisingly recent. The abuser can be male or female; however, it is much more common for the abuser to be male.

New Attitudes Toward Victims

For many years domestic violence victims stayed in their abusive relationships because they believed they had no other choice. The typical victim was an unemployed woman with minimal job skills and no ability to support herself and her children. She had no safe place to go. She knew cries for help were likely to be dismissed by others: "You must have done something to make him mad" or "It's your duty to abide by your marriage vows."

She knew her husband (her abuser) would track her down if she tried to leave, and probably beat her badly as punishment. She lived a terrible life of fear and pain, never knowing what might trigger an outburst leading to black eyes and broken bones. Sometimes the only reason a victim would seek help was to protect her children from the violence.

FACT

In the last twenty years the criminal justice system has become more sophisticated in its understanding and treatment of domestic violence. Significant money and energy have gone into educating law enforcement personnel about the dynamics of domestic violence. The cops no longer assume a woman struck by her husband must have done something to deserve it and walk him around the block to cool off. Now, they arrest him.

Today, laws provide protection to domestic violence victims. The laws of all states permit victims to get restraining orders by going to a courthouse and filling out a statement outlining the abuse. They can get a temporary restraining order without telling the abuser, and the order will stay in effect until a hearing, if the abuser requests one. The temporary restraining order excludes the alleged abuser from the family home until the hearing.

In many states, the court can order child support and spousal maintenance for the victim, helping the victim and the children to survive financially. The abuser can be ordered to stay out of the family home, giving the victim and the children a safe place to live. Sometimes the abuser is ordered to stay away from the children's schools and to have no contact at all with the victim. The prohibited contact includes all forms of communication such as telephone calls, letters, e-mails, and so on.

ALERT!

Most protection orders issued in domestic abuse cases are good for only one year. If the abuser continues to threaten harm or violates the terms of the order, it can be extended. It is rarely a permanent solution to the issues of the relationship.

Victims' Safety Net

Support networks for domestic abuse victims have developed, too. In many cities, victims and their children can stay in shelters for a few weeks while they look for housing and employment or wait for a court date to get a restraining order that will let them return to their home. Advocates trained in domestic abuse law, the psychology of abuse patterns, and the practicalities of finding housing, child care, employment training, and the money to pay for them work closely with the shelters and the courts. Often they accompany victims to the courthouse to help them fill out the necessary papers and attend hearings.

Many smaller communities and rural areas are served by hot lines reached by calling 911. These communities often have volunteer advocates who answer these calls and help victims find safe places to stay while escaping the abuse and the abuser. These advocates also accompany the victims to the courthouse to help fill out their papers, find temporary care for the kids, and help in other ways during this scary and dangerous time.

Many women who are abuse victims don't want a divorce or an end to the relationship—they just want the abuse to stop. Domestic abuse treatment programs and anger therapy programs are available in many communities. Some families and some relationships are saved by treatment and counseling; however, it's not uncommon for a spouse who is served with an Order for Protection to initiate a divorce proceeding.

The Most Dangerous Time

Statistics show the most dangerous time for a domestic abuse victim is when she's trying to get out of the abusive situation. During this critical time, community resources need to work together to keep her and her children safe. In recent years, criminal laws have expanded to include domestic assault and violations of civil, as opposed to criminal, restraining orders. Police are directed to take alleged abusers to jail if they see any evidence abuse has reoccurred.

FACT

Second offenses are more serious crimes. Criminal courts can order no contact between a victim and an abuser as a condition of getting out of jail. A criminal court judge also may want to know that the victim has been informed of the abuser's release, so the victim can take appropriate steps to be safe.

Victim Behavior

An odd psychology underlies the dynamics of domestic abuse. Some abuse incidents occur after too many drinks escalate a quarrel into a physical fight. By the next day, when both parties are sober, neither one wants to press charges. If one of the parties got arrested, the other wants him released from jail. Even in cases of repeated abuse not involving alcohol or drugs, the victim may refuse to help in prosecuting the offense.

For many years, a criminal case would fall apart if the victim refused to help. This victim behavior was very frustrating to police, to prosecutors, and to judges. Education helped cops, prosecutors, and judges to better understand victim behavior, but it didn't help them bring the abusers into the system and make them take responsibility for their behavior. Cops felt it was a waste of their time to haul abusers into court. Prosecutors were unhappy. Judges were upset.

Ultimately, these newly sensitized members of the justice team went to legislators and got the laws changed. Now cases can go forward without the victim's cooperation when other evidence—photos, observations of cops called to the house, or medical records—points to abuse. This change in the law has helped, but cases still have to be dismissed when the only evidence is the victim's testimony and the victim refuses to testify.

Abuse Victims Need to Take Precautions

As mentioned, the most dangerous time for a victim is when she takes action to get out of an abusive situation. The abuser's behavior can get very scary. For example, he is likely to file for divorce, hide as much of the marital estate as he can, and try to convince the kids their mother's immoral behavior has caused the divorce. This type of abusive dad is especially likely to persuade teenage sons to side with him against Mom. These boys have seen this kind of behavior from their dad for a long time and have come to believe this is how to treat women.

Too often, even this treatment of a woman who wants out doesn't appease the righteous abuser. He decides, "if I can't have her, nobody can have her" and takes steps to isolate or kill her. He may use the other ultimate weapon—the children—and run away with them. During this dangerous time, a victim needs to take all possible steps to protect herself and her children.

If you've been abused and seek a divorce, you should consider talking with a therapist. Emotions can be overwhelming in an abusive situation, and adding the emotional strain of a divorce can become too much.

Awareness Leads to Education

As awareness of the problem of domestic abuse has grown, community leaders have gotten funding for education programs—programs for people involved in the abusive relationship; programs for advocates, law enforcement, and the folks who take the cases to court; and even programs for judges.

Now, when police respond to a call for help, they don't take it lightly. Sometimes an advocate goes with the officers to provide information and support. If not, the officers give the victim information on how to get help. And, finally, more abusers are convicted. While some victims still fall through the cracks, and some abusers still kill the women in their lives, much more help and understanding is available for domestic violence victims today than even a few years ago.

It's very important to get some kind of a handle on domestic violence because it's learned behavior. Boys who see their dads control their moms with slaps, punches, and snarls tend to treat their own girlfriends and wives the same way. Girls who see their moms abused tend to grow up passive, accepting the victim role in adult relationships.

Emotional Components of a Divorce

Thankfully, for most people, the emotional component of a divorce doesn't rise to the level of emotional abuse. But emotions always are a part of the divorce process. Whether you're motivated by anger or sadness, you'll find yourself wanting to make the other guy hurt, too. It's appropriate to recognize your anger—it's not appropriate to act on it.

ALERT!

Be aware that you can control only your behavior. You may be surprised at how your spouse behaves or even at the behavior of the courts. You may be in for a long and miserable divorce, but still it will be shorter than staying married.

Unfortunately, emotional or physical abuse is a factor in many divorces. Divorce laws and laws addressing protective orders interrelate. If abuse is an issue for you, tell your lawyer. You may need to get a restraining order before you take the potentially dangerous step of beginning your divorce. If your spouse is emotionally abusive, take whatever steps you can to prepare your spouse for your announcement that you want a divorce. Try to treat your spouse with respect and civility, and don't let your spouse's behavior goad you into an angry response.

Chapter 11

Beginning the
Divorce Process

Yeou've decided divorce is the only option and now you're wondering how
does a divorce begin? What happens next?
How does the divorce move from the
"thinking about it" stage to the "making it
happen" stage?

Getting Started

First you'll interview several lawyers and select one who feels right to you (see Chapter 5). Let's assume you've found a good divorce lawyer and are ready to begin the process. Your lawyer will probably send you a form to complete on the history of your family and your marriage. You'll fill out the form and mail it to the lawyer, so that the lawyer can review it before your next meeting.

Your Marriage History

When you get together, you and your lawyer will first review and sign a retainer agreement. Then you'll review the marital history together. Your lawyer will help you understand what parts of your marriage history are important to the divorce process, and will also explain what parts are not legally important. For example, it's important that you inherited some property from your uncle during the marriage. It's probably not important that your spouse preferred reading a book in the evening to talking to you.

Listen to Advice, But Stay in Control

You will tell your lawyer what you hope to accomplish in your divorce, and your lawyer, being a good divorce lawyer, will tell you what parts of your plan are reasonable and what parts are not. For example, if you tell your lawyer you want custody of your children, but you work sixty hours a week and your spouse stays home with the children, your lawyer will tell you that unless something is seriously wrong with your spouse, you're unlikely to get custody. You need to listen to this advice. Many people spend a lot of money pursuing goals they can't obtain, usually because they're too wrapped up emotionally in the issue to see the reality of the situation. Try to operate with your head and not with your emotions. Your lawyer would rather not give you bad news, so when your lawyer does, pay attention.

Your lawyer may say you're entitled to more than you want. Think hard about this advice. Be sure you're the one who decides what you want. Sometimes pushing for more is what turns a divorce from friendly to hostile.

If your lawyer says you can get custody of the children by showing your spouse is emotionally unstable, think about whether you really want to do this. Would it be good for your children to drag their other parent through a battle about mental health? Suppose you actually got custody of the children. Are you prepared to take time off in the middle of the day to go to the doctor or the dentist or get your child to soccer practice? Be careful what you ask for.

ALERT!

After that first meeting with your lawyer, it's a good idea to rethink your objectives. Objectives need to be reasonable, obtainable, and based on reality. Revenge should not be an objective. It's a visceral response that may produce short-term results but long-term harm. While you may be able to hurt your spouse in the short term, what have you really gained?

Think about Timing

What about the timing of starting a divorce? Do you have any sense of how your spouse will react when served with divorce papers? Have you discussed this with your spouse, or will your decision to get divorced come as a big—and unpleasant—surprise? If you've both agreed to divorce, perhaps divorce papers can wait a bit while you, your spouse, and your lawyers discuss ways to resolve the issues. If you can work out a plan for living separately without using the courts, this will be less expensive and more likely to work well.

Anticipate Your Spouse's Actions

If your spouse doesn't want a divorce or is likely to be angry when you announce your decision either verbally or by serving papers, your strategy will have to be different. Some people do irrational things when they find out their spouse wants a divorce. They run and hide with the children. They empty bank accounts or run up huge credit card debts. You may need to take steps to protect your children, your assets, and your credit rating before you say anything. These are important issues to discuss with your lawyer.

Financial Documents

You and your lawyer will make a list of the documents needed to develop an understanding of your financial situation. Your lawyer will tell you which documents you need to verify your financial information. You will possess some of the documents, which you can provide easily, and your spouse will have some of the documents, which may or may not be easily obtained. Other papers may held by the bank or some other institution. You and your lawyer will develop a plan for getting all the documents, but remember, anything you can do to help collect the required documents will save your lawyer time, and save you money.

If your lawyer says that you need to round up certain financial information before you begin the divorce, get the documents right away. When you respond quickly to your lawyer's requests, you help move the process along. Your lawyer can prepare better, clearer papers if he or she has the necessary information.

Here's a list of basic financial information needed for a family with modest assets, including a house and retirement accounts:

- Recent paycheck stubs
- Recent bank statements showing checking and savings account balances and activities
- Recent statements showing retirement account values
- Current real estate tax bills
- Documents from recent home transactions (refinancing or appraisal)
- Debt balances as of the separation date or the current date if you haven't separated

To begin the divorce and set the process in motion, your lawyer will draft the required papers which are called a summons and petition, or sometimes simply a petition or complaint.

The Summons

This document tells your spouse he or she has thirty days to respond to the attached "petition for dissolution of marriage." The summons also contains restraining provisions such as neither party is to hide nor dispose of assets while the divorce is pending. In some states, a summons restrains parties from harassing or otherwise bothering each other. It may require the parties to keep all presently existing insurance in full effect and not to change beneficiaries. Some states require the summons to contain language encouraging the parties to use alternate dispute resolution.

Requirements differ from state to state, but serving a summons begins a divorce, unless you and your spouse file a joint petition. If you and your spouse have resolved all of your issues before you begin your paperwork, you may be able to skip the summons and prepare a Joint Petition and Stipulation that contains all the basic information of a regular petition and is followed by your agreement, or stipulation, and signed by both of you before a notary.

The Petition

The petition tells the bare-bones facts of your marriage. Each state has specific requirements about what must be in the petition, which your lawyer will know. The petition usually needs to include:

- Names, addresses, and birth dates of the parties
- Date and place of the marriage
- Children's names and birth dates
- Employment and income of the parties
- Real estate, with legal descriptions, owned by the parties
- Statement that one of the parties has lived in the state long enough to begin the divorce there
- Statement that the marriage is over, usually "irretrievably broken" in no-fault states
- Finding of fault in states that require it

- Amount of time parties have been separated (Some states require a minimum period of separation before divorce.)
- Other property owned by the parties (cars, boats, retirement plans, insurance)

After the petition sets out the facts, it then describes what the petitioner is asking for. This part of the petition is called the "prayer for relief." It usually asks that the marriage be dissolved, that the children live with one or both parents, that one of the parties support the other, and that the property be divided fairly and equitably.

The petitioner and his or her lawyer sign the petition, which in so doing indicates that the petitioner believes the information to be true, and that the lawyer recognizes his or her obligation to be ethical in drafting papers and in representing the client. The signatures are then notarized.

ALERT!

Never sign anything you haven't read or don't understand. This is a life lesson, but holds especially true in matters of divorce. Also, never sign your name to documents containing false information—you will likely be found out and the price you pay could be quite high.

Serving the Papers

"Service" is the legal term used when legal papers are delivered from one side to another in a case. Usually a summons must be personally served; that is, the papers must be handed to your spouse or to a person of a responsible age in your spouse's household.

Your lawyer will probably hire a process server—a civilian who works for a company that serves and delivers legal documents—to serve the papers to your spouse. If this is to be an amicable divorce, at least for now, your spouse may prefer to pick up the papers at your lawyer's office rather than risk being served in a public place.

Some states require divorce papers be filed with the court before they are served. Others have no filing requirement. Either way, the divorce begins when these papers are served.

When you want to use the court, you need to prepare and file the summons and petition and your motion papers. The court doesn't get involved in your life until you ask it to, and that's done by filing your papers.

FACT

When papers are filed with the court, the system kicks in and may take control of your divorce. You need to know the impact of filing any papers before you do so. You may be able to get the divorce going without filing, and you need to know which way is better for you.

An Affidavit

You may want a court order giving you the use of your home, a car, and a bank account during the divorce. Unless you and your spouse can negotiate the terms of this order, you'll need to prepare a motion asking for these things and explaining why you need them. To do this, you must prepare a document called an affidavit, which is a sworn statement you and your lawyer prepare telling the court why you need whatever it is you're seeking.

Persuading the Judge

For instance, if you have school-age children, you might tell the court you want them to live with you in the family home so that way their lives will be minimally disrupted, and they can continue to go to their school, play with their friends, and participate in their neighborhood activities. You might say you need the newer, bigger car to transport them safely. And you need the bank account to pay the monthly household expenses. You'll want to tell the judge the things you believe will persuade him or her to do what you want.

If you and your spouse disagree about a parenting arrangement—temporary or permanent—you'll need to make a motion asking a judge to decide. You'll need to prepare an affidavit explaining why your arrangement is best for the children. It's important to tell the judge in this affidavit how the children have been cared for up to this point, because judges tend to maintain the status quo for children. So if you've been their major caregiver, say so; if you haven't been, then you need to present a very strong case for making the change.

Be Prepared with Details

If you want to have joint custody of the children with your spouse, you should set out your proposal in detail. You should spell out the children's school schedules and provide the mileage between their school or day care and your and your spouse's residences and workplaces. You also might spell out the children's activity schedule in some detail. And, it would be wise to include your work schedule and that of your spouse. This practical information can help a judge form a workable plan.

FACT

If you and your spouse live far apart, the judge will probably try to avoid sentencing the children to life as commuters, and minimize the number of exchanges during the school week.

Restraining Orders

Is your spouse likely to behave badly when served with the divorce papers? Will she try to hide marital assets? Will he spend like crazy, running up big credit card debt? Might she run from the state with the children? If any of these are possibilities, maybe you need to serve some restraining orders when you serve the summons and petition.

If you decide you need restraining orders right from the beginning, by that decision you've also committed to going to court. Except in very unusual situations, courts won't sign an order presented by one side, called an ex parte order, without scheduling a hearing for a few weeks down the pike. The court will schedule a hearing so that both of you can be present and present your version of the situation. The ex parte order will prohibit both parents from taking the children out of the county until the hearing, and it may also say that neither party is to incur new debt or transfer any marital moneys and property until the hearing. Judges are much more comfortable signing ex parte orders that apply to both spouses.

To Court or Not to Court

Even if you don't need the ex parte restraining orders, you and your lawyer might decide you need some rules to govern behavior during the divorce. Say you're afraid your spouse will try to keep you from seeing the children, and you're also concerned your spouse will continue to spend money you don't have staying in a house you can't afford. You know your spouse will be really angry when the divorce papers are served, but you tried discussing your situation before going to a lawyer, and it didn't work out. What can you do?

Temporary Orders

You can try to negotiate rules that will govern your family's behavior during the divorce. If your spouse hires a lawyer, the four of you can meet to discuss a temporary arrangement. The lawyers can also develop a plan and present it to you and your spouse. You'll want to decide who will live in the marital home, when the children will be with each of you, how you'll pay for two homes, what funds can be used, what documents need to be exchanged, and what property needs to be valued by a third person.

If it's possible to negotiate a temporary arrangement, one of the lawyers will draft a document called a "stipulation for temporary relief" or "interim agreement," or whatever your court system calls it, for you, your spouse, and the two lawyers to sign. If you need a court order incorporating the terms of the agreement, one of the lawyers will get the order signed by a judge.

FACT

If you obtained an ex parte restraining order or your spouse is too angry and upset to meet and negotiate, you'll need a temporary court order that will stay in place until another temporary order replaces it or until the final judgment and decree is issued. To get that temporary order from the judge, you'll need to bring a motion.

Motions

Once you and your lawyer decide what you're going to ask the court to do, your lawyer will get a hearing date from the court administrators and draft a document called a motion (request). You are, in effect, moving (asking) the court for help. Court rules require that you also draft an affidavit, your sworn statement, to go with the motion.

The minimum amount of paperwork consists of the motion and affidavit. If you have issues that involve children, you will probably seek affidavits from friends and family who know about your skills and attributes as a parent. Given these issues and others you might have, your motion and affidavit may grow into a thick pile of papers very quickly. These papers have to be served on your spouse or your spouse's attorney, and the other side will probably respond with a motion and affidavits of its own. Your affidavits probably will upset your spouse, just as you'll probably be upset when you get your spouse's responsive papers, including responsive affidavits.

Now you have to respond to your spouse's papers with new affidavits. Then maybe your spouse responds to your responses. This is getting crazy! At some point the exchange of papers has to stop, so most courts set a deadline for filing papers, often five days before the hearing. Court administrators probably won't have time to get any papers filed into your court file only five days before the hearing, so you'll have to have copies delivered to the judge scheduled to hear your motion to be sure the judge has them.

Are you getting the picture here? Any idea how much money you've spent so far?

Programs about the Divorce Process

Before a motion can be heard, most states require parents to attend an educational program about the divorce process and about parenting during and after a divorce. So you and your spouse will probably spend several hours at the required program, which may include a meeting among you, your spouse, and a staff social worker to discuss and try to work out some temporary parenting issues. Any agreements you reach during this meeting can be put into an order that will be effective until the judge issues another order after a temporary hearing.

To help you battle the urge to take out your frustration and anger on a gazillion affidavits, purchase a punching bag. For every angry statement, retort, or sarcastic criticism you want to level at your spouse, hit the bag instead. Depending on how angry you are, you may just wear yourself out in one session. This is a great stress reliever and a way to relieve your frustration outside the courts.

It's an Emergency

Suppose you need help NOW. What can you do? If you use the normal court process, it may take weeks or more to actually get into court. Then you may have to wait for more than a month for the judge's decision. If you're already in financial trouble with no family to lend you money or you have a spouse who is behaving badly, you may be able to get an emergency order. This may be that extraordinary situation where the judge will issue an ex parte order that grants temporary relief.

If your lawyer believes it's possible to get such an order, you'll need to prepare all the paperwork already described, plus a plea for emergency relief that sets out why the judge should grant it. Your lawyer will prepare what's called an ex parte order, which he or she will take to the judge for signature before the papers are served on your spouse. As mentioned earlier, this order is called an ex parte order because only one side—yours—has appeared before the court. These orders contain hearing dates at which time both sides can speak on the issues. The major difference here is that the order does more than keep the kids in the county or freeze assets—it directs one of the parties to do certain things.

The ex parte order is a temporary order, justified because an emergency exists, and is usually valid only until the hearing. In addition to those provisions that apply to both of you, depending on the circumstances, the order may give you temporary use and occupancy of the house, use of a car, or temporary custody of the children. It may also order your spouse to pay you temporary support.

ALERT!

Judges don't like ex parte orders; somehow they feel unfair. Judges especially don't like orders that throw someone out of his or her house. You must really need such an order and be able to justify that need. Seek this extraordinary relief only if you must, and make sure an emergency really exists.

Order to Show Cause

If you're in dire need of financial help, but you and your lawyer don't believe you can get an emergency order, another possibility exists. A document called an Order to Show Cause can be used with the motion and affidavit papers. This document basically orders your spouse to court to show cause as to why your order should not be granted. For example, the Order to Show Cause may contain a provision ordering your spouse to pay you a specified amount of temporary support, and your spouse will need to explain why this shouldn't be necessary.

Your lawyer will take the Order to Show Cause along with all of your motions and affidavits to court to be signed by a judge. Your lawyer has an obligation to tell your spouse's lawyer that he or she is going to court to get the order signed. Not all courts in all states will issue such an order, but if your court will do so, it will provide you with some temporary financial help until a hearing can be held. The financial support will stay in place until the judge issues another order following your hearing.

Once you and your lawyer have determined that all the needed paperwork has been prepared, your lawyer will get the court order signed and the papers get served on your spouse. Different states have different requirements here, but all states require personal service of court papers that begin the divorce, unless your spouse chooses to accept service by mail or one of a number of other exceptions that may be applicable to your case. There are always exceptions—your lawyer should know about them.

The Temporary Hearing

If you've chosen to go to court, at some point you'll actually have to go to the courthouse for your first hearing before a judge. The last time you met with your lawyer you probably talked about what you should wear to court, and based upon your lawyer's advice, you selected clothes you would wear to an important and serious event, such as a funeral—conservative and sober. Your clothing also should be comfortable, but shouldn't detract from the words said by your lawyer or by you, should you get to say anything. You'll probably be pretty nervous, so you don't want to wear clothes that make you even more uncomfortable.

Men and women should dress appropriately for court. It's important to dress in a way that shows respect for the judge and the court. You want the judge to hear your lawyer and not be distracted by your outfit.

Before the Hearing

You and your lawyer will go to the courtroom where your motion is to be heard. Your spouse and lawyer will be there, too, and maybe your spouse's parent (for moral support) or your spouse's new love interest (just to get you upset). This ploy usually works. It's not uncommon for people waiting outside the court to lose control during this time of high stress and emotional volatility, so court administration usually assigns a number of deputy sheriffs to the family court. The presence of uniformed officers helps to keep things calm, and the officers are trained to respond quickly if folks get out of control.

It's best to come to court with only your lawyer and any expert who may present information at the hearing. Family and friends may increase the tension and be a distraction, and you need to be able to concentrate on the court hearing.

During the Hearing

Say your hearing is scheduled for 2 P.M. At 2:45 the judge's clerk pokes his nose out to tell you the judge will see you shortly, which turns out to be another half an hour. Finally, it really is time for your motion to be heard. You and your lawyer sit at one table before the judge's bench; your spouse and lawyer sit at the other. The judge appears, and everyone stands until told to sit. After that the clerk may announce the case, so the judge knows which file to look at.

ALERT!

Never bring children to a court hearing. Divorce is stressful enough for children without making them active participants in your war with their other parent. Courts do not look kindly on parents who bring their children to court.

The lawyers introduce themselves, and then your lawyer argues on behalf of your motions. Your spouse's lawyer responds. Maybe each lawyer responds to the other's arguments. After the judge has heard both sides, the judge usually tells everyone that he or she will take the matter under advisement and issue an order within ninety days. You're dismissed and leave the courtroom.

After the Hearing

Well, how about that! Your heart was beating a mile a minute, your future was on the line, and you didn't get to say a word. Not only that, your lawyer didn't point out all the lies in your spouse's affidavit and didn't even argue some of the points you thought were important. And the judge has ninety days to issue an order? What are you supposed to do in the meantime?

Your lawyer assures you the hearing went well, and tells you to be patient and wait for the judge's order. Thank goodness you were able to negotiate an order about seeing the kids before the court hearing.

The Judge Issues a Temporary Order

Eighty-eight days after your court hearing, your lawyer calls to say the judge has issued an order, and suggests you come to his or her office to review it. With a sinking feeling, you drop everything. The order is a disaster. It feels like the judge never read your papers or heard your lawyer's arguments. Your spouse gets the kids, the house, and most of your income. You never got to say anything to the judge.

Because you have to move out of the house and pay most of your income to your spouse, you'll have to move in with your parents or a buddy temporarily. How long is temporarily? You'll have to drive about an hour to your former home to see your children for two hours twice a week. You'll have to work as much overtime as you can to have some spending money for your visits with the children and to pay some rent. After reading the order, you don't feel much like working at all, let alone working overtime.

FACT

The productivity of wage earners tends to decline during the divorce process. Some judges and lawyers attribute this to the wage earner's desire to pay less support, but the process of divorce and reduced productivity really are connected. The stress of the divorce makes it hard to perform well on the job.

Usually you can't appeal temporary orders. This means you'll have to live with the judge's order unless you bring another motion that results in a different order. Some people decide that living with the order, however terrible, is better than risking an even worse result by going back to court. Others never tire of beating their heads against the wall, so they bring motion after motion, obtaining only an enormous bill for attorney's fees and the anger of the court. If you choose to live with the order, at least you have a framework within which to operate until the divorce is done.

Chapter 12

The Discovery Process

When you went to see your lawyer at the beginning of the divorce process, you talked about information needed to work out the final details of your divorce. The process used by lawyers to get information from the other side or from a third party is called discovery.

What's Included in Discovery?

Lawyers have an ethical duty to obtain information so that they can properly advise their clients. So, if the lawyers are in charge of your divorce, they'll want all the information that exists, for example, about the finances and property of the marriage. Here is some of the important financial information you may need to supply in discovery:

- Current employment and income, including bonuses, stock options, and other benefits
- Employment history, including past income, bonuses, stock options, and retirement benefits
- Business tax returns for several years if you're self-employed
- Value of businesses
- Personal tax returns for three to five years
- Checks and check registers for three to five years
- Documents for all real estate purchased and sold before and during the marriage
- Value of real estate
- Retirement benefits and assets
- Life insurance owned by the parties
- Value of special personal property, such as antiques
- Value of boats, cars, snowmobiles, and other vehicles
- Value of the animals, crops, seed and fertilizer, equipment, etc. if a farm is involved
- Monthly expenses claimed by both parties
- Mental health and other health histories
- Inheritances, gifts, and claims of nonmarital assets
- Marriage debts

Not everyone has all the stuff on this list, and not everyone needs to have all this information to make a reasonable settlement. But this will give you some idea of the kinds of information that might be requested.

Discovery When You're Both Cooperating

Getting information from the other side can take several forms. In a cooperative divorce, your lawyer can simply call or write your spouse's lawyer and ask for the information you need. Your spouse and his or her lawyer then will provide the information they have in their possession. Likewise, you and your lawyer will provide whatever information you have that the other side has asked for.

FACT

Sharing information is the least expensive way of getting the complete picture of your marital estate. The more information you and your spouse collect and exchange, the less you have to pay someone else to collect it. This means you spend less of the marital estate trying to figure out what it is. This leaves more for the both of you.

If neither of you has some of the information the lawyers say they need, if both of you cooperate, the information is easily gotten. Suppose you need the records for the last year on your spouse's VISA account. Your spouse can get the records or can sign an authorization permitting you to get the records. Suppose your spouse wants your medical records for the last five years, but your doctor won't provide them to anyone except you. Either you'll have to get them, or you'll have to sign a release permitting your doctor to give the records to your spouse. If you don't want the hassle of getting certain information, you can sign a release or authorization permitting the other side to obtain it. Then they can decide how much they want, and go after it or not.

Discovery When You Can't Cooperate

If you and your spouse can't work together to collect the information, your lawyer will need to use the muscle provided by court rules to get it. Often when parties are angry and hostile, they try to keep information from each other. But if you play hard to get with information the other side is entitled to have, you end up paying your lawyer to delay the inevitable. This is not in your best interests.

Interrogatory

In a contested process, the most common form of discovery is through the interrogatory, a set of up to sixty questions your lawyer asks your spouse to answer under oath. Your lawyer probably has a set of standard interrogatories, which he or she pulls out and adapts for each case. Lawyers call these boilerplate interrogatories. You and your lawyer should review the proposed interrogatories together to make sure they focus on information that is likely to be helpful to you in preparing your case. Preparing the interrogatories and reviewing the answers you get takes your attorney time. You pay for this time.

If your spouse serves interrogatories on you through your lawyer, take some time to prepare your answers carefully. Answer concisely and clearly all the questions that you can. If you don't know the answer, say so. Don't guess. If you answer the interrogatories one way, and further discovery provides different information, you will look as if you weren't being truthful.

ALERT!

When you fudge the truth, you have to remember just how you fudged for future reference. Not an easy task, especially when you're under the stress of a divorce. You don't gain anything by playing fast and loose with the truth when the outcome has so much impact on your future.

Depositions

Another form of discovery is called the deposition. Your lawyer prepares a list of questions for your spouse or a potential witness, such as a person who performed a custody evaluation or who valued your business. Then your lawyer sends a notice to your spouse's lawyer saying, in effect: "You are to show up on March 1 at 10 A.M. at my office for your deposition to be taken." Usually lawyers have already set the date by agreement, but the notice is required by court rules.

Sometimes if lawyers haven't set the date in advance, they do the lawyer's "deposition dance." One lawyer serves the other with the Notice for Taking Deposition. Then the other lawyer sends a letter saying that the date chosen won't work. After a series of letters, a date is finally selected. You pay for your lawyer's time, so try to encourage your lawyer to set the date by agreement to avoid the costly back-and-forth dance.

When your spouse's deposition is taken, your spouse, your spouse's lawyer, your lawyer, and a court reporter are present. You can be present, too, if you choose. Your spouse is sworn, and answers your lawyer's questions. Sometimes your spouse's lawyer objects to your lawyer's question and then proceeds to make a legal argument. The lawyer does this to preserve his or her objection. If the transcript is later used in court, that lawyer may ask the judge to rule on the objection, with the purpose of keeping that particular question and answer out of court. Everything said at the deposition is taken down by the court reporter and later transcribed for both sides and for the court.

Reasons for a Deposition

The deposition's purpose is to obtain information needed to resolve issues. Sometimes it can be used to find out what kind of a witness your spouse will be, to impress your spouse with what a sly fox your lawyer is, or to catch your spouse in some misstatement that can be used at trial. Some chronic liars are exposed by the deposition; on the other hand, some good, honest folk are scared into saying things they don't mean. The deposition will cost you the fees of your lawyer and the court reporter, and maybe the fees of your spouse's lawyer.

On a rare occasion some useful information can be obtained at a deposition. Once a client announced at her deposition that the only person she hated more in the world than her husband was her husband's lawyer, the one taking her deposition. Is that useful information? No, it's a waste of time.

Handling a Deposition

If your spouse's lawyer takes your deposition, answer the questions clearly and concisely. If you don't know the answer, say so. Answer only the question that's asked, and pause briefly before giving your answer to give your lawyer time to object. Do not volunteer information. If you stick to the questions, your lawyer can give you guidance and object to questions he or she believes to be improper. Your lawyer can advise you not to answer a question, but your lawyer can't protect you if you blurt something out.

Your spouse's lawyer may try to use the emotional stress of divorce against you by tempting you to argue or make outbursts that could hurt you. If your temper is flaring, take a moment to breathe deeply and think about what you're going to say before responding to a question.

Using Experts

Some information needed to settle your divorce might not be readily available. For instance, if you need the value of your home or business, you'll need to hire an expert to figure it out. Ordinarily, you wouldn't have this value available unless you had recently done some refinancing or sold or purchased the home or business. Or maybe you need an expert to help you come up with the best parenting plan for your children. Maybe you need an expert because your spouse hasn't worked more than part time for several years, and the two of you need to know what your spouse's earning potential is and how to achieve it. Or maybe you need someone to figure out your stock options or the investment you made in rental properties with inherited money.

All these areas call for the opinion of an expert: a licensed certified public accountant, a realtor, a psychologist, a business evaluator, or a rehabilitation counselor. In short, you need a person who has expertise in areas where you need help.

Working Cooperatively Is Best

If you and your spouse work cooperatively, you can agree on the experts to use. If you can select one in each area where you need outside expertise, and can agree to accept the report of that expert, you can save a ton of money. First of all, you pay only one person rather than two. Second, you will get a neutral opinion—one not favoring either side—on which to base your settlement. Third, you don't get the court involved, thereby avoiding a possible third opinion.

Valuing a Professional Practice

Let's assume you and your spouse agree to work with one expert— often called an independent neutral—to come up with a value for your spouse's dental practice. You tell your lawyers you want to hire an expert with knowledge of dental practices, and each lawyer produces the names of two or three experts. You may ask for the experts' credentials, so you have some basis on which to choose.

You and your spouse pick the expert. You tell the expert what you want, and you provide the expert with the information he or she asks for. The expert gives you his or her best opinion, and you plug it into the balance sheet you're preparing. This may sound pretty simplistic, or too good to be true, but it really does happen.

Divorce lawyers develop a short list of experts who can be trusted as independent neutrals in cooperative divorce situations. These neutrals can be of immense help to you in valuing your assets.

Dueling Experts

Contrast this with the litigation approach to using experts: You tell the expert that you "know" the practice is worth a bazillion dollars, that your spouse cooks the books, and that your spouse has intentionally cut back work over the last year to reduce the practice's value. You give the expert a bottom line from which to work. "The practice must be worth at least $500,000," you say. Since you're the one paying the expert, is it any surprise that the expert comes up with a value of $550,000?

Well, your spouse hires an expert as well. Your spouse tells the expert the economy has slowed and demand for your spouse's specialty, orthodontics, is down because it's elective. The practice really is worth only the value of the used equipment, your spouse says, and the business can't be worth more than $50,000. It may even have a negative value. Since your spouse pays the expert, is it any wonder your spouse's expert develops a value of $34,000 for the practice?

ALERT!

What numbers are ringing in your mental cash register at this point? Fees for the experts, fees for the lawyers, fees for a court reporter. Clearly, this valuation is getting very expensive. It may cost more than the dental practice actually is worth.

At this point, you have some options. Your lawyer can take the deposition of your spouse's expert to see if there are any weaknesses in the expert's analysis. Your lawyer may well want your expert to be present at the deposition to help ask the right questions. This, by the way, is a legitimate use of a deposition. You and your lawyer want to know what the other side's expert will say at trial, and whether the expert's opinion can be challenged.

Your side and your spouse's side may decide to hire a third expert, chosen by the first two experts. You may even take the issue to the court. The judge may decide a third opinion is needed, that of an independent neutral. Why didn't you think of this earlier?

A Contested Court Hearing

At some point you bring competing experts and their reports to court for a contested hearing on the value of your spouse's dental practice. It's fair to assume the judge knows nothing about dental practices, beyond what's involved in getting his or her teeth cleaned on a fairly regular basis. On top of that, neither expert is a scintillating speaker, and your lawyer doesn't do much to make your expert interesting, so the judge pretty much snoozes through the daylong argument.

When the dust settles, the judge determines a value somewhere between $34,000 and $550,000. As long as the judge can come up with a reasonable explanation for the value, it will pass muster with the appellate courts. But chances are, it probably will be a value neither party agrees with.

After all that, here's what you end up with: expert reports costing anywhere from $15,000 to $50,000 apiece; a day in court for two experts and two lawyers costing anywhere from $3,000 to $15,000 each; plus a stress level measuring off the charts while this litigation is going on. Why punish yourself and your family? If you use an independent neutral from the beginning, you can get the information you need for a lot less time, money, and stress. Most important, you'll end up with a real number that can contribute to a workable settlement.

Vocational Rehabilitation Counselor

Suppose your spouse has been unemployed or working only a few hours each week since your first child was born. It's clear from family expenses your spouse will need to work full-time to generate income to support two households. Or, while you can afford to support your spouse and children now, you feel at some point your spouse should become financially independent of you.

You and your spouse can choose to use a vocational counselor as an independent neutral and put your energies into implementing the recommendations. Of course, you also can each hire a vocational counselor and fight about what career your spouse should pursue and how long it should take him or her to become self-supporting.

What if your spouse has a college degree in some esoteric field like art history and has never used this education for employment. What are your spouse's skills and interests? If neither of you can answer these questions, you may want to hire a vocational rehabilitation counselor. These experts usually work in the unemployment field, but some have expanded their practice to divorce. They usually administer a battery of tests to learn interests and skills, and have current information about the job market. They can put together this information to make recommendations, which often include getting training or additional education.

Financial Evaluators

If you need to get a handle on your cash flow, you may want to use a certified public accountant (CPA) or other financial expert. A CPA can show how tax implications of certain actions can cost or save you money. If you and your spouse can work together in this area, you really can do yourselves a favor. So much money is spent arguing over net income, the tax consequences of paying spousal maintenance, the proper 401(k) deduction, and so on, that there's not much left over to actually live on. If the same money and energy can go into putting together a workable plan, everyone loses less.

Real Estate Professionals

Realtors can give you a good idea of what your real estate is worth, and so can real estate appraisers. Most appraisers' values tend to be on the conservative side, because appraisers usually start out with a lending institution, which generally wants to conserve its risk obligation. Realtors, on the other hand, may give your property a higher value, hoping you'll choose to work with them in selling your house. Realtors can also give you a bottom-line cash-to-seller analysis. This will tell you what you could realistically expect to receive if you sold your property. This information may help you decide whether your property should be sold but isn't always helpful in determining its value.

Experts and Children

You can use experts a number of ways to resolve custody issues. Your lawyer will know the skills and reputations of many psychologists and social workers with expertise in helping divorcing families create workable parenting arrangements. Your lawyer can assist you in hiring the person best qualified to help you accomplish your goals.

Determining Your Goals

For starters, you need to decide whether you want to negotiate a plan with your spouse, or whether you want to decide what's best for the children yourself? Do you want an expert assessment of your skills and strengths as a parent? Would you rather take your spouse to court and fight over custody? What you want will influence whom you hire. Obviously, if you and your spouse can sit down and rationally work out a plan, you don't need an expert. If you agree in principle but are bogged down in details, you might want to work with an expert experienced in developing parenting plans.

ALERT!

Use the information you get from the expert to help resolve divorce issues rather than having the expert testify before a judge who probably has little or no knowledge about the issue and is likely to make a decision you won't like. This costs you in time, money, and frustration.

Psychologists and Family Services

If you and your spouse want to do the right thing for your kids but are too angry and hurt to sit down and talk it through, you can hire a psychologist with expertise in parenting and children's needs. The psychologist can be a buffer between the two of you, helping put your ideas into words that are constructive rather than destructive.

Where can you get help? Catholic Charities, Lutheran Social Service, and Jewish Family and Children's Services have social workers and psychologists on staff. And larger communities often have a family services arm of the court system to help with parenting plans and custody evaluations. Sometimes, these people move into private practice after gaining experience in the public sector. Lawyers who work with these folks on a daily basis come to know their strengths and weaknesses. When hiring an expert to help with parenting, you'll want to use the same approach as hiring your lawyer or personal therapist.

FACT

You'll also need to consider costs. Will your insurance cover any of the psychologist's fees? Rarely. Public agencies cost less and may be able to provide all the help you need. Experts with the best reputations don't come cheap, so their use should be reserved for really difficult parents with high conflict and dysfunction, or for those who need just one or two meetings to put together a parenting plan.

An Independent Neutral

Let's suppose you and your spouse can't reach an agreement about parenting after the divorce, and you really can't sit down and discuss the issue. But at the same time, you both really want to do the right thing for your kids. So you wisely decide to hire an independent neutral expert to conduct a custody evaluation.

This person will probably meet with the two of you to get basic information about you and the family. The custody evaluator may ask you to fill out and return a questionnaire that may contain a section asking for your custody proposal. In addition, the expert may ask each of you to take a psychological evaluation or other diagnostic test to check out your mental health. The expert will also meet with your children to get a sense of who they are, how well they're adjusting to the divorce, and any special physical or emotional needs they may have. The custody evaluator will come to your home to see what it's like and to see how you and the children interact in the home setting. The expert may also meet with you and the children in a professional setting. The expert will talk to friends and family, too.

When the custody evaluator has collected the needed information, all of you will meet to hear the recommendations. If you're then able to settle, the evaluator will write up your agreement and send it to your lawyers. If you can't settle, the expert will write up a custody evaluation and send that to your attorneys. One of the attorneys may decide to take the expert's deposition, to see whether the report can be challenged, or whether to hire a second expert. This is much more time consuming, and this means it will be more expensive.

Going to War

If you and your spouse choose the ultimate custody war, you'll each hire an expert and duke it out before a judge at some point. A custody battle is the ultimate failure of the system to meet the needs of divorcing families. It's expensive, it's very stressful, and it's harmful to the children. And, after a week of bashing each other in court, you'll still be expected to somehow make the judge's ultimate decision work.

FACT

The discovery process is intended to give you and your spouse information that will enable you to resolve your issues. If you ask the right questions, hire experts you trust, and listen to your lawyers, you should be able to reach a reasonable resolution without a trial.

Use Your Time Wisely

Discovery's purpose is to gather information. If you and your spouse believe you can work out a settlement, you'll need to know just what the two of you have in order to divide it up. You'll need facts about your finances and property. You'll need to focus on what constitutes a fair and equitable division of property and a reasonable plan for taking care of your children.

On the other hand, if you're pretty sure you and your spouse can't work out a settlement, you'll need to know more than the extent of the marital estate. You'll need to know whom your spouse will use as trial witnesses, and what kind of witnesses your spouse and experts will be. You'll need to know what theories appeal to the judge who will hear your case. You'll also need to prepare to be a witness yourself. You'll need to focus on your spouse's weaknesses and possible prior misstatements, any bad judgment your spouse has shown regarding finances or the children, or whatever is at issue between you.

You can expect to spend a considerable amount of time and money conducting the discovery needed to bring your divorce to trial. A lot of discovery won't feel very uplifting. Some people are able to stay angry and vindictive long enough to really want a trial; some calm and reasonable people simply get stuck on an issue and need a third person to decide it; but most people calm down at some point and choose a less destructive alternative. Ⓔ

Chapter 13

Custody and Visitation

Custody and visitation are the traditional words used to describe parenting during and after the divorce. These words sound unpleasant and inappropriate for talking about rearing the children. The word *custody* carries the connotation of ownership or incarceration, and *visitation* is what you do at a funeral home. Nevertheless, these are the words found in the statutes across the nation.

Parenting Arrangements

Parenting arrangements or *parenting plans* are phrases used to describe how you will care for your children after the divorce. These plans come in as many variations as there are creative parents to develop them. However, when courts make parenting decisions, they follow traditional patterns. Courts do not do much creative work. Their job is to resolve disputes, not try to second-guess parents in conflict.

You don't have to like your ex-spouse, but for the children's sake, try to show respect for him or her. Co-parenting cooperatively will be a lot easier if you can maintain a respectful relationship, and this is in the best interests of your children.

There are five terms the court uses to designate custody:

1. **Legal custody.** This describes major decision-making about your children, including their education, religion, and health care; the decisions about where the children will go to school, what church they will attend, and who will provide medical and dental care are legal decisions.
2. **Physical custody.** This refers to the actual time a child spends with a parent. It can be sole or joint.
3. **Sole custody.** This means one parent is in charge.
4. **Sole legal custody.** This means one parent decides where the children go to school, picks their religion, selects their doctors and dentist, and decides if any elective medical or dental care, like braces on their teeth, will be obtained.
5. **Joint legal custody.** Also called shared legal custody, this means parents make major decisions about their children together.

Information about the Children

Most states' laws provide that both parents are entitled to information about their children regardless of the custody designation, unless such information could endanger a child. Information about the children might be withheld from an abusive or very angry parent who has made threats to take the children. Even so, such a parent would retain the right to see the children in a supervised setting. Parents have the right to know where the children go to school, where they worship, and the names of their doctor, dentist, and orthodontist.

Both parents have the right to get school notices, attend parent-teacher conferences (not necessarily together), and participate in school activities. They are entitled to copies of their children's report cards. Both parents are entitled to see their children's medical and dental records and to talk to the health care providers.

Children in Therapy

Many children whose parents are divorcing end up in therapy. The children may be having difficulty with the divorce or with the behavior of one or both of their parents in the divorce context. Courts don't have the authority to order parents to get their children into therapy. However, many parents send their children to a therapist, often because the children's behavior becomes worrisome or difficult during a divorce.

FACT

Allegations or evidence of abuse may cause the court to issue restraining orders that prevent the abusive parent from going to the child's home, school, or place of worship. However, even abusive parents are entitled to see their children's medical, school, and therapy records. Unfortunately, some abusive parents use this information to try to continue to control their spouse, to the child's detriment.

Many therapists ask parents to sign a confidentiality agreement stating that conversations between a therapist and child are private. Therapists believe they can be more helpful to children if the relationship is not a part of the divorce, especially if it is one that goes to court.

Be aware that if you do go to court, the judge may order the therapist to turn over his or her notes and records to the parents. Exposing your child's confidences, shared in the belief that they were private, can have a devastating effect on your child's mental health.

Joint Legal Custody

Parents with similar values usually can agree on major decisions for their children, if they can put their hurt and anger aside and focus on the children. However, parents involved in major power struggles usually can't make these decisions together. Also, in families where domestic abuse has occurred, most states' laws prohibit imposing joint legal custody on parents. The parties may choose joint legal custody, but they will have to persuade the judge this arrangement can work in spite of the abuse.

Many states' laws include a preference for joint legal custody, unless a good reason for sole legal custody exists. Good reasons for sole legal custody include domestic abuse, an uninvolved and absent parent, or a parent's mental illness.

ALERT!

While your energy may be focused on working out a co-parenting arrangement that works for everyone, you shouldn't forget about the former in-laws. Grandparents, aunts, uncles will want to visit with the children as well.

Developing a Workable Parenting Plan

If you are parents, developing a workable parenting plan is the most important part of your divorce. As discussed elsewhere, the children of divorce suffer the most serious and long-lasting consequences from conflict between their parents over them. Parents can do a much better job than the judge in putting together a workable parenting plan, because parents know, deep down, what's best for their children. When parents can see past their anger, hurt, and pride, they can create a workable plan because they have all the facts. The judge almost never has all the facts. You should continue to take responsibility for your children by making your own parenting plan.

Physical Custody and Visitation

A parent who has sole physical custody has the children most of the time. The other parent has visitation (that awful word again). To get away from visitation, the words *access* or *parenting time* are often used.

FACT

Often the visiting parent is unwilling to contribute funds over and above the court-ordered child support. However, research shows that when parents decide together to send kids to private schools or camp or music lessons, they often agree to share the costs of these enriching childhood experiences. When parents work together, the children benefit.

Parenting Time

Parenting time comes in many flavors. Often children spend every other weekend and one evening each week with the noncustodial parent. Sometimes they spend less time with one parent during the school year and a chunk of time with that parent during the summer. When parents live in different states or far apart in the same state, they may choose a schedule that minimizes the complications of getting from one home to the other. The children may spend the school year in one home, the summer in the other, and half the school holidays with each parent. When a parent and a child share a special interest, they can participate in an activity together and have their time together determined by the activity schedule.

Parents with emotional problems that make them unstable, parents who have abused their spouse or the children, and parents who have threatened to run away with the children may have their visitation supervised by a third person to protect the children and the spouse. Sometimes the supervisor is a family member; sometimes an agency in the community provides supervision.

Joint Physical Custody

Joint or shared physical custody can take many forms. Some children spend alternate weeks with each parent. Some spend Sundays through

Tuesdays in one home, Thursdays through Saturdays in the other, and alternate the Wednesdays. Some divorced parents have the children stay in the family home, and they—the parents—move in and out.

Shared parenting plans work only when the parents can put their animosities aside and focus on what's best for their children. Obviously, these parents will have frequent contact with each other and will have to work cooperatively to coordinate schedules, locate lost book bags, and make sure one of them picks up the children from activities. They also will need to live fairly close to each other. Obviously, joint custody is not for all parents.

FACT

The children of divorce who grew up in a traditional custody arrangement where Mom had custody and Dad had visitation consistently report that they would have liked more time with their fathers. Children appear to have strong relationships with their mothers, regardless of the custody arrangement. But the children have a need for more contact with their fathers.

Joint custody is not for all children, either. The children are in emotional turmoil because of the divorce. They may have a hard time remembering a complex parenting schedule and sometimes go to the wrong house, a very traumatic experience. Joint physical custody is usually not a good plan for very young children. When parents live within blocks of each other, get along well, and have well-adjusted children, joint custody works well. However, it can also work under less than optimum circumstances when the parents are motivated to put the interests of their children first.

Children's Preferences

The children of divorce prefer joint physical custody. When these children are interviewed as young adults, they are clear in their preference for joint custody. And, by joint custody, they mean equal time with each parent. Apparently, the next best thing to having their parents stay married is having them stay equally involved in their lives. The complications created by the logistics of joint custody are much less important to the children than maintaining parental contact.

Negotiate or Litigate?

As with all aspects of a divorce, you'll end up with a more workable parenting plan if you put it together. You can take into account your schedules, your children's special needs, and the strengths each of you bring to your role as parent. Parents who develop their own parenting plan put their energies into implementing it. This means your plan has a higher likelihood of success than one imposed on you by the court.

When you litigate, you turn decision-making over to a judge, who is a stranger. The only things the judge knows are the things you tell him or her. A judge is likely to hear mostly negative things, as each of you strives to emphasize the other parent's weaknesses. As discussed previously, a major source of a judge's information is the affidavit you submit with your motion for custody of your children.

Hypothetical Custody Litigation

Let's look at one little piece of custody litigation. Suppose the parents, Jack B. Nimble and Suzie B. Qwik, have two children, Julie and Jack Jr. Suzie has announced she wants a divorce, and she and Jack have a huge argument. Jack leaves the house and moves in with a coworker who lives across town, a forty-five-minute trip during light traffic. Suzie serves Jack with divorce papers. Jack responds by scheduling a court hearing to get custody of the children. (Remember, as we have discussed elsewhere, you have to prepare an affidavit to go with a motion.)

Take a look at the two sample affidavits that follow, one from Jack and one from Suzie. These are composites of affidavits culled from many hearings. After you read these, try to put yourself in a judge's shoes. What would you do with this information if you were the judge? Next, look at the "translation"—the judge's probable interpretation—of these affidavits. With any luck, you'll figure out what information is helpful and what will come back to bite you. Then you'll know what to put into an affidavit, if you ever have to prepare one.

Dad's Affidavit

STATE OF MIND   DISTRICT COURT

COUNTY OF CONFUSION   FAMILY COURT DIVISION

Jack B. Nimble, being duly sworn, on oath deposes and says [this is legalese],

1. I am the petitioner in this divorce proceeding.
2. I make this affidavit in support of my motion for custody of my children, Julie and Jack Jr.
3. My spouse and I have been married for 11 years. Julie is 10 and Jack is 8.
4. Since the children were babies, I have been much more involved in caring for them than their mother has been. When they were little, I got up with them in the night. I got up with them in the morning and made their breakfast before I left for work. I read them stories before I tucked them in at night. I coach Julie's soccer teams and Jack's baseball teams. I have always been available for the children. They are closely bonded to me.
5. My spouse has been an inconsistent and unstable mother. She never got up with the children when they woke during the night. She likes to sleep in, so she never made breakfast, either. One reason she likes to sleep late is that she spends a lot of her evenings out with friends, bar hopping and partying. I usually go to bed by midnight, and often she hasn't come home by the time I turn in.
6. I'm not much of a cook, but my spouse, who theoretically is home all day, never cooks. She buys premade dinners, or we order pizza or Chinese. My spouse doesn't have time to cook because she is out playing cards or shopping or going to her various groups. She is never home and is pretty much unavailable to me and the children.
7. It's bad enough my spouse is never home. On top of this, she is setting a very bad moral example to our children. She drinks, smokes, and has had several affairs. Sometimes she goes to the casinos where she drinks, smokes, meets men, and gambles. Now she is involved with our next-door neighbor's twenty-year-old son. This is very embarrassing for our children as well as humiliating to me.

8. My spouse really isn't much interested in the children. She has her own life and just wants to be free to fool around and do her thing.

9. Although my spouse doesn't work outside the home, she doesn't work inside the home, either. She is a lousy housekeeper. Stuff is strewn all over. Most of the time I end up doing the wash, so the children and I will have clean clothes. We use paper plates for our takeout food, so we don't have to wash dishes.

10. In short, my spouse should move out of the house because she can't afford to live in it and doesn't take care of it.

11. I should be given temporary legal and physical custody of the children and stay in the house with them.

Signed, Jack B. Nimble

Mom's Affidavit in Response

STATE OF MIND   DISTRICT COURT
COUNTY OF CONFUSION   FAMILY COURT DIVISION
Suzie B. Qwik, being duly sworn, on oath deposes and says,

1. I am the respondent in this divorce, and I submit this affidavit in response to my husband's affidavit and in support of my motion for custody of our children.

2. First of all, I would like to say my husband must be living on another planet with another family. His affidavit is an incredible distortion of reality.

3. He states he got up with the kids when they were babies. Well, I'm here to tell you I breastfed both babies, and he never got up to feed them because he wasn't equipped to do so.

4. He says he gets breakfast, read to the children when they were younger, and put them to bed. Yes, he did those things, maybe once a month.

5. He never really coached soccer or baseball. Once in a while he would attend a game and yell at the children a lot.

6. He accuses me of partying, staying out late, and having a boyfriend. In the last year I have gone out evenings because our marriage is in

such bad shape I need to spend time with friends. The kid next door mows our lawn because Jack can't find the time and helps me with heavier tasks around the house. For Jack to say we are having an affair is crazy. Jack is so jealous and controlling.

7. I hold our home together. Jack works 60 to 80 hours a week. He is gone from early in the morning before anyone else is up, until 8 or 9 at night. When he comes home, he grabs something to eat and goes into his study to work some more. No wonder he thinks we eat only fast food; he is never home for dinner.

8. Jack provides the money to run our household. I provide everything else. He never has anything nice to say to the kids and me. He is forever putting me down. If I don't do things his way, he can be very nasty. He can be scary, too. He has threatened to hurt me more than once.

9. I think Jack has a serious drinking problem. Often when he comes home at night, he reeks of alcohol. He has been arrested for drunk driving. He has a stash in his study and drinks while he "works" in there.

10. If Jack really thinks he has a strong bond with the children, he is living in fantasy land. He spends so little time with them, they really don't know him. I would be willing to bet he doesn't even know the names of the children's teachers this year.

11. Jack also has never taken the children to the doctor or the dentist. I drive them to their activities. I make sure they have appropriate clothes, get regular haircuts, and do their homework. Jack has no clue about the children's lives.

12. Jack has moved in with a woman he knows from work. He has been trying to insinuate her into our children's lives. He accuses me of setting a bad moral example. Talk about the pot calling the kettle black!

13. I should have custody of our children. Jack should pay enough support to me and the children, so we can stay in the house. The children have grown up in this house; it is the only home they know. They need some stability during this stressful time.

14. I am sure Jack loves our children. He should spend time with them and get to know them better.

Signed, Suzie B. Qwik

What the Judge Hears

Now, try to put yourself in the judge's robe for a few minutes. What information do these affidavits provide? What information is missing? If you had to issue a temporary parenting plan, what additional information would be helpful? The judge will probably interpret these affidavits—based on considerable experience with divorcing parents—something like the following.

It's clear that the parties are angry. Dad has used his affidavit to take shots at Mom by attacking her skills as a homemaker and a mother. Mom's response shows she is stung by his criticism.

The parties have very different perspectives about their marriage. Taking their affidavits at face value, it sounds as if the children are on their own most of the time. Dad's working long hours, and Mom's out partying. It's more likely that the events both parties describe as everyday occurrences happen once in a while, not all of the time. It's likely that Dad works some long hours because he is the primary wage earner, and that Mom goes out with her friends now and then because she is lonely.

If your ex-spouse or former in-laws badmouth you to your children, resist the urge to do the same. If your children are witness to a name-calling battle, they may feel as though they should choose sides. If the badmouthing doesn't subside, try to talk it out with your spouse or former in-laws.

Mom has raised the issue of alcohol abuse. While she has provided no hard evidence, it would be a good idea to address this issue immediately. A chemical dependency evaluation of both parties will either confirm Mom's claim and, perhaps, get the abuser into treatment or put it to rest, so that it doesn't keep showing up in later affidavits.

Both Suzie B. Qwik and Jack B. Nimble want to be involved with their children. This is good. Dad is just realizing how important his children are to him, and it would not be surprising if he decided to cut back on his work hours to spend more time with the children. While the children will certainly benefit from more time with their father, the resulting income reduction will make finances really precarious. If Dad's salary is reduced, Mom will probably have to go to work, which will mean she'll be less available to the children.

The parties have not provided useful information about the real routine in their household before the separation. The only way to get this information may be to get a custody evaluator involved. Often the judge will issue an order maintaining the status quo until the evaluator provides more information about the family and recommends an ongoing parenting plan.

The parties have provided little financial information. However it's clear that somehow they've managed to survive financially until the hearing. The judge may issue an order designed to keep the mortgage paid and food on the children's table until a custody evaluation is completed. The judge will probably order the parents to provide specific financial information at the next hearing.

Miles Apart

What the parties thought they said and what the judge heard is miles apart. It was clearly very important to Dad to tell the judge his spouse is behaving badly, that she was not fulfilling her role as spouse. It was important to Mom to tell the judge her husband was not fulfilling his role as parent and companion. But neither party told the judge what the judge needed to know. How do they really parent their children? What kind of schedule would work for the family, taking into account everyone's activities, the distances between the parents' homes, and the demands of work and school?

Decisions That Please No One

The judge now has the impossible task of forming a schedule with no useful information. Many judges sidestep this task by sending families to an arm of the court that has different names in different states. It may be called court services, family services, or social services. Courts in counties with small populations probably won't have these services available, so the parties will have to hire someone in the private sector to work with them.

If a judge can't avoid making a decision, the judge will probably do one of two things: Either give Mom sole legal custody of the kids with an every other weekend visitation schedule for Dad, or give the parents joint legal and joint physical custody. This would be a temporary order until trial.

ALERT!

While this order is called a temporary order, do not be deceived. The court is most unlikely to change the parenting arrangement at trial, unless circumstances change dramatically.

Mom and Dad didn't want either one of these options, but now they're stuck with the judge's decision unless they can persuade the judge to change his or her mind. The kinds of things that make a judge change an order are primarily negative. One of the parents has a mental breakdown, one of the parents goes to jail for drunk driving, or one parent abuses the other or the children. Without some dramatic change, the order will stand for the duration of the divorce, unless the parents themselves can agree to a different arrangement.

How Courts Decide Custody

Suppose Jack and Suzie didn't learn their lesson. That is, they didn't learn the importance of making their own decisions about how they will rear their children. They've been unable to work out a plan and now they've taken their case to the judge.

Factors to Consider

The custody statutes of each state tell its judges how to decide custody cases. That is, the law gives the judge a set of factors to consider including:

- Determining who is the primary parent; that is, the parent who was more responsible for the day-to-day child care

- The plan the parents want
- Reasonable preference of the child, if the child is mature enough to express a preference [This is tricky. Psychologists tell us not to ask a child which parent he or she wants to live with, as this is putting too much pressure on the child who is already stressed out because his or her parents are getting a divorce. Usually preference is explored indirectly, by asking the child about his or her activities, favorite things to do with each parent, and the like.]
- Relationship among the child, siblings, parents, or other significant person
- Child's adjustment to home, community, and school
- Permanence of the parents' respective living arrangements
- Nature of the family ambience in each proposed home
- Mental and physical health of the parents and children
- Length of time the child has lived where he or she is now living and the importance of maintaining that continuity
- Child's cultural background
- Impact of abuse on the child, if domestic abuse has occurred

In addition, if parents are seeking joint legal or physical custody, the judge needs to know how well the parents can cooperate, what methods for resolving disputes they will use, and whether it would be harmful to the child if one parent had sole custody. This latter factor deals with whether a sole custodian would support and encourage the relationship of the child with the other parent.

Interviewing the Children

In a custody trial, each parent presents evidence on the factors the judge is to consider. The judge may request an interview with the children in his or her office to get input from them. Some states even mandate that a judge interview the children. The lawyers may submit questions to the judge that they want asked. The judge makes a record of the meeting, but this record is not made available to the parents. It may be used to clear up a misunderstanding about what took place during the interview; however, the record will only be made available to the attorneys.

ALERT!

The parents are not present at the interview. However, their lawyers may be present, if they so request and the judge agrees.

Moving with Your Children

Concern that your spouse may want to relocate to another state with the children may be a strong motivator in seeking a shared parenting arrangement. Suppose you and your family live in Oregon, and your spouse has family in Kansas. Your spouse is having trouble finding a decent job, and you don't make enough to support two households. Your spouse may be strongly tempted to return to the nest under such circumstances. The laws about moving, or removal, vary from state to state, but it's harder for one parent to move a significant distance with the children when the other parent has a major role in their lives.

To Move . . .

Again, laws vary from state to state. In some states, the parent who wants to move has to show the court the move is in the child's best interests. This means the parent who wants to move has a legitimate need to move. For example, an employer makes relocation a condition of keeping a job; the custodial parent has an extended family and support system in a distant state; or the custodial parent is having a hard time making ends meet in the state where the divorce is taking place. The parent seeking the move will need to show she or he has done research on housing and schools and, most important, that the moving parent has a plan for the child to maintain contact with the other parent.

Or Not to Move?

Other states put the burden on the parent who is not moving. This parent will have to show the court why the move is not in the child's best interests. The parent who is remaining will need to show that the child is integrated into the community, that the child has a close and important relationship with the parent who is not moving, that the move will be harmful to the child's stability, or that the other parent doesn't really have to move.

Either way, if you're concerned that a move may be lurking under the surface of your divorce, you may want to seek at least joint physical custody to make it harder for your spouse to take the children to a distant location. Be sure to discuss this concern with your lawyer.

Not Sure the Child Is Yours?

Sometimes a question arises about the parentage of one or more of the children. Mom gets mad at Dad and tells him he's not the father. While Dad may take this with a grain of salt, given that Mom made the accusation when she was angry, the seed of doubt has been planted. What can be done?

Today, sophisticated DNA testing can determine parentage of children to a 99.99 percent probability of paternity. While blood testing still is used, most agencies that test for paternity collect a saliva sample from the mother, the child, and the putative father. From these samples it is possible to determine whether Dad is really, biologically, Dad.

The question of what you do when you discover your three-year-old isn't your biological child is a tough one. If you're the only father this child has ever known, you still may want to be Dad because you have a strong psychological bond. Or not. Courts are divided on how to handle this issue, so you'll need to discuss it with your lawyer.

Chapter 14

Child Support and Spousal Maintenance

When you and your spouse separate, there will be two households to support. The spouse with the greater income will contribute to the support of the spouse with less, or no, income. The contribution is usually in the form of child support and support for the spouse, called spousal maintenance or alimony.

Child Support

If you have children, you have a responsibility to support them. In most states this obligation continues until the children marry, die, join the military, finish high school, or otherwise become emancipated. Some states end the obligation at age eighteen; others extend it to age twenty-one. Ask your lawyer about the law in your state.

Historically, child support orders varied widely from state to state and from county to county. Child support was based on the reasonable needs of the child and the payor's ability to pay. This arrangement gave judges a lot of discretion in determining child support awards. Often the spouse ordered to pay child support didn't pay, so households with children experienced significant reductions in living standard.

Creating Guidelines

In the 1980s, Congress responded to growing concerns about the impoverishment of children of divorce and the increasing number of single-parent families on welfare. Congress passed child support enforcement amendments that required all states to develop guidelines by October 1, 1987, or risk losing the federal contribution to their welfare programs. Needless to say, states responded, and today all states have child support guidelines.

Three Primary Approaches

At present, there are three primary approaches implemented by different states to determine the amount of child support. Some states use a percentage of income approach. These states have developed a chart that includes the income of the payor, the number of children, and the percentage to be paid. Depending on the state, the percentage may be applied to gross income or to net income. It could be 25 percent of income for one child, 30 percent for two children, and so on. This approach, which makes certain assumptions about the payor's ability to pay child support, is based on a formula rather than on the child's needs.

Other states use something called an income shares approach that considers both parents in developing a formula. Again, the formula may be applied to gross or net income, and is based on numbers more than on needs.

A third approach, called the Melson formula, requires the court to determine the basic needs of each parent, and then set the child support. But because the majority of states use a percentage of income approach, most of the current child support discussion is focused on determining the income of the payor.

FACT

Parents can't waive child support. The law says that child support is a child's right, and no parent can take this right away. Child support can be reserved, that is, not paid for a period of time because of overall financial circumstances or because of the parenting arrangement.

What Is Income?

Income can come from many sources. Most employed people are paid a salary, while some self-employed persons pay themselves only when their business makes enough money to do so, thereby controlling the timing and amount of their income. Some people receive investment income, either from dividends paid by stocks or from profits made by investing in the stock market. Some people own investment property, such as an apartment building, and receive rental income. Some people had a good job last year but quit when the marriage fell apart. The court may impute income to them (ascribe a certain amount to them as if they were still working).

Reading Your Pay Stub

If you work for wages, you get paychecks with a pay stub, which provides a lot of information. It shows your gross income before anything is deducted. It shows your deductions and your rate of withholding. For example: M-3 means "married with three exemptions." Your pay stub shows what you get paid per hour for regular time and overtime, how often you get paid, and how many hours you worked the last pay period. It will show whether you are paying for health and dental insurance, and whether you've invested in a plan that enables you to set aside pretax dollars for paying medical and dental bills. Your pay stub also shows how much from each paycheck goes into your retirement plan.

All of this information is important. First of all, it tells you how much money you earn each pay period. If you're paid weekly, you can multiply your net pay times fifty-two and divide by twelve to get your monthly income. If you're paid every two weeks, multiply by twenty-six and divide by twelve to get your monthly income. Because most budgets are computed on a monthly basis, it's helpful to compare monthly income to monthly expenses.

Your spouse gets to see your paycheck stubs, too. If you're socking away a large percentage of your pay into retirement or over-withholding so that you get a tax refund at year's end, you can be sure your spouse or your spouse's lawyer will notice this right away.

If you're self-employed or otherwise unable to predict your income (due to commissions, bonuses, etc.), you may need to look at W-2 statements for several years to develop realistic income figures.

Other Income

If you have investments, they may generate income. (If they don't, you may need to make some changes!) Stocks pay dividends and bonds mature. Some people buy and sell stocks, and others buy and sell real estate. If you invest in a new venture, you might lose money the first few years, which you can take as a deduction on your taxes. Understandably, your spouse will want to keep an eye on this venture, but it's unlikely you'd invest in a business if you didn't expect it to make money at some point.

Social Security

If you or your spouse are near retirement age, you'll want to figure out your eligibility for social security benefits. When people have been married for more than ten years, the nonworker spouse is eligible to receive half the earner's social security. The age of eligibility will depend on when the earner entered the job market. As society ages, the age of eligibility goes up.

If you or your spouse becomes disabled and eligible for social security disability benefits, your children may be eligible for benefits, too. While most courts take the position that these benefits are not a substitute for child support, this money is available to help take care of the kids.

FACT

Supporting two households after divorce is complicated stuff. You need a lawyer who knows your state's laws and can help you develop a support plan that stretches the dollars. Divorce lawyers know how to do an analysis called the FinPlan that can help pinpoint optimum levels for child support and spousal maintenance. They can also tell you what mix of child support and spousal maintenance the Internal Revenue Service will accept.

Imputed Income

Say your spouse had a good job during the marriage. Angry now, your spouse quits and refuses to look for a new job. If you take your spouse to court for child support, the court may well determine that because your spouse earned $10 an hour on that job, your spouse has the ability to earn $10 an hour. The court imputes this income to your spouse and orders child support accordingly. Or, say you decide to change jobs and take one that pays less and provides no overtime. The court may use your previous earnings as the basis for the support order, imputing to you the ability to earn the amount you earned before.

Imputing income can create a financial mess. When orders are based on what the court believes you can do, rather than what you're actually doing, you can fall behind in your support obligation quickly. And the spouse relying on the support order will not have the money needed to pay bills.

One purpose of imputing income is to encourage the unemployed or underemployed payor to find a good job. Another is to maintain a consistent child support obligation, so that when the payor does get a decent job the accumulated back payments, called arrears, can be collected for the benefit of the children.

Deviating from Guidelines

Most judges treat child support guidelines as if they were carved in stone, but they were intended to be a starting point for child support orders. Judges are reluctant to deviate from the guidelines because they have to make written findings in support of any deviation. Making findings is a lot of work.

Going Up

If you want the court to issue a support order that is higher than the guidelines, you will have to give the court a reason. Perhaps you have a special needs child who requires twenty-four-hour care. Maybe throughout the marriage you and your spouse were able to send the children to private schools and summer camps. Circumstances should not change for the children unless there isn't enough money to maintain past benefits.

Coming Down

You may want the court to deviate downward from the guidelines. You may be supporting a child from a prior marriage. Ordinarily that support obligation would be subtracted from your income before applying the guidelines. Perhaps you have a new child with another person, born during your separation from your spouse. Courts take the position that your first family comes first, that you took on this new obligation with knowledge of your existing one. Rarely will the court reduce your support to enable you to take care of a new child.

Joint Custody and Child Support

Child support guidelines assume one parent has sole physical custody of the children. When parents share physical custody equally and have comparable incomes, child support is often reserved, meaning neither pays support to the other. The parents share the costs of health insurance and child care.

If one parent earns more than the other, that parent probably will pay child support to the parent with less income. Some states have adopted formulas for determining child support in these cases. The smaller income is subtracted from the larger one with the remainder divided by two, to reflect that the children are with each parent half of the time. This formula can produce a harsh result for the lower-income parent, but it's easy to compute and, therefore, appealing to courts.

If you and your spouse choose a shared parenting arrangement, you can also decide how you will finance it. If you and your spouse make an agreement about support, you're not bound by the guidelines; however, the court will have to approve your agreement. Ideally, each household should have similar income available to meet the needs of the children. When one household is rich and the other poor, the imbalance may undermine the shared parenting plan.

FACT

Statistics show that visitation and custody influences the payment of child support. Those parents with joint custody are more likely to pay child support than those who do not have custody or visitation rights.

Enforcing Child Support Payment

A major reason the federal government got involved in family law was to enforce court orders for child support. Prior to 1980, collection rates were abysmal, and child support orders were mere pieces of paper. Today, income withholding is used to collect most child support. An employer deducts child support from the payor parent's paycheck and forwards it to the state collection agency, which then sends it to the payee. The employer is obligated to notify the state agency if the employee quits his or her job. The employee is obligated to notify the state when reemployed, and the new employer has an obligation to check for and honor existing support orders.

Parents ordered to pay child support can be tracked by social security numbers from state to state and even outside the United States. The Uniform Reciprocal Enforcement of Support Act authorizes one state to enforce another state's orders. County or district attorney's offices have a division devoted to child support collection where a parent having trouble collecting child support can go for help, whether or not the parent receives public assistance.

Health Care Costs

Most states require the payor parent to maintain health and dental insurance for his or her children and to contribute to child care costs. Many parents take a look at the health care available through their respective employers and select the best coverage. They may agree to split the cost of insurance coverage and any uncovered medical expenses for their children, or to prorate costs based on their relative incomes. If parents don't agree, the court will order the payor parent to maintain the health insurance.

Heavy Hand of the Law

Courts have several weapons in their arsenal for the person who doesn't pay court-ordered support. The judge may find the person in civil contempt of court and put that person in jail for civil contempt, provided the judge gives the "contemnor" the ability to get out of jail by paying the support owed, or by paying part of what is owed and contracting to pay the balance.

ALERT!

The court can revoke the driver's or professional license of a non-paying ex-spouse as well as his or her passport. When all else fails, the non-paying parent may be subject to criminal charges.

Spousal Maintenance

Child support is largely determined by statutes that have formulas for figuring out the amount of support to be paid. Statutes also set the rules for spousal maintenance, or alimony, but the judge determines the amount to be paid. Spousal maintenance is a payment from one spouse to the other for the recipient's support. If the parties litigate this issue, a judge has discretion to decide the amount and duration of a spousal maintenance award.

FACT

In Texas, spousal maintenance is available only when the parties have been married at least ten years. And then, it is limited to a maximum of $2,500 a month for three years. Homemaker spouses try to get out of Texas for their divorce. Payor spouses try to get in.

Taxable Income

An important characteristic of spousal maintenance is that it is paid with before-tax dollars. If you're the payor, when you do your income taxes, you deduct spousal maintenance payments off the top before determining your gross taxable income. This means it's much cheaper to pay spousal maintenance than it is to pay child support, which is paid with after-tax dollars. For instance, if you're in the 40 percent tax bracket, your spousal maintenance costs you 60 percent of its face amount.

Spousal maintenance is taxable income to the recipient. Usually a person who receives spousal maintenance has little earned income and is living in the house with the children, and thus gets a deduction for the mortgage interest and as head of household for tax purposes. The recipient spouse usually has a minimal income-tax liability; therefore, paying spousal maintenance can stretch a family's dollars. It's an important tax-planning tool.

Some Alimony History

Before 1950, courts routinely awarded homemakers, typically female, lifetime spousal maintenance, unless the woman had misbehaved, committed adultery, or abandoned the marriage, for example. At that time, most married women were unemployed and totally dependent on their spouses for support.

After the women's liberation movement, judges' attitudes toward spousal maintenance changed, and the awards dried up. This was particularly difficult for the fifty-five-year-old woman who had never worked outside the home. A judge was likely to give her $400 a month support for ten years, even if her spouse could afford to pay substantially more. The harsh results of these court decisions led to yet another turnaround. Today courts again are awarding lifetime spousal maintenance to spouses who have been career homemakers, and the awards are usually sufficient to enable these dependent spouses to meet their financial needs.

Temporary Maintenance

Spousal maintenance can be temporary or permanent. Most states' statutes give judges some guidance here. Temporary spousal maintenance is often awarded in a shorter marriage where the homemaker spouse had a decent job before children were born and, with some educational updating, can get back into the job market.

When the parties can't agree about temporary spousal maintenance, they may hire a rehabilitation counselor to evaluate the skills, interests, and employment opportunities of the spouse seeking maintenance. This counselor can provide guidance to the parties and, if necessary, to the court on what it will take to get this spouse back in the job market and self-supporting.

You may be tempted to make your spouse pay alimony for reasons other than financial need. Again, try not to let your emotions get the best of you. It's better for all of those involved if you can work on a way to become financially independent and move on with life.

Permanent Maintenance

When a court is asked to decide permanent maintenance, statutes provide guidance. Most state laws set out certain requirements—a long-term marriage, or if the marriage is less than ten years, a very good reason the homemaker spouse cannot reenter the work force. Maybe young children are at home or the spouse has serious health issues. A judge is directed to determine whether the spouse seeking maintenance lacks enough property to generate independence or is unable to provide adequate self-support.

When a judge decides the maintenance amount, he or she must consider the standard of living enjoyed by the parties during the marriage, the payor spouse's ability to pay, sacrifices made by the homemaker spouse in terms of giving up a career, and the ability to provide for retirement. Some laws state that if a judge can't conclude a homemaker spouse will someday be self-supporting, the judge should award permanent maintenance. The obligation to pay spousal maintenance usually ends when the payor dies or when the payee dies or remarries.

Sometimes spousal maintenance is awarded for a specific number of years. Either party can seek modification of spousal maintenance before that term ends.

Modifying Support Orders

Child support and spousal maintenance payment orders can be modified if the financial circumstances on which they are based change. The payor parent may get fired—a possible basis for a temporary reduction in child support. One of the children may run off with the circus—another reason to reduce child support. Maybe a person receiving spousal maintenance finishes a college refresher course and gets a good job, which may be a basis for reducing or reserving that person's spousal maintenance. The person paying spousal maintenance may retire and seek a reduction or termination of the support obligation.

Keep in mind also that retirement benefits may be treated differently depending on the specific facts of a case. If a couple in their forties is getting divorced, retirement benefits probably will be treated as property—marital assets to be divided. If the parties are in their late sixties, they may be receiving pension benefits, which are then treated as income. The law is clear: Pension benefits are either assets or income, not both.

It is of critical importance to be sure that your judgment and decree contain very specific information about the financial basis for child support and spousal maintenance provisions, so that changes in circumstances are clear. If a lot of years pass between entry of the decree and a motion for modification, everyone could forget the basis for the original order.

Preparing a Budget

You will need to prepare a household budget to help you and your spouse figure out appropriate support levels. Some people keep track of monthly expenditures with a computer program such as Quicken. Others have no idea what they spend each month. Those who keep records need only add up a year's worth of grocery bills and divide by twelve to get an average monthly grocery expense. Those with no clue need to start keeping track immediately or get the household check registers for the past year or two to develop a sense of household spending.

The Family's Standard of Living

Budgets are important to establish the family's standard of living during the marriage. If your family has sent the children to private schools, taken several vacations each year, or dined out often, these expenditures should be reflected in check registers and credit card bills. If you need to take the issues of child support and spousal maintenance to court, you'll want to show the court the family's standard of living during the marriage.

Use real numbers when you prepare your budget. This is not the time to put together your dream budget. When your budget exceeds the combined incomes of the two of you, anyone will know something is not right here. Judges go to the grocery store, too. A judge will not be pleased if you pad your budget. A judge needs you to provide helpful information, and you will get a better result if you do so.

ALERT!

Even though you may be accustomed to living the high life, this doesn't mean you'll be able to continue such a lifestyle following the divorce. Nearly all divorcing couples must create budgets and alter their spending habits.

Accepting Responsibility

When you got married, you agreed to accept responsibility for your spouse and any children you might have. This responsibility continues for both parties even though the marriage ends. To the extent that some parents are reluctant to meet their obligation, state laws require the payment of child support and set out guidelines for the amount to be paid. State governments have financial stakes in making sure child support gets paid—if you don't support your children, public moneys may be needed to do so. Spouses also have an obligation to take care of each other, in marriage and in divorce. This obligation is less clear-cut than child support because it is assumed adults can take care of themselves. So, spousal support is dependent on the facts of each case.

Child support and spousal maintenance can be adjusted as the financial circumstances of the parties change. While the divorce is final, support is subject to review until the obligation to pay it ends altogether.

Chapter 15

The Marital Estate and How to Divide It

We've talked about the emotional divorce and the legal divorce, and we've considered how you'll parent children during a divorce. Here and there you've seen references to marital and non-marital property and equitable division of property. Now it's time to take a closer look at these financial pieces of a divorce.

The Marital Estate

The marital estate is the property you and your spouse have accumulated during marriage. Nonmarital property is the money and property you bring into the marriage, the money and property you inherit, the money and property given to you by someone outside the marriage.

Sounds simple, and sometimes it is. Suppose when you got married, you really didn't have much stuff. You had recently completed school and started a job, but were still living at home. About the only things you had were a computer, your bicycle, some camping gear, and an old car that wasn't worth much but got you where you wanted to go. Your spouse had a cell phone, a bed, and a table. Family and friends gave you things as wedding presents: sheets, towels, silverware, a blender—typical wedding gifts. Your parents gave you some money that you used to pay rent on an apartment. At this point, the sum total of your marital estate was the gifts you received as wedding presents. The items you brought into the marriage, modest as they were, were yours before the marriage, and would be labeled premarital.

FACT

Some people are under the assumption that common law marriages are subject to the same laws as traditional, lawful marriages. This isn't necessarily true. While some states do recognize common law marriages, others don't. It's best to check out your state's laws to better understand your rights following a breakup of such a relationship.

If your marriage ended that first year, you would probably divide up the wedding gifts by each taking those that came from family or friends. If your premarital stuff was still usable, you probably took it as well. Chances are you would move back in with your folks and start over. Pretty simple indeed. Many brief marriages are this simple, so if your marriage lasted only a short time, consider going to your local self-help center and doing the divorce yourselves.

A More Complicated Situation

Say the two of you have minimal possessions when you marry, and you receive some nice wedding presents. During your marriage you work for a small start-up company that hits it big. Your salary increases rapidly, and soon you're making more money than you ever dreamed of. Your spouse has a decent job, too, but makes a lot less than you do. To help you out in the beginning of your marriage, your parents give you some money toward the down payment on a house. After you begin to earn some serious money, you and your spouse also buy two new cars and a time-share in Florida. Eventually you buy new furniture and take some great trips, charging some of the furniture and all the trips on your credit cards.

The Good Years

After a few years of the good life you both decide to add children to the picture, so you have two children, two years apart. The little company you work for continues to flourish, and you get bonuses consisting of money and stock options. Because you have the big income, you two decide your spouse will stay home with the children. Although you spend most of the money from your job, you do put some aside in retirement funds and play around in the stock market a bit. After you've been married eight years, your spouse's favorite uncle dies and leaves him $10,000 that he invests. You two buy a duplex to rent out and use the rental income to pay the mortgage and maintenance on this property. Your spouse does the hands-on managing of the property, including some repairs.

Divorce on the Horizon

While working on the duplex, your spouse develops a relationship with one of the tenants. Your spouse buys the tenant gifts and pays for them with the credit cards issued in both your names. One day you happen to open the VISA bill and discover a charge for a watch you've never seen. When you confront your spouse, your spouse admits the affair, at which point heated words are exchanged, and your spouse leaves the house.

Breakdown of Marital Assets

Staying with this hypothetical situation, the house may or may not be a total marital asset—it depends on the character of your parents' gift for the down payment. Typically, parents give money to the happy couple, but when the happy couple is getting divorced, the parents sometimes remember they really gave this money to their child alone. Often the only proof of the parents' intent is to whom they wrote the check. If they wrote it to both of you, their gift will be considered a gift to both of you, and the entire house is a marital asset. On the other hand, if the check was made out to you alone, you can claim your parents gave you this gift, and this contribution to the value of the house would now be considered nonmarital property.

If you decide to divorce, you need to know about the potential financial consequences. For starters, what is the marriage property, the marital estate? All the things you purchased during the marriage using the money both of you earned are marital property. That would include the cars, the time-share, the duplex, the furniture, the retirement funds, and the stocks you bought with your income.

What about your spouse's inheritance from his uncle? It sure looks like a gift. Let's suppose your spouse actively played the stock market with that money, buying and selling on a regular basis. In some states the active management of funds would define any increase in their value as marital property. But if your spouse simply bought GE stock, for example, and let it sit there, any increase in value would be characterized as passive, and the entire amount, including the original gift, would keep its nonmarital status. If your spouse put the stock into both of your names, however, the stock would change from nonmarital to marital.

Still Another Scenario

Let's change our facts a little. Suppose you owned a house before you got married, and shortly after the marriage you sold it to buy another, using the money from the sale of your house to buy a new family house. For the next eight years, you and your spouse made mortgage, tax, and insurance payments from money earned during the marriage. At the time of the divorce, the house is worth a lot more than you paid for it. In such as case, many states will give you a nonmarital interest in the house from that initial investment, providing you have documents clearly showing you moved the money from your first house into the second.

ALERT!

Think about what you want to fight for. The person who wants to make a nonmarital claim has the burden of proving it.

How Do Courts Divide Property?

The answer is, "it depends." Many states are equitable division states, which means marital property is to be divided equitably. This usually means fifty-fifty, but it leaves the court with some discretion to decide what's fair. (It's always a bit of a worry when a judge has discretion.) In community property states, marital property, called the property of the community, is always divided equally. Some states still retain the concept of fault in their divorce laws. Therefore, if one party in the marriage has behaved badly, as defined in the law, he or she can be punished by getting less of the marital property. It's important to know your state's laws before you begin a divorce.

ALERT!

If you bring property into the marriage or inherit property during the marriage and want it to remain yours, keep it clearly separate or keep very good records of how it's used, otherwise it will become marital property to be divided with your spouse should you divorce.

Create an Inventory

To divide your property, you first need to know how much you've got. Get an inventory form from your lawyer or use the Asset Summary Sheet in Appendix B of this book, and make a list of all your property. If household goods and furniture are an issue for you, make a separate, detailed list of this property. If you're still living in the house, go to each room and itemize the things in it. If you're not living in the house anymore and don't have your possessions committed to memory, you may need to get permission from your spouse to walk through to write your list. If you own antiques, paintings, sculpture, china, sterling silver, crystal, or other items of significant value, you may need to have them appraised. In most communities, experts who mostly handle estate sales can value these items.

It's very helpful if you and your spouse can agree on a date of valuation. If all property is valued as of about the same time, you will be comparing apples with apples. If you can't agree, and your lawyers can't agree for you, the court will choose the date of valuation. This date is usually the date of the pretrial hearing or the trial itself. If you've been in the divorce process for some time, the values you have may be old, so they will need to be updated to the date the judge selects. If you have a lot of property, this becomes an expensive process.

FACT

The furniture in your home is considered used furniture and is now worth much less than when it was new, even if you paid a lot for it. (Kind of like when you drive your new car off the lot and it becomes used.) Now your furniture's value is in its usefulness. Ask for those items that will minimally furnish your new place and let the rest go.

Asset Summary

Take a look at the asset summary following and you'll see a list of items showing your values and your spouse's. Our example puts both yours and your spouse's values all on one document to make it easier to understand, but they would be two separate documents in real life. This asset summary is meant to give you an idea of what should be included and what you need to know about each item. For more detail, look again at the Asset Summary Form in Appendix B.

Asset Summary

Asset	Wife's Values	Husband's Values	Values Stipulated for Settlement Only
Personal Property			
Furniture	$5,000	$10,000	$8,000
Furnishings	1,000	3,500	3,000
China, silver, crystal	12,000	18,000	15,000
Jewelry and furs	3,000	15,000	9,000
Homestead (purchase date)			
Market value	380,000	478,000	400,000
Mortgage	[213,000]	[213,000]	—
Second mortgage	[43,000]	[43,000]	—
Net equity	124,000	222,000	144,000
Apartment building (purchase date)			
Market value	609,000	463,000	528,000
Mortgage	[350,000]	[350,000]	—
Net equity	259,000	113,000	178,000
Sweat equity	—	68,000	—
Lake cabin (purchase date)			
Market value	400,000	315,000	380,000
Mortgage	[12,000]	[12,000]	—
Net equity	388,000	303,000	368,000
Back taxes	—	—	
Boats and vehicles			
Fishing boat and trailer	7,500	6,000	6,000
1999 Lexus			
Market value	28,000	17,000	21,000
Encumbrance	[12,000]	[12,000]	—
Net value	16,000	5,000	9,000

Asset Summary (*continued*)

Asset	Wife's Values	Husband's Values	Values Stipulated for Settlement Only
2000 Honda Odyssey			
Market value	18,000	29,000	23,000
Encumbrance	[19,000]	[19,000]	—
Net value	[1,000]	10,000	4,000
1997 Harley-Davidson			
Market value	—	18,000	—
Encumbrance	—	[18,000]	
Securities			
240 shares GM stock (purchase date)	—	See market quote	—
Bank accounts			
Savings	minimal	minimal	—
Checking	minimal	minimal	—
Life insurance			
Company/Policy number			
Face amount	25,000	125,000	—
Cash surrender value	**2,000**	—	—
Loan	—	—	—
Retirement accounts			
Deferred comp./ account number	—	319,000	319,000
Company/Plan name	—	—	—
Owned by	—	—	—
Profit sharing	—	—	—
Pension	—	—	—
Keoghs	—	—	—

Asset Summary (*continued*)			
Asset	Wife's Values	Husband's Values	Values Stipulated for Settlement Only
IRAs	—	—	—
Business interests			
Name	To be determined	—	—
Type	To be determined	—	—
Ownership interest	—	—	—
Debts			
VISA	21,000	17,000	17,000
MasterCard	8,319	8,319	8,319
Discover	2,870	3,100	2,870
Sears	300	—	300
Loans to parents	15,000	—	—
Total	—	—	28,489

What does this all mean?

If the parties are pretty far apart on values they've given to a number of items, it's a good bet the items on which they've placed a lower value are the items they want. For instance, if the wife wants to keep the house, she'll want it to go into the overall property division at a lower value, so she gets more of the other property.

Surprise!

Often the parties learn new information by looking at the asset summaries their spouses prepare. For example, you may learn for the first time that taxes on your lake cabin haven't been paid for the last two years. You thought that your spouse had taken care of this. Or maybe this is the first time you've heard your spouse is claiming a nonmarital interest in the house. And where did this "loan to parents" come from? That was a gift, you thought. And, can you believe it? He went out and bought a motorcycle.

Sweat Equity

What is this "sweat equity" item? Here are some examples. The person who put in a lot of work on real estate that you own together may claim the property is worth more because of this work. This is probably true, but courts rarely credit a spouse who put out this effort. Sometimes a spouse will use this argument to try to create an interest in the other party's nonmarital property, which usually doesn't work, either. Another way the sweat-equity argument arises is when one of the parties has refinished antiques and wants credit for making them more valuable. Courts are seldom persuaded by the sweat-equity argument.

Bring in the Experts

The parties who filled out the asset summary did not have their major assets valued by an expert. Instead, they assigned values based on guesses or what someone told them. Maybe they went to a marine store and priced new boats, or to the local gift shop and priced silver. Perhaps their realtor buddy gave them a ballpark number for houses in their area. If values given to the items on the list are all roughly equal, then it probably won't be necessary to involve an expert. However, if the values placed on certain items are vastly different, these items should be valued by a neutral third person or, if you litigate, by two not-so-neutral experts.

Words about Debt

The date of valuing assets may not work as the date for establishing debt. You may have frozen your joint credit cards shortly after you decided to divorce and can use balances as of the date both of you stopped using the marital credit cards.

You may be overwhelmed by the amount of debt you are left with following the divorce. Before you turn to bankruptcy, consider consumer credit counseling services or debt consolidation companies to help you get out from under the weight of money owed.

One of you may not have been able to get a separate card. This is probably unlikely in this day and age, when credit cards are sometimes issued to the family dog, but possible. So you continued to use the marital credit card. If you used credit during the separation because your spouse wasn't providing financial support, the reasonable debt accumulated for living expenses may be your spouse's responsibility. Your determination of the marital debt will need to be based on your particular circumstances.

Values for Settlement Purposes Only

After you and your spouse prepare your inventories, you should schedule a four-way meeting between both of you and your lawyers. Before the meeting, each side can provide the other with documentation that has been collected—things like recent property tax statements, investment reports, and statements from retirement accounts, life insurance, and bank accounts. If you refinanced your home recently, you may already have a house appraisal in your file along with other lender documents that might be helpful.

The First Meeting

So, using the asset summary we reviewed earlier, you meet at one of the lawyer's offices and you and your spouse take a look at each other's summaries. (Remember there will be two lists, one with your values and one with the values assigned by your spouse.) Look for areas of possible agreement. For those items that show important differences, try to seek a solution. For example, you can look at Blue Book values for the vehicles and narrow your differences. You can agree to use independent neutrals to obtain values for other items, such as the real estate and the business. Set a timetable for getting these values and schedule a second meeting.

A Second Meeting

Assume the real estate appraisals and business valuation have been completed in a timely fashion. (This may be a big assumption, but there's really no point in meeting if the reports aren't done.) At this second meeting, put your energies into trying to develop that third column labeled "values stipulated for settlement only." This label means you're not bound by these numbers if you're unable to reach agreement and negotiate a complete property division.

More Work to Be Done

You may be able to agree on all the numbers except for the business valuation done by the independent neutral. Now you'll need to hire your own expert, and your spouse will probably want to hire an expert, too. So, you hire the new experts and, after two or three months, they submit their reports. It's possible the two new experts have come up with a business value close enough to the first value, so that you now can agree. If not, you may choose to litigate this issue only. It's not a perfect result but better than taking all your property issues to court.

ALERT!

While money certainly matters, it isn't worth going to war over. If you and your ex-spouse spend all your resources fighting over values and settlements, you may very well having nothing left to fight over once all is said and done. Negotiate whenever possible.

Final Division of Assets

Assume you have been able to create that third column. The next step is to decide who gets what. With any luck you'll be able to negotiate a division of the major items of marital property. Take a look at the following Proposed Division of Assets form.

Proposed Division of Assets		
Asset	Wife	Husband
Homestead	$144,000	—
Cabin	—	$368,000
Apartment building	—	178,000
Furniture	45	35

Proposed Division of Assets (continued)		
Asset	Wife	Husband
China, etc.	15,000	—
Jewelry and furs	9,000	—
Boat and trailer	—	6,000
Lexus	—	9,000
Honda	23,000	—
Harley-Davidson	—	18,000
Stock	Half	Half
Debt	—	[28,489]
Business	—	—
Cash equalizer	25,000	[25,000]
Grand total	**529,500**	**529,011**

You put in the agreed-on values for the property items, according to who gets what. When you total the values in each party's column, you may find that one of you is getting significantly more than the other. If this is the case, you will need an equalizer. In the example, the husband needs to pay his spouse a cash equalizer of $25,000 to make the balance sheet come out even.

It's wise to split as few assets as possible, unless they're easy to divide. You can split your stock holdings easily, if they're publicly traded. Dividing the shares of a closely held corporation may be more difficult. If it's the family business, you need to think about whether it's a good idea to each retain an ownership interest after the divorce. In our example, the Proposed Division of Assets sheet still doesn't show a value for the business, but proposes alternatives for dividing it. In this example, each spouse will retain half of the stock in the business and share earnings fifty-fifty. Otherwise, they will have the business valued and set up a plan for one spouse to buy out the other over time. The cash value of the life insurance was so modest, the parties may have decided simply to maintain the insurance for the benefit of the children.

QUESTION?

What is an equalizer?
An equalizer can be a cash payment or a division of another asset, such as a retirement fund, that makes the final division close to fifty-fifty.

Personal Property

You may have noticed that household goods and personal property aren't addressed in detail in the asset summary and property division. Lawyers and judges hate dividing personal property. It's not uncommon for the parties to have pages and pages of inventory and to become quite irrational about getting their stuff. Too often the cost of dividing personal possessions exceeds its value, and of course, there's a reason for this—the parties aren't really fighting over stuff; they're still caught up in their power struggle and inability to let go.

Personal property can be divided a number of ways. If you can agree on the list, you can draw straws to see who chooses first, then select items on a rotating basis until they're divided. (You can agree to make copies of family photos and share the cost.) Or, you can have an auction: Each of you makes a list of the property you want with its value; then each of you can buy items on the other's list at the price noted.

Do your best to divide your possessions yourselves. Only you know the underlying emotional attachments and significance of your things. To the lawyers and the judge; it's just stuff that can be replaced easily.

Dividing Retirement Benefits

Many different kinds of retirement accounts exist. The most common general categories are defined benefit plans and defined contribution plans. In a defined benefit plan, the plan will pay you a specific amount per month when you retire. The amount may depend on your retirement age. For example, it may be a smaller amount if you retire before age sixty-five.

A defined contribution plan is one in which you invest a specific amount each month from your paycheck during your employment, which may or may not be matched by your employer. These funds are invested and, you hope, increase in value over the length of your employment. When you retire, you can select among various options as to how you will receive these funds. You can take a lump sum amount or elect to receive monthly payments. If you put pretax dollars into a deferred compensation plan, you'll have to pay taxes on these moneys when you receive them.

Wherever possible, divide assets in their entirety. Splitting retirement accounts requires that additional documents be prepared after the divorce. If one of you keeps an interest in real estate awarded to the other in the form of a lien, you will have to deal with each other when that lien interest is due. A clean break makes it easier to move on with your life.

Qualified Domestic Relations Order

Some retirement accounts, such as 401(k)s, can be divided by a Qualified Domestic Relations Order or QDRO (pronounced "kwadro"). Your lawyers need to draft the QDROs after the divorce is final. These documents direct an employer to divide and later pay out the retirement funds according to your agreement. If one of you dies before the QDROs are submitted and approved, the retirement funds may be dispersed differently from your agreement.

ALERT!

If you agree to use QDROs as part of your asset division, make sure they are drafted immediately after the divorce is final. You may lose money you planned to live on in your old age if your ex-spouse dies before the QDRO has been drafted and approved by his or her employer.

A defined benefit plan can't be divided by a QDRO, and neither can retirement funds for military personnel or for people who work in the public sector. You and your spouse will have to agree on a division of the payments when they begin, and agree on a surviving ex-spouse provision. If retirement funds can't be divided, you may have to use other assets to make an equitable property division. Or, you may choose to divide payments when they are made. A potential danger here is that the recipient may not live until retirement, or may die soon after the payments begin, leaving the ex-spouse high and dry.

Social Security Benefits

If you and your spouse have been married for more than ten years when you divorce, you are entitled to receive a percentage of your former spouse's benefits. You may want to check with social security administrators to find out what those benefits might be. This knowledge might encourage you to stay in the marriage a few more months to make it to the ten-year mark. But note that you can either receive social security benefits in your own right or through your spouse, not both.

A Second, Third, or . . . Marriage?

If you're marrying for the second time, you may want to take specific steps to protect the assets you acquired during and after your first marriage. If you come into this second marriage with a lot of property, you'll want to talk to a lawyer about preparing a prenuptial, or before marriage, agreement. The purpose of a prenuptial agreement is to protect assets both for yourself and for your heirs—children you have from your first marriage, for example.

A prenuptial agreement lists your property and your beloved's property. It makes specific provisions for how this property will be divided in the event of death or divorce. For instance, you might agree that if the marriage lasts less than three years, each of you takes back all your property, one of you pays the other a cash settlement of so many dollars, and you both move on. If the marriage lasts more than ten years, you might agree that different terms apply.

Doing a "Prenup" the Right Way

If you decide to use a prenuptial agreement, you need to do it right. Often prenuptial agreements are challenged when the parties divorce, and courts end up throwing them out as unfair or signed under duress. If your agreement throws your formerly beloved out in the cold with only the clothes on his or her back, the court will want to avoid such a harsh result. If the agreement was signed the night before the wedding, and your spouse now claims you threatened that the marriage was off unless the agreement was signed, the court will probably find duress. If you had a lawyer and your spouse didn't, the court will be hesitant to enforce the agreement, if the terms are questionable.

ALERT!

Prenuptial agreements need to be prepared carefully. Both parties need to be represented by lawyers who review the document. Both parties should fully disclose all their assets, and the terms of the agreement should be fair. The agreement should be signed well before the wedding.

Other Protective Measures

If you enter into a second marriage without a prenuptial agreement, you may want to take other steps to protect assets you bring into the marriage. The problem here is, when folks think about marriage, they seldom think about protecting their property. In the best of all possible plans, you would have your house, and any other real estate, valued the month of the wedding. You would make copies of bank statements and investment or retirement account values for that month. If you owned a business, you would have its value documented at that time as well.

People almost never do this; it seems so heartless and crass. When they divorce, they have no idea what their stuff was worth when they got married, and they can't compare those values with present-day values. Remember, if you want to establish a premarital interest in anything, you have the burden of proving it to a judge. Tracing nonmarital interests gets only more complicated as you bring more assets into a marriage. If you don't keep good records, you won't be able to show where your money or property went, and you won't be able to make a nonmarital claim.

Impact of Bankruptcy

Bankruptcy law is a specialized area. Be aware that it's a potential hazard. If your spouse decides to file for bankruptcy during the divorce, you'll need to consult with an attorney who specializes in bankruptcy law, if your own lawyer doesn't have this expertise. Do this right away to protect yourself and your assets. A bankruptcy proceeding puts a stay on your divorce proceeding. If your spouse discharges the joint credit cards and other debt, the creditors can come after you, and you may need to join in the bankruptcy.

ALERT!

Child support, spousal maintenance, and other obligations "in the nature of support" are not dischargeable in bankruptcy. Be sure to have language in your divorce decree that labels the payment of certain obligations as "additional support." Be sure the decree spells out that you are to be held harmless from those obligations your spouse is to meet.

If your spouse files for bankruptcy after the divorce, your property settlement may be totally undone. Again, you need to act quickly with the help of a competent bankruptcy lawyer. You'll be unable to collect your property settlement during the automatic stay of the bankruptcy. If the final divorce decree made your spouse responsible for various debts and obligations, they may fall back in your lap. Make sure your divorce decree has language that protects you against this possibility.

The process of determining and dividing the marital estate is simple and straightforward when your assets are few and clearly marital or nonmarital. If you've been married a long time and have acquired significant property, both from your own efforts and through gift or inheritance, the determination and division becomes more complicated. If you've kept good records, the job is easier. If you don't have documentation for your nonmarital claims, you may be better off treating your property as marital and putting your efforts into dividing it equitably. Try to think of personal property as just stuff that can be replaced. Avoid spending more than it is worth fighting over it.

Chapter 16

Moving Toward Trial

At some point after you file the summons and petition beginning your divorce, the court system will decide it's time for you to come to court. Court administrators or a judge's clerk will send a notice to both sides setting a pretrial hearing date. You and your lawyer will need to meet and prepare for going to court.

Why Have a Pretrial Hearing?

Courts use the pretrial hearing to get organized for the upcoming trial. Your court will have its own set of rules and forms for the hearing. The forms must be completed, sent to the other lawyer, and filed before the hearing. The court will expect you and your spouse to have completed all discovery, lined up all witnesses, developed trial strategy, prepared a settlement proposal, and discussed settlement. Judges, like litigants, have a lot of unmet expectations.

When a pretrial notice arrives at your attorney's office, you probably won't be ready to go to trial. Remember our discussion about discovery in Chapter 12? Your experts may be waiting for documents from your spouse or for information from outside sources. For example, suppose you've hired an expert to evaluate your spouse's ability to become employed. Your expert may have requested a psychological evaluation of your spouse, but that evaluation hasn't been completed, so your vocational expert can't complete the report.

ALERT!

Lawyers like to blame courts for the perception that divorces seem to take forever. The judge's view is that lawyers are rarely ready for trial when a date is first set. It's more common for the lawyers to ask for a continuance (rescheduling) of the court date than it is for the court to need a continuance of the hearing.

Are You Ready for Pretrial?

What if you're really not ready? Of course, you and your lawyer will need to discuss whether you should ask for a continuance of the pretrial or go unprepared. This decision depends a lot on your judge, and also on whether the same judge will handle both the pretrial and the trial. There are two lines of thought here. Some judges feel they shouldn't preside over both the pretrial and the trial. They base this on the fact that settlement discussions may occur at the pretrial that might influence trial decisions. Other judges feel they should handle both. They believe they can be much more persuasive at pretrial if the parties know they also will hear the trial. For example, if a judge tells you how he or she feels about an issue at the pretrial hearing, the judge sends a clear message about how he or she will decide at the trial. This message can help the parties settle.

To Go or Not to Go

If your judge is a stickler for the rules, you should not go to the pretrial unprepared, because you don't want to make the judge angry and possibly negatively influence his or her later decisions. If your judge is more flexible, you could go to the pretrial and use it as an opportunity to get a feel for the judge's perspective on issues. Again, when the judge gives you his or her take on certain issues, the judge gives you tools to move toward settlement.

Deciding to Settle Your Divorce

There's some evidence that simply going to the courthouse encourages settlement. Judges like to say a chance to settle exists every time parties come to court. It's true. Pressure of the upcoming trial and fear of the unknown is strong. You could get vibes you don't like from the judge, and you may finally understand you'll be letting this person make decisions that will affect your future. You may well decide negotiating a deal is a good idea.

Narrowing the Issues

Whatever your decision—going to pretrial or asking for more time—you and your lawyer may decide this would be a good time to meet with the other side. You probably don't need to have all discovery done to talk settlement. At the very least, you may be able to reach some agreements and clarify disagreements. Lawyers call this narrowing the issues.

A list of agreements and disagreements can help you focus on preparing good, clear information in areas of contention, so you and your lawyer can prepare an organized argument for the court. You're much more likely to persuade the judge if he or she understands what your side is saying. You might be surprised at how often lawyers confuse a judge. No wonder judges' decisions often seem miles off the mark.

Try not to let your emotions get in the way while trying to settle. You should always stay focused on your objectives. Present the issues in a clear manner and suggest a realistic resolution.

Partial Agreement

If you have a conference with the other side and reach some agreements, one of the lawyers will draft a partial stipulation. This document sets forth agreements made at the meeting, and is signed by both parties and their lawyers. It becomes part of the court file. Be sure you read the stipulation carefully before you sign it, because you'll have a very hard time changing agreements afterward. Lawyers write in legalese, so if you don't understand parts of the agreement, be sure your lawyer explains them.

If something in the agreement is different than what you thought you'd agreed to, discuss this new wrinkle with your lawyer. If it's not a major deal, maybe you'll want to accept it rather than jeopardize the rest of the agreements. However, if it is a major deal, don't sign the agreement until this item has been dealt with to your satisfaction.

Most court rules require divorcing parties and their lawyers to discuss settlement before a pretrial hearing, but they often don't get around to it. Some judges will assess fines if spouses haven't gotten together to talk before pretrial. Other judges will require the parties and their lawyers to use the pretrial time to discuss settlement, then set a new pretrial date.

Pretrial Paperwork

Paperwork required for pretrial hearings differs in each state, but it's also similar. In general, the court wants basic information about the parties, children, and assets, including a financial statement similar to one you might fill out for a bank loan. It can be another trip down the Wonderland rabbit hole to put financial statements of the divorcing parties side by side. Are these people from the same family? The same world?

When parties prepare court papers, they often develop an advocacy mindset. This means they massage data to work to their advantage. A business owner puts its value at nothing; the owner's spouse says the business is worth big bucks. A spouse uses income figures from a prior job, or from before a recent raise, to minimize his or her income. You get the picture.

Budgets

In addition to the financial statement, you'll need to prepare a budget. Again, *budget* and *wish list* are not the same thing. Often one party's budget exceeds the total family income. It's important to prepare a real budget based on prior spending and including changes brought about by the divorce. For instance, the family home may have been sold, so each party could afford to own a home. The monthly mortgage payments for each party are now different. Mom had been staying home with the children but has gotten a job. She now has an income, but the family now has child-care expenses as well.

Sticking with Reality

Finally, each side prepares a settlement proposal. Again, this isn't time for a wish list or the time to get your spouse upset all over again. It's time to make a realistic settlement offer based on all the information you've obtained during discovery and based on all the information in your gut. For instance, if the custody study recommends that Mom be the primary parent because you work long hours away from home and she's always been there for the kids, you know in your gut she's a good mom and will take good care of your children. You also know you love your job and can make a lot more money to support the kids than your spouse can. Use your head and accept the recommendation. Now is not the time to propose you be the primary parent.

ALERT!

Some resolutions may be hard to swallow, especially if it involves your children. But now is not the time to throw a fit and fling threats at your ex-spouse. Such a tantrum might very well validate some of the findings and cause even more problems. If it's something you feel very strongly about (having looked at it from a realistic point of view), discuss it with your lawyer.

Going Ahead

Let's say you and your lawyer decide to attend the pretrial even though you're still waiting for a report from your vocational expert. Your attorney figures the judge may be annoyed but won't assess sanctions, or fines, so you and your lawyer prepare as much of the required paperwork as you can.

When you get to court you tell the judge that you and your spouse have an issue about her employability, but that you can't say much more because you're still waiting for the expert's report. At the same time you include a reasonable settlement proposal.

Your lawyer tried to set up a meeting with the other side before pretrial but was unsuccessful, and you have yet to receive any papers from the other side. Finally the other side agreed to meet at the courthouse an hour before the scheduled hearing, so at least you'll be able to tell the judge you've met to discuss something.

The First Scenario

Here is one possible scenario. You, your attorney, and the other side find a conference room at the courthouse. In the hour before the scheduled pretrial, you make some agreements. When the judge's clerk checks with you at the appointed hour, you say, "We're making progress," so the clerk suggests you continue to negotiate, which you do for another hour. Now the clerk tells you the judge no longer has time to see you and gives you a new pretrial date. You're pretty disappointed you didn't even see the judge but glad that you've made some settlement progress.

The Second Scenario

Or, pretrial could go like this: You meet at the courthouse a few minutes ahead of time. The judge's clerk calls the attorneys into the judge's office, called chambers. You and your spouse sit uncomfortably on benches outside the courtroom for what feels like forever. Finally the lawyers come out to tell you what the judge has said, and the four of you now talk a bit, using the judge's input to resolve some issues. The lawyers go back to see the judge, and this time they come back with a new date for a second pretrial.

Lawyers love to go into the judge's chambers without their clients. They can snipe at each other there: "He hasn't sent me his pretrial statement or answered my interrogatories." "She doesn't return my phone calls." They can also tell the judge they could settle the case if their clients—that's you—weren't so unreasonable. After exchanging war stories about other cases, they discuss your case for a few minutes and come back with the judge's wise words. Trouble is, each lawyer may hear those words differently. Because you weren't there, you're in no position to question what your attorney tells you.

FACT

Trial doesn't always mean gathering in a courtroom and hearing testimony. It also can mean preparing written arguments with supporting documents on unresolved issues, and submitting them to the judge by a certain date. The judge also may give each side one chance to respond in writing to the other's arguments, with a due date for these responses as well. Then the judge will review the written submissions and decide.

Staying in Control

An experience like this will help you understand that by going to court you lose control of your divorce. Think how it felt to sit in the corridor while your lawyer met with the judge. They were talking about your life, your future, and you weren't able to provide input or even meet the judge. If you go to trial, you'll turn all decision-making over to the judge. How scary is that? Compromise looks better and better.

Judges like to have clients and their lawyers work on a settlement, so they'll usually let you take all day to try to resolve issues. Because you'll experience a letdown feeling if you never see the judge, you'll want your lawyer to ask the judge's clerk if all of you can go into chambers at the appointed hour. If you all hear what the judge has to say, you'll all get the same direction, which may help resolve or at least narrow issues. And you'll at least meet the judge who is probably going to try your case, and get some sense of what he or she is like.

Be assertive about meeting with a judge. If a judge resists meeting with everyone in chambers, ask that the meeting be held in the courtroom with everyone present. It's disrespectful for a judge and lawyers to talk about you and your future without you present. Don't let them do it.

A Typical Pretrial Hearing

Here's how many pretrial hearings play out, so try to imagine yourself going through these motions. You and your lawyer arrive a few minutes before your pretrial is scheduled. You're dressed conservatively to show you respect the process and the judge. You haven't brought friends along, although you may bring your accountant in case you need his or her expertise. Your spouse shows up with a lawyer and an entourage: mother, sister, best friend, and new significant other. You all go into the courtroom and sit in the spectator seats.

Inside the Chambers

The clerk comes through a door at one side of the judge's bench and makes sure everyone is present. The clerk asks for copies of documents that are supposed to be in the court file but aren't, while your spouse's lawyer sputters a bit about the slowness of the mail and the fact he failed to bring copies with him. (Remember, you haven't seen these papers, either, because they aren't ready.)

You've told your lawyer you want to be present for whatever happens, so your lawyer asks if all four of you can see the judge. You all go into the judge's chambers and sit around the judge's desk as the lawyers explain the issues to the judge. Because you're present, they can't badmouth you or indulge in war stories on your time meter. The judge may give you useful information such as, "Unless there is some information I haven't seen, I am disinclined to award spousal maintenance in this case" or "I can't find any documentation for this nonmarital claim. If there is no proof, there is no claim." These kinds of observations can be very helpful.

ALERT!

Men should never wear caps or hats in the courtroom or judge's chambers. Women should not show cleavage or wear a lot of noisy jewelry. Wear clothes that show you respect the judge. They like to be respected.

Proper Behavior

Remember, you're a guest in a judge's office, so show respect. Judges like old-fashioned good manners, so be polite to your spouse. And don't bring your enormous briefcase full of divorce papers into chambers. It makes you look obsessed with the divorce. In addition, don't speak unless the judge asks you a direct question, and then answer only the question the judge asks.

After meeting with the judge, you're sent to a nearby conference room to discuss settlement. Activist judges are likely to keep you talking until your lawyers report nothing more can be settled because of missing information. If both sides are missing information, the judge probably won't impose sanctions. If only one side has failed to bring required documents, the judge may impose fines but make them conditional. (For example, if the case settles within the next thirty days, the fine will be forgiven.)

Too often one party is stuck on the behavior and actions of the other and unable to think of resolving issues for the family's benefit. You can be sure the judge will pick up on this, and you won't look good.

Still Moving Toward Trial

At the close of negotiations, everyone (except your spouse's entourage) troops back into the judge's chambers and reports on progress or lack thereof. The judge or the judge's law clerk takes notes, maybe on a laptop computer, or the judge directs one of the lawyers to prepare the pretrial order. The order will spell out any agreements, set out a schedule for completing any unfinished discovery, set a date for exchanging exhibit and witness lists, and set any sanctions for failing to complete tasks on time.

The judge may schedule another pretrial hearing depending on the judge's preferences. Some judges really like to try cases. They like sitting up on their benches, hearing testimony, making rulings on evidence, and appearing wise. These judges probably will set a trial date after one pretrial hearing.

On the other hand, some judges really don't like to try cases at all. They have trouble making decisions, especially in divorce cases. They'll give you every opportunity to settle your case, and may schedule several pretrials. If that doesn't work, they'll give you time to discuss settlement on the day of trial, then probably reschedule the trial.

Last Chance to Settle

Some wise judges realize divorce trials mean all other alternatives have failed—that the parties won't take responsibility and the buck has stopped in the judge's courtroom because someone else has to make the decisions. These judges probably will schedule a second pretrial with some serious sanctions for failure to exchange necessary documents. These judges will enforce sanctions because they know you can't settle the case if you don't have the information you need. Judges who understand divorce dynamics try to get the parties to make as many of their own decisions as possible. They then work with the divorcing spouses and their lawyers to devise a plan for resolving any remaining issues.

It's All about Preparation

The pretrial hearing is a tool to prepare for trial. It makes lawyers complete their preparation, gets everyone organized, and sets the trial rules. It's common for the parties to reach agreement on at least some issues at the pretrial. In fact, if you and your spouse have completed discovery, you're likely to resolve all the issues of your divorce at this time. (E)

Chapter 17
The Trial

A judge has an image of the perfect trial. At the perfect trial, lawyers are well prepared. Parties present only relevant evidence and give the judge the information he or she needs. The attorneys give the judge the proposed findings they brought with them. Everyone goes home. The judge renders a decision well before the ninety days are up. Now, back to reality.

Final Preparations

Again you'll need to meet with your lawyer to decide on a final witness list so you can provide it to the other side before trial. The time varies from state to state but assume witness lists need to be exchanged at least a week before trial.

If you're contesting custody, your witness list will probably include family and friends, but your lawyer will streamline this group of witnesses. The judge assumes family members and friends are going to say nice things about you, so their testimony is noteworthy only when they don't (or if your spouse's family has good things to say about you). Select a family member who has seen both you and your spouse with the children and can provide recent information. Then select one really good witness from among your friends, which is probably enough, because the judge doesn't need to hear six people say the same thing. Choose the friend who'll be the most effective and who really knows you and your children well.

ALERT!

Make sure your lawyer meets with the witnesses who will testify at the trial. Your lawyer needs to get a feel for these witnesses and how they will present themselves to the judge. Then he can narrow the list to those who will do the best job for you.

Double-Check Financial Information

For financial issues, you'll be using experts. If you haven't been able to agree on independent neutrals, both sides will bring their experts to the trial. You and your lawyer need to review the experts' testimony with them ahead of time. If your experts are interesting and easy to understand, they should be given ample time on the witness stand. If they're dull, although very bright, you may want to limit their testimony to explaining charts and exhibits clearly and concisely. You don't want to bore the judge, but you do want the judge to understand your position.

By the week before trial you should have your spouse's budget, current income information, vocational evaluation, if requested, and a good sense of the assets of the marriage. You can use this information to decide whether to offer your spouse maintenance. If it's pretty clear you'll have to pay maintenance anyway, you may be able to negotiate a deal that works well for both of you, rather than letting a judge decide.

As you and your experts prepare for trial, you'll be able to see whether you can prove your position on certain issues. If your experts can't convince you, they can't convince the judge. On the other hand, if you see the weaknesses in your argument, you may choose to give in on those issues and focus on the areas where you're strong. Giving away something you don't really have may produce some movement toward settlement from the other side as well.

In many states, parties can change their names as part of a divorce. You should decide before the trial whether you want to change your name at this time. Some parents choose to keep the same name as their children while they're in school.

Use Current Numbers

Both sides need to give the judge up-to-date financial information. Recent pay stubs, the most recent tax returns available, and current stocks and real estate values should be in your lawyer's file, ready for court. If you and the other side haven't agreed on a date for valuing assets, it's possible the court will use the pretrial or trial date. You need to have values as of both dates. If you want the judge to use a different date, you'll need a persuasive reason.

The judge can select a valuation date, if you haven't agreed on one. If stock market values have been fluctuating widely, real estate prices have been booming, or some other factor has affected your holdings' values, the judge will want to pick a valuation date that doesn't create a crazy result. The judge will want to use a value that is valid at the time she makes her decision.

Review Your Exhibits

Exhibits are the documents given to the judge during the trial. They include budgets, financial statements, expert reports, charts, graphs, and medical records. Exhibits are intended to validate testimony and, sometimes, to flesh it out. Your trial will go much more smoothly and you will please the judge if both sides meet beforehand to review exhibits.

During this review, it'll be clear to the lawyers that some exhibits are going to be received by the judge, no matter how much they object. It's in everyone's best interests to stipulate, or agree, to admit these documents. As one side presents its case and these exhibits are offered into evidence, the other side can simply say, "stipulated." This saves a lot of time during the trial, and judges like trials that move along. Stipulating that a document can be part of the trial record does not mean you agree to the contents of the document.

Laying Foundation

Some documents won't be automatically admitted. For example, if you want to get certain bank records into evidence, you have to establish their authenticity. In lawyer language, this is called laying the foundation for the records. Ordinarily, this would mean you have to bring the record keeper to the courtroom to testify these are indeed your records from the bank where he or she works. The other side knows you can get the bank employee to come to court with the records by issuing a subpoena duces tecum, which is Latin for "Show up with the stuff." So your spouse's lawyer might well agree to waive his or her foundation objection to the bank records. That way you don't have to pay for the subpoena, for getting it served, and for having the guy from the bank come to court.

Laying foundation for an exhibit can be unnecessarily expensive and time consuming. The judge will be irritated, and it's rarely to your advantage to irritate a judge. However, both sides will probably have exhibits that will require bringing a person to court to lay foundation. Lawyers will be happy to negotiate a deal here: "I will waive my foundation objection to your bank records, if you will waive your foundation objection to my medical records." This way neither side has to bring a witness to authenticate the records. And the judge will be happy. A happy judge will do a better job of listening to evidence.

If you're using charts and graphs as exhibits, take a hard look at them. Do you understand them? If you don't, what makes you think the judge will? Only present exhibits to the judge that will help the judge understand issues and your position on them.

ALERT!

Sometimes litigants bring a storage box of canceled checks to court as an exhibit. No judge has time to go through this box of checks. If you really want the judge to know about the checks, prepare a summary, with the actual checks as backup for verification. A judge is far more likely to review a summary than to delve into a box of old checks.

Making Agreements or Stipulations

We just talked about the lawyers meeting to review exhibits and to make agreements about getting them into evidence. Lawyers can stipulate a number of things prior to trial. They can put together a statement of the facts—including all of the facts to which both sides agree—and reserve the right to argue about any contested facts. They can even agree about which facts are contested.

Lawyers can agree to have witnesses testify out of order, which can be a bit confusing, but it's far better than spending a lot of time arguing about it. For example, say you have a doctor witness who is available only Thursday afternoon, but your spouse's case probably will be presented Thursday afternoon. The lawyers can agree the doctor can testify when she shows up at the courtroom. In addition, it can be very expensive to have the doctor wait around to testify, because he or she will bill by the hour, just as other experts do.

Lawyers can agree to have a witness testify by deposition or video deposition. Suppose an expert who can help explain your business's value has just gotten a contract to work in Bali for six months. Obviously, it would be too expensive to bring that person back to trial, so his or her testimony can be preserved in a deposition where the lawyers conduct direct and cross examination as if they were in trial. Similar testimony can be presented by conference call, too.

Stipulations to exhibits, facts, valuation dates, and the order of witnesses are important aids to making the trial go smoothly. However, they can happen only if the lawyers meet prior to trial and reach these kinds of agreements. If real issues need to be litigated, it's probably wise to stipulate the less important stuff and focus on these disagreements. In other words, pick your battles.

ALERT!

If your spouse's lawyer sets your teeth on edge, try to remember that this lawyer, like yours, has a job to do here. Part of a lawyer's job may be to get you upset, so don't play into the plan. Bite your tongue and stay calm.

The Big Day Arrives

Let's say you, your lawyer, and several bankers' boxes of documents arrive at the courthouse a few minutes before the trial is to begin. (Be sure to arrive early, since you'll need some time to unpack and get organized.) Then the other side arrives, at which point your spouse's lawyer beckons to your lawyer. The other side has a last-minute settlement proposal, so the lawyers huddle. When the judge's clerk appears to ask if everyone is ready, the lawyers ask for a few minutes to talk. Now what?

A Last-Minute Proposal

Your lawyer comes to you with the other side's proposal. The offer is good only if you agree not to go to trial. If the trial starts, all bets are off. What should you do?

In the best-case scenario, you spent a lot of the night before trial clarifying your bottom-line position. You now can evaluate the proposal with that bottom line in mind. If you didn't do that, you'll need to huddle with your lawyer to review the proposal. If it's reasonable, you should probably accept it, or make a reasonable counterproposal. A settlement, even on the courthouse steps, is usually better than letting a judge decide.

Trial Attire

We've talked about this before. Again, use common sense. If you don't have any, consult with your lawyer or your lawyer's paralegal. If you want the judge to think you're poor, don't wear all your best and brightest jewelry. If you want the judge to think you're a good mom, don't dress like a prostitute. Wear comfortable clothes because you'll be in an uncomfortable setting all day long. You don't need the added discomfort of shoes that are too tight or a stiff starched collar. And remember, a judge can see your legs and feet under the counsel table, so be sure your socks match.

FACT

Most courts prohibit food and beverages in the courtroom, but they will provide water at your table. Do not bring soda or munchies, and, absolutely, do not chew gum. Judges are truly offended by gum.

Who Should Come to Court?

Do not bring children to the trial. Judges do not let children testify, and probably won't let them listen to the trial. If the judge wants input from the children, the judge will talk with them on a day other than the day of your divorce trial. If you bring the children, they'll have to sit outside the courtroom, and if they are young, someone will have to sit with them. They will be both bored and stressed, guaranteed.

Limit your entourage. Don't bring your new love interest, unless that person is going to testify. Then, have that person there only for testimony. Usually judges won't allow witnesses to sit in a courtroom until after they've testified. Keep that in mind when you ask people to come to your trial. If you want your best friend to be there for moral support, remember that your friend can be in the courtroom only if he or she isn't going to testify or has already done so. Think about how much of your personal life you want to share, even with your best friend.

Judges Rely on Their Eyes and Ears

Judges notice what people wear and how they behave, and draw conclusions from these observations. A rich guy who comes to court dressed casually in a cashmere sweater and Gucci loafers sends a message. A spouse who gives off intimidating vibes will give a judge information about the relationship. A spouse who uses every opportunity to bad-mouth the other person tells the judge he or she isn't letting go of the relationship and moving on. Maybe that person is going to make sharing responsibility for the kids impossible.

Judges like reasonable people who take reasonable positions. Judges notice who makes the trial take longer. While they don't consciously punish these people, decisions on close issues may be influenced by their frustration with them.

Remember that it's always best to negotiate whatever you possibly can. You may not get exactly what you want, but at least you'll maintain some control over the issue instead of allowing a third party complete control.

Opening Statements

Let's assume the last-ditch settlement effort failed, and the trial is about to begin. Most civil cases begin with opening statements from lawyers, but these seldom are used in divorce courts because a judge hears cases without a jury, except in Georgia and Texas. However, opening statements are a good idea because they make each side state its perception of issues. Sometimes after hearing opening statements the parties agree on some issues (to their surprise)—usually because the lawyers haven't met and conferred like they were supposed to—and then won't have to introduce evidence on issues they agree on.

Trial Paperwork

You, your lawyer, and your lawyer's staff have prepared a mountain of documents for the trial.

At a minimum, these documents will include the following:

1. **Exhibits.** There should be four copies of each: one for the judge, one for each lawyer, and one for the witness who will testify about and from the document. Often, lawyers prepare loose-leaf folders of exhibits for the judge. One volume contains agreed-to exhibits; another holds the ones the other side may object to.

2. **A trial notebook prepared by your lawyer.** This contains your lawyer's opening statement and testimony outlines from your witnesses, sometimes including questions your lawyer plans to ask. The notebook will also include questions to ask the other side's witnesses and strategy reminders.

3. **Proposed findings to submit to the judge at the close of testimony.** Proposed findings are your version of what the judgment and decree should look like, based on the evidence you intend to present to the judge. It's really your final argument to the judge put into the form of the judgment and decree. Preparing proposed findings helps you and your lawyer organize the evidence you want to present at trial. Judges find a well-prepared proposed findings helpful when it's time for them to prepare a decision in your case.

Procedure and Evidence Rules

You hired a lawyer in part to navigate your divorce through the legal process. Your lawyer knows the procedure and evidence rules–your lawyer better, because it's a given you don't know them. Focus on the content of the testimony, and let your lawyer flex legal muscles on your behalf.

Procedure Rules

Procedure rules apply to how things are done in the legal process. For example, some papers have to be served personally while others can be served by mail. These rules govern how many days before a scheduled hearing you have to serve papers on the other side. They're the rules that say every time you serve a motion, it has to be accompanied by an affidavit. They're kind of a cookbook on how to make a lawsuit.

Evidence Rules

Evidence rules govern information admissible in court. Family courts frequently apply one such rule called the foundation rule. Say your lawyer wants to ask your tax expert about the significance of a specific line on your tax return. The lawyer first must show the expert has the necessary knowledge to do this. This is called laying foundation.

FACT

A counselor may not be able to testify about what your spouse said unless your spouse has given a release to provide the information. Otherwise, it may be considered privileged, like communications between a lawyer and client.

Another evidence rule, called the hearsay rule, also is used often. This rule says you can't tell the judge what someone else has said unless that person is going to testify. So, you can tell the judge what your spouse said because he is a party to the divorce, will hear your testimony, and will be able to respond. But you can't tell the judge your marriage counselor said your spouse was behaving irrationally. If you want this information to come in, the marriage counselor will need to be a witness.

Testifying at Your Divorce Trial

Ordinarily the petitioner, or plaintiff, goes first. If your spouse is the petitioner, your spouse's lawyer may call you as the first witness. This is a tactic some lawyers use to unnerve the other side and perhaps get the person to say things he or she will regret. Be prepared for this possibility. Don't panic. Take deep breaths. And remember your lawyer will give you a chance to expand on answers you give during cross-examination.

Direct Examination

When it's your turn, your lawyer calls you to the witness stand. You swear to tell the truth and then sit down in the witness chair. Your lawyer starts the questioning, which is called direct examination. The first few questions will be preliminary: your name, address, age, and employer. These questions help you get adjusted to testifying. After that, your lawyer takes you through the outline you and your lawyer prepared. If some facts don't make you look so good, you should be the one to introduce them, if possible. You know your spouse will if you don't. If you can bring up the bad news first, you can give your perspective and maybe soften its impact.

Cross-Examination

When your lawyer finishes his or her questions, your spouse's lawyer will conduct cross-examination. Your spouse's lawyer will try to ask questions that can be answered only "yes" or "no." If you want to explain your answers, the lawyer probably will say, "This question calls for a yes or no answer." Sometimes a judge will let you explain, but if the judge doesn't, don't get upset. Your lawyer will give you a chance during redirect examination.

Rules for Testifying

If you can follow these rules when you testify, you'll do a better job.

1. **Listen to the question, then answer it.** Don't volunteer additional information. Answer the question asked. Don't begin an answer about your behavior with, "My spouse . . . ."
2. **Pause before answering questions to give your lawyer time to object.** If two people talk at the same time, it's a nightmare for a court reporter or a tape recorder to sort out who's talking.
3. **Look at the judge when you speak.** This is the person you want to hear you. Your lawyer already knows what you're going to say.
4. **Don't try to match wits with your spouse's lawyer.** Your lawyer's been doing this for a long time, or at least longer than you have.

This is your lawyer's turf. You may win a skirmish but lose the war with smart retorts.

5. **Don't argue with the attorneys or the judge—especially not the judge.**
6. **If you need a break, ask for it.** If you need to regain your composure, need a drink of water, or need to use a bathroom, don't hesitate to speak up.
7. **If you and your spouse have children, always refer to them as "our" children—never "my" children.**

Testifying in court is scary and stressful. It's important to remember you're trying to give the judge information to help the judge decide contested issues. The judge doesn't have to like you. And the judge really isn't interested in your spouse's small failings in housekeeping, cooking, or ironing unless they resulted in the health department or social services getting involved. Tell the judge what the judge needs to know, then stop.

When the Other Side Testifies

Have a pad of paper and pen ready. If the witness says something you disagree with, make a note. Don't elbow your lawyer or whisper in his or her ear, because this will distract your lawyer from following the testimony. Let your lawyer do his or her job.

ALERT!

The judge will watch you while your spouse testifies. Remember that the judge pays attention to nonverbal as well as verbal communication. Try to let your reactions be genuine. Don't make faces.

When your spouse's lawyer finishes examining the witness, you and your lawyer can confer briefly before your lawyer begins cross-examination. This is the time to have your lawyer review your notes on issues on which you and your spouse may have very different perceptions of certain events of your marriage. This may be a part of why you're getting divorced. Try not to hiss, "That's a lie!" Sometimes it is, but sometimes it's a different perception.

Where Does the Time Go?

A typical court day runs from 9:30 A.M. to noon, with a fifteen-minute morning break. Courts typically resume at 2 P.M. and run until 4:30 P.M., with a fifteen-minute afternoon break. Judges usually hear motions or have sentencings first thing in the morning, which may take longer than scheduled and run into your trial time. Same thing for the afternoon motion. What's more, those fifteen-minute breaks can stretch into thirty minutes or more. And, if the judge has an obligation after work, he or she may want to stop promptly at 4:30 P.M. If you're lucky, you'll have four hours of actual trial time during a court day. Of course, you'll pay for at least eight hours of attorney time!

Weeks may pass between court appearances for your trial. It would be wise for your lawyer to keep good written notes, and even order a transcript of prior sessions. You and your lawyer will need to prepare good findings at the end of the trial because the judge will have a hard time remembering too.

Suppose your case is set for a two-day trial. You start late on the first day and are about 60 percent of the way through the case by the end of the second day. The judge doesn't have time to hear the rest of the testimony the following day, plus your attorney has another trial starting then. So the judge and the lawyers confer and end up agreeing to finish the trial about sixty days from now. At this rate, it may take several months to complete your trial.

After all the testimony is in, the judge has ninety days in most jurisdictions to issue a decision. Often attorneys ask for the opportunity to submit written final arguments and a proposed judgment and decree. They usually get another couple of weeks to do that. The judge's ninety days doesn't kick in until all papers have been submitted.

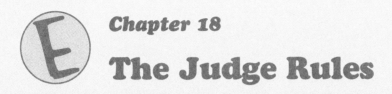

Chapter 18

The Judge Rules

The trial is over. The attorneys have submitted all arguments and the judge is considering the case. When will the judge decide, and what will you do with the decision once you get it? You'll need to review the decision with your lawyer to determine your next move. You're almost finished.

Can You Hurry a Judge?

As you already know, a judge has a specific time period to issue a decision. This usually is ninety days from the date of the last submission. Some judges get decisions out quickly, while some issue decisions on the ninetieth day. Some don't do their work on time. The waiting can be nerve-racking.

FACT

You now have time to reflect on your trial. You and your lawyer may sit down and review what went well and what went poorly. You are very nervous about what the judge will decide. You can make a settlement proposal to the other side, even at this late stage of the process. The certainty of a final resolution outside of court may appeal to your spouse as well.

Further Delays

The temporary orders in effect when you went to trial remain in effect until they're changed by another order. However, sometimes it's necessary to get an order changed while you're waiting for a judge's decision if, for example, you lose your job or your spouse gets one. The new circumstances require a motion with all the paperwork—affidavits and any exhibits.

If you bring a motion after trial but before a final decision, you can expect a further delay in the final decree. The judge first will have to rule on the motion. If the motion's substance changes facts presented at trial, the judge will probably treat it as a new submission and recompute the ninety-day period from the date of the motion hearing.

Facing a Dilemma

If a judge doesn't issue a decision within the allotted time, you can't do much about it. In most states, when a judge endorses a paycheck, he or she is also signing a statement saying no work is overdue. Although a judge's paycheck can be withheld if the judge is not in compliance, your attorneys probably don't want to be whistle-blowers if decisions are late. They have to work with this judge in the future. It's a dilemma.

Finally, the Judge's Decision

Your lawyer may call to tell you about the decision, or may just mail it to you. Read the decision carefully, then read it again. Write down your questions and concerns, and then schedule a meeting with your lawyer. You should meet within a week of getting the decision because there are time limits on challenging it. The judge's decision will usually be in three parts: the findings of fact, the conclusions of law, and the order.

Findings of Fact

In findings of fact, a judge makes decisions about facts contested at a trial. These findings reflect which witness the judge believed. Sometimes when two experts present evidence, a judge will rely on the evidence he or she understands better. When witnesses present very different values for something, such as a business, a judge is likely to select a value somewhere in between. If you and your spouse do a lot of mudslinging and foster care isn't an option for your children, a judge will have to decide which of you is the lesser evil, and make findings to support that choice.

Conclusions of Law

From the findings, a judge will draw legal conclusions. A legal conclusion would be something like this: "From the findings about the parties as parents, I conclude that it would be in the best interests of the children to live with their father." Or, like this: "From the facts presented at trial, I conclude the wife has met her burden of proving she has a 30 percent nonmarital interest in the house." When a judge talks about meeting the burden, the judge is saying a person has provided enough evidence to support a claim.

The All-Important Order

Judge's orders are derived from the findings of fact and the conclusions of law. For example, the judge finds that Dad is the one who provides stability and nurturing for the children. From this finding, the judge concludes it would be in the best interests of the children to live with their father. Considering the best interests of the children, the judge issues an order saying something like this: "Dad is granted (or awarded) sole physical custody of the children."

FACT

"In the best interests of the child" is a legal standard. U.S. appeals courts have issued decisions to explain just what this means. In some ways, a judge has to take the position of "All-Knowing Parent" to decide just what is in the best interests of your children.

When the findings, conclusions, and order are stated separately, you can follow a judge's thinking pretty easily, even if you disagree with it. In some courts, a judge prepares a document called Findings of Fact, Conclusions of Law, Order for Judgment, and Judgment and Decree. In such a document, findings and conclusions are combined in one portion, and the order simply says "Let Judgment Be Entered Accordingly." This means you and your lawyer have to go through the findings to make sure the judge got the facts right, then review those same findings to ascertain the legal conclusions. This is pretty confusing, and it's why you hired that good divorce lawyer.

In some courts, after a judge makes a decision, he or she directs one of the lawyers to prepare the judgment and decree based on the judge's findings and conclusions. Both lawyers sign off on the document saying it's consistent with the judge's order, but this doesn't mean they agree with the decision. If the lawyers have to prepare the judgment and decree, this lengthens the process.

An Unwelcome Decision

Chances are you'll be unhappy with a judge's decision. In fact, some judges say they know they've done a good job when both sides are unhappy with a decision. What they're really saying is that mutual dissatisfaction reflects the impartiality of the decision.

On the Lookout for Mistakes

When you and your lawyer review the judge's decision, be on the lookout for certain things. Did the judge get the facts right? Did the judge make computation errors? Did the judge confuse the parties? Did the judge make enough findings to support his or her conclusions? Does the judge have a basis for facts he or she found after hearing contested evidence? Parts of the judge's decision may reflect the use of judicial discretion, where the judge interprets the evidence after considering words, documents, and behavior. Remember, what the judge sees in the courtroom influences his or her interpretation of the evidence.

Did the judge make a legal error? Here you'll have to rely on your lawyer. And, if the judge did make an error based on the law, does this mistake support a motion asking the judge to reconsider? Can the mistakes be corrected easily by conferring with the judge? That is, would the other side agree to these changes, too, because they're clearly the result of confusing the parties or making a computation error? Do the mistakes require going back to the trial judge before considering an appeal? Can you go back to the trial judge? Should you appeal?

ALERT!

Don't get cocky if you find that the judge has made a mistake. This doesn't mean you'll end up getting what you wanted. A mistake may be corrected, but the outcome may be different from what you expect.

Conferring with the Judge

If a judge has made obvious factual errors, such as a mathematical error in computing child support or getting the parties mixed up, your lawyer and your spouse's lawyer can correct these by conferring with the judge. If the judge is willing, this can be done by conference call. If correcting these errors leads to an outcome the judge didn't intend, the judge may want to have a hearing about these errors, with arguments on what the outcome now should be.

If the judge believed your spouse instead of you, you'll have a hard time getting the judge to change his or her mind, even if you can correct certain factual errors in your favor. On top of that, appeals courts are very reluctant to reverse trial court judges' decisions when these decisions are, in effect, a judgment call (rather than a legal error) on the trial judge's part. This is that judicial discretion concept. Unless a trial judge was clearly wrong, an appeals court will affirm a trial judge who has had the advantage of seeing witnesses and determining their credibility.

You might consider making your spouse a new settlement offer, a better one than before trial but still preferable to the judge's decision. If the judge was skating on thin ice in the decision, your spouse may choose to settle rather than let the courts take another shot at both of you.

Here's an example. You might offer a to pay your spouse a lump-sum payment instead of paying monthly alimony. Your spouse could invest the money and live on the income. The two of you wouldn't have to deal with each other every month and could move on with your lives. Plus, spousal maintenance wouldn't depend on your staying alive and employed.

Back to the Trial Judge

If you and your lawyer think the judge made mistakes that support an appeal, you probably should first ask the trial judge to take another look. This is called making a motion for amended findings or a new trial. Some states make such a motion a precondition for appeal. The appeal is based on denial of a new trial, assuming the judge denies the motion, and that's a pretty safe bet.

In a motion for amended findings, you'll raise the issues you would raise on appeal. You might argue the judge simply didn't make enough findings about your parenting skills to deny custody. Or you might argue the judge ignored some important evidence, but this is a little chancy because the judge might flat-out say he or she didn't believe that testimony. Or you may cite other cases to show the judge applied the law incorrectly.

Should You Appeal?

After the judge rules on your motion, look at the whole picture to decide whether to appeal. If you got most of what you wanted from your motion, maybe you should pick up your marbles and go home, because appeals courts are unpredictable. Appeal only if the trial court missed a very big issue, and your lawyer says you have a good chance to prevail.

FACT

Judges hate to be reversed by appeals courts. Appeals court decisions are public, and all the lawyers and other judges can read them. Your judge will take your motion for amended findings seriously and may make corrections in response to your motion.

Otherwise, it's too expensive in time, money, and emotions to prolong your divorce by another year or so. Yep, that's how much time you're looking at.

Rules of Appellate Procedure

The Rules of Appellate Procedure give you a specific time limit to appeal a judgment. You'll need to decide fairly quickly whether to appeal because you'll need to accomplish a lot in the sixty to ninety days allotted. You need to order a trial transcript from the court reporter, which, if the trial was long, will take awhile for the court reporter to type up—and you're probably not the only case wanting one. Your lawyer needs to put exhibits into order and write an appellate brief. And you need to submit certain papers in a specific format dictated by the Rules of Appellate Procedure for your state.

If you're the appellant, you will prepare all your papers, submit them to the appellate court, and serve them on the other side. The other side, called the respondent, then has a chance to respond. When all the paperwork (yours and the other side's) has been submitted to the appellate court, the clerk of that court will schedule oral argument. The lawyers then go to the court to make spoken arguments and answer the appellate judge's questions about their positions. You're permitted to attend oral argument, but you won't be permitted to say anything.

The appeals court will issue a decision within six months or so. Yes, that's a long time. While you're waiting to get on with your life, you again may consider making a settlement proposal. Negotiating a settlement is always an alternative.

While you should always consider negotiation, don't give in to issues you feel strongly about just to be done with it. Spending so much time in the courts may be a tactic your ex-spouse is using to wear you down. Maintain focus on your objectives and think through negotiations before signing on the dotted line.

Appeals Court Outcomes

There are three possible outcomes from an appeal. The appeals court may affirm the trial court's decision, which means that, unless you appeal to your highest state court, the trial court decision stands. Or, it may affirm part of the decision and reverse another part, issuing its own decision where it reverses the trial court. If this happens, you can appeal this kind of decision, too, to the highest appellate court of your state. And finally, the appeals court can reverse and remand (send back to court) all or part of the trial court's decision. When it remands a portion of the trial court's decision, it sends it back to the trial court for another hearing. (Got all of this so far?) It would be possible to have that hearing, get the trial court's decision, and appeal again. And again. And again. Some people develop a new career called "The Divorce" instead of moving on with their lives.

When a case is appealed to the highest court, the issue presented is: Did the appeals court make a mistake? The high court can affirm the appeals court or reverse it. It also can send the case back to the trial court. It probably would be possible to spend the rest of your adult life in the courts, if you had enough money and nothing else to do.

Implementing the Final Order

At some point, the case will be over. Even when the judgment and decree is final, work still needs to be done. Some decree provisions require you to do something to implement them. For example, if the court has awarded you the house, you'll need to get the title transferred into your name. To do this, you get a certified copy of the judgment and decree along with a Quit Claim Deed signed by your ex-spouse, and take both these documents to your county's Registrar of Deeds or Registrar of Titles (it depends on whether property is Torrens or Abstract) where the title transfer is processed.

If you agreed to remove your ex-spouse's name from the mortgage and take over payments for mortgage, insurance, and taxes yourself, you'll have to refinance your home. To ensure this happens, you may be directed to hold your ex harmless should you not meet this responsibility. This means you'll reimburse your ex-spouse for any and all loss or harm you may have caused him or her because you didn't make the necessary payments.

ALERT!

Though you may breathe a huge sigh of relief once the divorce is final, it's probably at this time that you'll feel the effects of prolonged stress. Your muscles may ache, you may feel nauseated, or you may just want to crawl in bed and stay there for the next three years. Take care of yourself (physically and mentally) and these effects will soon subside.

Suppose you got the house, and your spouse got a lien against it for a specific amount. That lien will be due and payable at some point, maybe when your youngest child turns eighteen or maybe after a set number of years. When you pay off the lien, you'll want to get a Quit Claim Deed giving you the property free and clear. If you sell the property before paying off the lien, you will have to pay the lien from the proceeds of the sale.

New Names and Titles

You'll need to transfer titles to cars, boats, trailers, or snowmobiles according to decree terms. Usually you and your spouse can simply sign off on the title documents and apply for new titles. If you changed your name, you'll need to change your social security registration as well as the name on all your accounts—bank, credit, and utility—and apply for a new driver's license.

Money Matters

If the decree divides retirement funds, your lawyer may need to draft a Qualified Domestic Relations Order for each account that is to be so divided. Each employer has different requirements for this order, so your lawyer will have to contact the company's legal department to get the appropriate form. Other retirement money may be divided by providing a certified copy of the judgment and decree.

The decree will order child support and spousal maintenance, if warranted. You may have had a support order in place while the divorce was pending. Perhaps you and your spouse had an informal arrangement to pay support that didn't involve the formal system.

If income withholding is in place when the decree is issued, you'll only need to give the new numbers to the employer or the agency that implements the withholding. If payments are being made directly and you want withholding, you'll have to make arrangements to get it set up. Usually it takes several months between the request and the implementation. You'll need to pay the agency or your ex-spouse directly during that time.

Is It Really the End?

With any luck, you're now finished with the legal divorce. If you had to go to trial, you've invested several years, a lot of money, and your sweat and tears in the process. Unless you and your ex-spouse learn to resolve issues through negotiation, you may meet again in the halls of justice as your lives and circumstances change. Ⓔ

Chapter 19

Being Parents after a Divorce

Y ou've read the chapters with information about legal and physical custody and children's needs at different developmental stages. Now that you're divorced you need to develop your plan for being parents to your children until they're legally adults. Of course, you hope the plan continues to work after the children are legally adults, but at that point you're on your own.

Creating a Plan When You're Friends

The courts can serve as your backup only as long as the children are considered dependent under the law. Most state laws label children emancipated when they reach eighteen, marry, join the military, or finish high school. When one of these things happens, the courts lose jurisdiction over the children, because the legal system loses the ability to make decisions about them in this context. However, a few states retain jurisdiction until the children reach age twenty-one, so you need to check your state's laws with your lawyer.

On Friendly Terms

Assume for a moment that you and your spouse are on reasonably friendly terms. You can talk to each other on the phone about the children, and you've been flexible, trading weekends to accommodate activities and special events. If you both show up for your son's baseball game, you can even sit together and cheer. This is terrific. Your ability to work together bodes well for the ongoing mental health of all members of the restructured family.

ALERT!

All parents need to have a written parenting plan. Even when you and your spouse get along well and can operate under a flexible, reasonable, and liberal plan for visitation, you may disagree at times. When you do, a written parenting plan can serve as the tie breaker, the fallback position to resolve the disagreement.

Be Realistic

As you design a parenting plan, you and your ex-spouse need to consider the practicalities of implementing it. For example, you may both philosophically agree that the children should spend as much time as possible with each of you, so you're considering taking the kids half of each week. But does this fit the needs and wishes of your children? And can you make this happen? How does it fit in with the reality of your work schedules? For example, if you plan to exchange the children on

Wednesdays after school, this means you have to keep Wednesday afternoons clear for the foreseeable future. Can you? Nothing is more devastating for a child than to be left waiting at the schoolhouse door while all his or her little friends hop on buses or bikes to go home.

And what about weekends? To keep your division equal, you'll need to exchange the children on Saturday evening or Sunday morning. Religious commitments may make this awkward. In addition, this would mean neither of you would have a full weekend with the children. This may or may not be a problem, but you need to think about it.

FACT

You can include the use of a parenting consultant in your divorce decree. You can give the person you choose authority to resolve parenting disputes between you and your ex. You will pay less than it would cost to go to court to settle your disputes about the children, and you can get your dispute resolved immediately.

Creating a Plan When You're Not Friends

Now assume you and your ex-spouse don't get along well—you're both still angry and find it hard to be civil to each other. But despite your animosity, you both want to create your own parenting plan, rather than let the judge decide. What can you do?

You can enlist the help of a third person, a mediator or a parenting consultant, to help formulate your plan. You've already learned a bit about mediators, so if you use one, be sure to pick a person who knows about children's needs as well as divorce laws. A parenting consultant usually is a mental health professional with experience working with divorcing parents. This person understands the developmental needs of children and the dynamics of relationships between parents who still are hurting and angry. A parenting consultant can propose a plan that you can review with your lawyer to make sure you're not creating legal pitfalls down the road.

Nonverbal Communication

In addition to having a parenting consultant available to resolve disputes, you can use a children's notebook, a book in which you communicate with each other about the children. You can tell the other parent what happened during the week, any illnesses that require medication, or any special concerns. You can, in effect, keep each other up-to-date about the children without meeting face-to-face or talking on the phone. A children's notebook works as long as both parents use it properly and not as another opportunity to take shots at each other. Remember, it's about the children.

Additional resources are available on the Internet. For a fee you can subscribe to a service that lets you do your scheduling and discuss the children online. One such service is *www.ourfamilywizard.com*. Communicating and scheduling by computer is fast, efficient, and can help keep the focus on the children.

Considerations for Angry Parents

Even though you're angry with your ex-spouse, you really don't want your anger to harm your children. You must consider their needs first and take into account each child's age and developmental levels. For example, if you want to minimize your ex-spouse's involvement with the children and maximize your own, ask yourself if this fits your children's needs. Because you and your ex-spouse are hostile, you also need to consider how you'll exchange your children. Exchanges at each other's home may be problematic, especially if angry exchanges turn into front-yard battles. If that's a possibility, try making exchanges where you don't even see each other, such as pickups at school or day care, providing you pick up the children on time and don't get into arguments with teachers and care providers. In your situation, a minimal number of exchanges each week is a good idea, because the fewer opportunities you have to find fault with each other, the better.

Parental conflict—often with children in the middle—has the most harmful long-term effects on the children of divorce. Whenever possible, parents need to keep children out of their conflict.

If Distance Is an Issue

What if you or your ex-spouse has moved to a different state? Here again, parents who can work together have more options than those who are dependent on a judge's decision because they can't get along. You may choose to split the year into school and nonschool segments, making one of you primary parent during the school year and the other parent primary during school holidays. Then all you need to work out is how to get the children from one place to the other, how and when to have telephone contact, and who gets the children on which holidays. If you can negotiate a plan, you can figure out a way to make it work.

Some parents alternate years with children. This plan may meet parental needs, but it's very hard on children, because they have to change schools, make new friends, and adjust to new routines every year. High school–age children need to attend the same school throughout whenever possible.

Details, Details

Once you and your ex-spouse agree on a parenting plan, you'll need to look at the details. The first detail is exchanging the kids, which is a two-part issue: when and where the kids are exchanged (time and place), and who will provide transportation.

Exchanging the Kids

If parents live near each other, many simply pick up their children from their ex-spouse, take them to their home for their scheduled time, and then bring them back. So long as this can be accomplished without angry words between the parents and the need to call the police every other week, this is by far the simplest arrangement. This has the additional advantage of making sure they get to your home on time. You aren't stuck waiting and worrying when the children are late.

Some parents who have a hard time getting along pick up their children at school or day care, which means only one parent needs to be involved. However, it's extremely important that the parent who picks up the children is on time or, at the very least, calls when running late. Nothing is more frightening to a child than to feel abandoned . . . again. Some parents who tend to be unpleasant and angry with each other might consider exchanging their children at a public place, where the presence of others usually helps keep angry parents from acting out. Fast-food restaurants seem to be a popular choice.

Really out-of-control parents sometimes use an exchange service. One parent delivers the children to this service thirty minutes before the other is to pick them up, and then leaves. Staff at the service care for the children until the other parent arrives. Using such a service means setting the exchange times during the agency's hours, and, of course, paying for the service, usually on a sliding fee scale based on your ability to pay. Yet another price of high-conflict parenting.

Exchanges can be a very emotional time for all involved, especially at first. But you must remember that you're the adult. The sooner you learn to accept the new situation, the easier it will be on your children.

Importance of Being on Time

If you and your ex-spouse live near each other, transportation can be worked out more easily than if you live far apart. Often the visiting parent picks up the children from the custodial parent's home, then returns them after the visitation time. This works well if the visiting parent shows up on time, or calls if running late.

Some parents are deliberately late with pickups and returns. Perhaps they're unconsciously still angry and expressing it by screwing up the schedule. You should know that arriving late for pickup is as hard on the kids as it is on the waiting parent. It resurrects old fears of being abandoned and prolongs the amount of time they have to worry about separating from the custodial parent. Be on time! Nothing is sadder than the child at the window, waiting, waiting, waiting.

A major issue that sends parents back to court over and over again is failure to meet the times set in the schedule. The cost of being late can be many dollars in attorney fees.

ALERT!

Experts agree that younger children should not spend long periods of time without seeing the other parent. If you have young children and want to do what's best for them, you may want to postpone a long-distance move (if at all possible) until they're a little older.

Distance Complicates Logistics

When you and your ex-spouse live far apart, logistics are tougher. Schedules have to be carefully planned. Weather can make travel difficult or impossible. And transportation costs are higher. To lessen these problems, some parents choose to meet halfway between their respective homes and exchange the children at a local restaurant, so they have a comfortable place to wait. Other parents alternate making the round trip from one home to the other. This works well when the driver has family or friends near the other parent's and can combine the exchange trip with a visit. If one parent does all the driving, the other may help pay for gas and maintenance on the vehicle that carries their kids. Sometimes, the visiting parent comes to the city where the custodial parent lives and stays with friends or relatives, so the visit can take place on the children's home turf.

It's fairly obvious that distance makes consistent contact with children more difficult. However, because almost all children want a relationship with both parents, the extra effort is important. You may want to think about the impact of distance before you choose to move, and make that move only when no other choice is available.

Sad to say, a lot of parents use the exchange as an opportunity to be nasty to each other, and the kids are stuck in the middle of arguments, threats, and other unpleasant behavior. If you care about your children, you'll make the extra effort to keep them out of your conflict. If you care about yourself, you'll make extra efforts to get past the conflict, too.

Phoning Your Kids

What about talking to the children on the telephone? Again, if the parents are civil to each other, they usually can agree to reasonable telephone contact. They can agree on some general parameters for calls, like between 8 A.M. and bedtime. Other parents need a specific schedule for calls, like Tuesday evening between 7 and 8 P.M.

Abusing Telephone Calls

Sometimes a parent calls to bad-mouth the other one or to tell the children how lonely he or she is. Sometimes one parent refuses to put the children on the phone, saying they aren't there or are in bed, or interferes with telephone contact in other creative ways. Sometimes an angry parent records telephone conversations between the children and the other parent, or listens in on an extension phone and make nasty remarks. It's no wonder some children avoid calls from their absent parent.

Other Alternatives for Contact

Today alternatives to the telephone exist. E-mail makes frequent contact with your child possible and allows you to have private conversations with your child that aren't time dependent or intrusive. While it's not the same as hearing your child's voice, it's a good substitute. Also, with cell phones, you and your child can talk to each other when the other parent is somewhere else, giving you the opportunity for a private, pleasant exchange.

Whatever method of contact you use with your children, try to keep conversations focused on their activities and interests. You sabotage communication when you use it to complain about the other parent or to lay guilt on the child for not spending more time with you.

Surviving Holidays

Then, there are holidays. Reasonable parents figure out ways to share holidays, so children can develop traditions with both sides of their family. Unreasonable parents fight over birthdays and major holidays and make everyone dread what should be happily anticipated events.

Be Reasonable

Some parents alternate holidays, while others celebrate the same holidays with their children every year, either to develop traditions or to accommodate traditional family gatherings. If Christmas is a big event in your ex-spouse's family, you might agree to divide the winter school break so Christmas falls in the ex-spouse's half every year. Then you and the kids can develop your own special event for your half of the school break. Kids don't object to celebrating a major holiday or birthday twice. It's the parents who have a hard time with this.

Sometimes a holiday may fall during the other parent's scheduled weekend. For example, your spouse might be scheduled for the first weekend in every month, which in September ends up being Labor Day. You're supposed to have the kids on that holiday, so what do you do? Reasonable parents switch weekends. Unreasonable parents insist on their time, regardless of how crazy it makes the weekend for the children and, of course, for them.

Cozy, But Not Too Cozy

Some restructured families get along well enough to celebrate holidays together. This is great because the children get to have a pleasant holiday with both parents present. If no disputes erupt and everyone focuses on the event, the strategy can be a pleasant experience for everyone. But beware of giving your children false hopes about your family reuniting.

FACT

Children never give up hope that their parents will get back together. When you share an activity with your ex-spouse and the children, be careful to avoid fueling that fantasy. Be friendly, but be clear that you're moving forward with your lives separately.

New Family Members

As you move on with your life, it's possible you'll develop a new relationship, even remarry. (After you've given yourself sufficient time to live singly, of course.) You'll want to use good judgment in introducing your new love to your children. For one thing, you want to be sure this relationship is likely to be permanent before encouraging your children to get to know and love the new person. It will be very hard for children to become attached to this new person, only to have this person disappear.

It's probably not a surprise that a new relationship can change an amicable relationship with your ex-spouse. Maybe the ex still had thoughts about getting back together and now has to accept that this won't happen. Maybe the ex-spouse sees your new love as trying to take his or her place with the children. Whatever the reasons, your ability to cooperate may evaporate.

This is one reason it's so important to have a written parenting plan to enforce when you need it. With any luck, your ex-spouse will adapt, and you can go back to reasonable and liberal. If not, at least you have a written schedule and can stay out of court.

Some Final Thoughts

When parents amicably negotiate a parenting arrangement, they can put together a plan that works. They can take into account distances, work schedules, family traditions, special activities, and everyone's needs. They can build flexibility into their plan and agree to make changes as their lives change and as their children's needs and interests change.

As children get older, they tend to get very busy with school, activities, and friends. In fact, teenagers often aren't very interested in spending time with their parents. As things change, reasonable parents work with the realities of their lives and their children's lives. These are the people who stay out of court and stay in charge of their lives. On the other hand, angry parents have a much harder time focusing on reality and on their children. All they want to do is hurt the other parent, regardless of what that may do to the children. They take their custody issues to court, over and over again, because they can't cooperate in developing a parenting plan. Often, they aren't really interested in rearing their children anyway. They just want to make life miserable for their ex-spouses.

See if you can put this whole parenting thing into perspective. Your children will be grown and on their own before you know it. The years that fall within the court's jurisdiction are a small percentage of your years as a parent. You can lay a positive foundation for many years of enjoying your children and grandchildren after they become adults. Or not. The choice is yours.

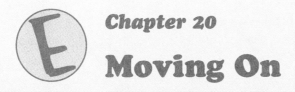

Chapter 20

Moving On

It's really over. Your divorce is final, and one way or another you have your judgment and decree. If you negotiated that decree, you can hit the ground running toward a new life. If you went to court and suffered through an appeal or two, you may be less ready to move on. Regardless, it's time to turn from the past and look toward the future.

Tying Up Loose Financial Ends

Before you leave the system behind, you need to pay your lawyer. If you and your lawyer are still friends—yes, that's really possible—you don't want to jeopardize that friendship. After all, you'll have other legal matters to address, such as changing your will, setting up trust funds for your children, or drafting a prenuptial agreement the next time you get married. And, unfortunately, it's always possible divorce issues will erupt again. If you maintain a positive relationship with your lawyer, you can call upon him or her for new needs. You'll save time and money because this lawyer already knows a lot about you and your history.

The divorce decree may order your ex-spouse to pay part or all of your attorney fees, but if your spouse doesn't obey this order, you may have to go back to court to get a judgment against your spouse for unpaid fees. However, the bottom line is you are responsible for the bill (recheck your retainer agreement to make sure). If your ex fails to pay, you'll have to, and then try to collect from your ex.

Resolve Issues Promptly

If you have issues with your lawyer, resolve them as soon as possible. The first step is to talk with your lawyer directly, so make an appointment to review whatever is troubling you—your file, your bill, your lawyer's handling of certain issues. Don't hesitate to ask your lawyer hard questions, such as "Why didn't you raise the issue of my spouse's mental health history?" Or, "Why are these phone bills so high?" Remember that the smallest increment many attorneys bill for is one quarter of an hour, meaning that a five-minute telephone call will be billed as one-fourth of an hour, or fifteen minutes. The fee agreement should spell this out. Did you call your lawyer a lot? Were you always calm, rational, and easy to work with? Take a hard look at your role in generating fees.

Making a Complaint

After you've discussed your concerns with your lawyer, you still may feel your lawyer didn't satisfactorily answer your questions. You may believe your lawyer's behavior was unethical, or you discover billing statement discrepancies. Maybe your lawyer can't account for funds that were to be held in his or her trust account during the divorce. Maybe your lawyer hasn't forwarded to you the property settlement—the check your ex says was sent to the lawyer weeks ago.

FACT

If you still think your lawyer's fees are too high, you can go to fee arbitration. Your local bar association can tell you how to set it up. Usually a fee arbitration committee is made up of lawyers and nonlawyer citizens who listen to each side and make a decision. Their decision is binding—that is, final—and you'll have to pay whatever fee the committee determines.

These are issues for the Lawyers Board of Professional Responsibility. However, you should evaluate your concerns carefully before making a complaint to be certain your complaint is valid. Dissatisfaction with trial results, a lawyer's inconsistent return of telephone calls, or insensitivity to your emotional response to the divorce are reasons to hire a different lawyer in the future, not reasons to make an ethical complaint. Over half the complaints made to the board come from divorce cases, but the board finds cause to go forward in very few of these complaints. Even so, unfounded complaints take up a lot of lawyer and board time, so be sure your complaint is legitimate. If it isn't, let go and move on.

Other Litigation Expenses

If you hired any experts for your divorce, you probably have to pay bills for their time, too. There's the accountant, the home or business appraiser, or the private custody expert, or any other expert who testified in your behalf. Making necessary arrangements to get these people paid is an important step in getting on with your life. The fewer reminders you have of the past, the easier it will be to look toward the future.

Talking to Your Children

Now that the divorce is over, you're ready to have a heart-to-heart talk with your children. With any luck, your own psyche is in pretty good shape, and you can tell the kids again that the divorce wasn't their fault. Tell them you love them—you can never do this too often. You can emphasize that your ex-spouse is a good person who loves them, too, and explain the parenting arrangement that has been worked out. If your kids are of appropriate maturity, ask them for input and help in making the schedule work.

ALERT!

Never give papers from the divorce to your children to read, or leave them out where the children can find them. Children have enough to deal with. Don't enmesh them in the adult details of a divorce.

Mending Fences with Your Ex

Let's assume you and your ex-spouse have no children and that, after dividing your assets, neither of you has an obligation to make monthly payments to the other, either as spousal maintenance or as part of your property settlement. If that describes your situation, you're in a good position to move on. You may be leaving the relationship on a friendly footing, or you still may be harboring bad feelings from the breakup and divorce experience. If you do want to clear the air, you can always go to a counselor who does exit counseling. Perhaps you can have a last supper together, reminisce about the good times, commiserate about the bad, and part on a friendly basis. Or not. Only you can decide whether it's important to mend fences.

On the other hand, if you have children, you'll have to deal with your ex until death—yours, hers or his, or the kids'. Under these circumstances, at least you'll want to have a civil relationship with your children's other parent. Of course, counseling is always an option, but in your day-to-day interactions with your ex, you can do a number of things, and avoid doing others, to improve dealings between you. For example, if your ex has primary physical custody of the children, here are some do's and don'ts.

1. Do pay any support on time and in full.
2. Don't send support checks with the children.
3. Do spend time with your children on a regular, consistent basis.
4. Do pick up and return the children on time. If you're going to be late, notify the other parent.
5. Do tell the other parent where you and the children will be if you're taking them on a trip. Write down an address and telephone number and dates of the trip.
6. Don't say negative things to your ex-spouse when exchanging the children. Be respectful and pleasant.
7. Don't show up at your ex's home unannounced. Respect boundaries.
8. Don't say things to the children such as, "I can't take you to the movies, because your mother has all my money."
9. Do work with your ex-spouse to pay for extras for your children like camp and music lessons. After all, these things benefit your children.
10. Do try to find housing near the children's primary residence, to make commuting easier, and to make it easier to be on time for picking up and returning the children.

Recent literature suggests an apology often goes a long way toward healing past hurts. So, even if you believe it was all your ex's fault, you might consider saying, "I'm sorry."

If you have primary physical custody of the children, here are some do's and don'ts:

1. Don't have the children ask your ex-spouse for the child support.
2. Don't schedule activities for the children that interfere with their time with the other parent.
3. Do encourage the children to contact the other parent on a regular basis.
4. Do make sure the children are ready to leave when it's their time to go with the other parent.
5. Don't threaten to prevent the children from seeing the other parent in

an attempt to get your ex-spouse to do something like pay for hockey or ballet lessons.

6. Do give the other parent complete information about the children's schools, doctors, dentist, orthodontist, and church.
7. Do share activity schedules so the other parent can attend games, practices, and recitals.
8. Do list the other parent on all school and medical records and church registrations.
9. Don't try to change your children's names.
10. Don't raise adult issues when exchanging the children. Be respectful and pleasant.
11. Don't try to move the children's home a long way away from the other parent. Long-distance parenting is hard on everyone.

These do's and don'ts address many of the issues that most often upset and make parents angry with each other. Be aware of the sensitive spots, and do your best not to pour salt into old wounds. Try to remember your ex-spouse is your children's other parent, a person you once loved and wanted to be your children's mom or dad. Try to remember conflict is the number one cause of problems for children of divorce. You're using negative energy when you stay angry and upset.

ALERT!

A major factor in getting on with your life is getting along with your children's other parent. The parent who continues to relive old hurts and angers harms him- or herself and the children. Ongoing anger drains your energy for no useful purpose.

Building a New Nest

You're now ready to begin a new life, and the question becomes, do you want a new place to live? The answer is probably yes, if you moved out of the house when you and your spouse separated. At that point you may not have thought very hard about housing. You may have hoped for reconciliation or award of the family home, so your current housing wasn't a big issue. But even if you're now living in the house you lived in during your marriage, you may be ready for a change for a variety of reasons. Now's the time to decide.

While you should look upon your new life as a great adventure and an opportunity to meet your goals and make your dreams come true, don't go overboard. Especially if you have children, there will always be something tying you to your former life. If you try to cut those ties, you'll likely regret it in the future.

The Marital Home

If you were awarded the family home in the divorce, you were given a mixed blessing. Often the family home is an affordable choice. The mortgage payment may be more manageable than comparable rental housing, and the children don't have to adjust to a new place and, possibly, a new school. On the downside, this home is where the marriage fell apart and may hold some unhappy memories. The home may need repairs and maintenance beyond your budget. You may be wise to sell the house and use the proceeds to start over in a place that is truly yours.

Bear in mind that you might not be able to replace the marital home with one of equal quality if you can't qualify for a big enough mortgage.

Distance Matters

If you decide to look for new housing, think about where the other parent is living and about the impact of distance on your shared parenting. Parenting is a full-time job, so if you can share this responsibility, both of your lives will be less stressful. Every parent needs time for him- or herself. Often the only time you get for yourself is when the children are with the other parent. If you live far from each other, the other parent may not be able to spend time with the children on a regular and frequent basis. When the commute time is under half an hour, each parent can more easily meet his or her share of the parenting responsibility.

Sharing Housing

When divorced parents have little money, they sometimes have to live with their parents or share housing with a friend. It's not uncommon for the parent with the children to move home with the folks some distance from where the family lived before the breakup. Now the visiting parent has both a long commute and a frosty reception from former in-laws when coming to see the kids. Not a very inviting prospect. No good solution may present itself here, except to encourage telephone and e-mail contact in those long periods between visits. Even if you don't have primary responsibility for the children, you may be financially strapped after paying support and monthly debt obligations. You may not have enough money to rent a place of your own, so you, too, may have to move back home or share an apartment.

Whether you're the custodial parent or the visiting parent, it's important to find housing that enables the children to stay with you overnight. They need to have their own beds and some privacy. It's not a good idea to share sleeping quarters with them. Sleep on the couch or put a sleeping bag on the floor, if you have to. And make sure your roommates know about and accept having children stay with you on a regular basis.

Living with a New Love

If your roommate is your new romantic relationship, you need to tread very carefully. Your children are adjusting to the divorce, and they may not be ready to accept a new person in your life. You may need to ask your honey to be absent when the children are with you, at least for a while. It takes a special person to put children's needs first.

Get Back to the Future

You've found a place to live and have furnished it so it feels like yours. You've established a routine that includes work and the children. Now, what are you doing for yourself? On those evenings when the children aren't with you, do you go home, flip open a beer, turn on the TV, and vegetate until bedtime? Do you call your ex-spouse and leave nasty messages on his or her answering machine? Do you call the children and tell them you're lonely?

It's normal to feel sad after a divorce. It's normal to be angry. It's even normal to feel sorry for yourself. For a while. As we talked about in an earlier chapter, divorce is a lot like experiencing the death of a loved one. Only here, the loved one didn't die, and now you don't even like that person very much. It's easy to keep the wound open by dwelling on the past.

ALERT!

Following the pain of divorce, many people are eager for acceptance. Therefore, it is easy to "fall in love" with the first person who shows interest in you. Though your feelings may seem true, remember that you're on the rebound and emotionally fragile.

Take Inventory

With time, you may even revise history to make yourself the undeserving victim. For instance, as you nurse your second or third beer, you feel more and more angry or sad, so you call your ex-spouse hoping to aggravate him or her, or maybe cry on his or her shoulder. Your ex, however, is out for the evening, and Grandma is watching the kids. How sad that you spent so much energy focusing on your ex-spouse when you were so far from that person's thoughts.

If you find yourself stuck in the past, it's time to take inventory. Who are you, and where are you going? What choices are open to you, and what are the consequences of these choices? If you can't do this yourself, consider working with a counselor or therapist to develop a plan for breaking free of the past and really starting that new life.

Testing the Waters

You're finally ready to think about life beyond the couch. The first step is to realize living alone is okay. For some of you, this may be a totally new experience because you went from living at home with your parents, to living in a dorm or an apartment with a roommate, to living with your spouse. At first, life on your own may feel really strange; however you can learn to luxuriate in time that is yours alone. Once you're adjusted to your single status, you're ready to look for new adventures.

What if you've never taken time to develop hobbies or interests outside work and family? A whole new world is out there, waiting to be discovered. Most communities offer adult education classes in subjects ranging from drawing to French to woodworking. Many local school districts publish their offerings quarterly. Health clubs offer classes, too. Their offerings range from exercise programs like Jazzercise to competitive athletics such as tennis. Many religious organizations sponsor programs just for singles ranging from social activities to speakers on investing your money to nurturing your children.

Taking such classes is a way to develop new interests and to meet new people. The choices are many, and the cost is usually modest. You just need to take advantage of the opportunities out there.

FACT

Getting off the couch and getting involved in activities is good for your mind and your body. Active people generally have better health and a more positive outlook on life. When you feel good, you communicate positive things to others. Your children will notice, and so will people who could be potential new relationships.

Involve Your Kids in New Interests

In addition to developing interests for yourself, you can look into new activities involving your children. Kids are a great excuse to do things you might be embarrassed to do on your own, like going to the zoo or a Disney movie. You and your children might learn a new skill together, like golf or playing the piano. Competing with a parent is often an incentive for children, and, to your surprise, you may find yourself having fun, too. Participating in activities with the children helps avoid the Sugar Daddy—or Mommy—syndrome where visiting parents just take their kids out and spend money on them or give them stuff. Giving of yourself is much more meaningful than loading up your kids with material things.

A New Relationship?

If you began a new relationship before ending the marriage, your spouse probably didn't react well to being replaced. Your spouse's anger and hurt may have increased the hostility level of your divorce. The relationship that triggered your leaving the marriage may or may not survive the divorce.

Introduce your new love slowly, and be patient. Testing the waters with some casual activities including your new love can be helpful in gauging the children's level of acceptance.

Take It Slowly

In any case, it might be wise to give yourself some time alone before reentering that relationship or beginning another. A new relationship has its best chance for success if you're feeling okay with yourself. If you get involved with someone new to show your ex-spouse you're still desirable or to fill those empty evenings, you may discover you haven't traded up. Amazingly, people tend to select new spouses who are much like the original model. You may want to take some time to figure out just what you want in a new companion and what characteristics of Spouse Number One led to the marriage's end.

Again, Consider the Children

For those of you with children, you need to be candid and up front with your new love about the importance of your children. If that person doesn't have children, chances are he or she will want some. Do you have the energy and financial ability to support a second family? Under the law, obligations to your first family take precedence over any new obligations you take on.

If your new love does have children, how they will fit into the equation? You'll need to introduce your children to a new person in your life and a whole new set of siblings. If your children see your love as having caused the divorce, they may be pretty hostile. Even if you stay single for a while, they may resent the new love taking your time and attention away from them, so be sure to focus your energy on making the children feel safe and loved.

Second Marriages

If you remarry, continue to be sensitive to your children's reaction. Sometimes they're really happy to have this new person as part of the family. Sometimes they're not. It may be wise to establish guidelines with your new spouse regarding the children. Discipline can be an especially sticky issue. If the kids know you're the only one who will enforce rules, they can make your new spouse's life a living hell.

ALERT!

Do not require your children to call a new spouse Mom or Dad. They already have a mom and a dad. Little kids will be confused. Big kids will be resentful. Your ex-spouse will be mighty angry.

A second marriage is harder than a first, and national statistics show an even higher percentage of second marriages fail. Second marriages have new stresses brought about by circumstances resulting from the dissolution of the first marriage. Your new spouse may push you into fighting for a different parenting arrangement. A lot of new wives pressure their husbands to go after joint custody. Or your new spouse may resent supporting your children, and pressure you to take your ex-spouse back to court for more child support. Whatever the pressures, you need to stay in charge in your second marriage, just like you needed to stay in charge in your divorce.

If you wait until you're ready, if you establish open lines of communication with those important to you—your new spouse, your kids, your ex—and if you stay in charge, you stand the best chance of success. Ⓔ

Appendices

Appendix A
Glossary

Appendix B
Worksheets

Appendix C
Resources

Appendix A
Glossary

action: The legal name for a lawsuit.

administrative process: A court hearing using a commissioner or hearing officer; often used in setting and collecting child support.

affidavit: A written factual statement sworn to under oath; a required companion to a motion.

agreement: A written document setting out areas of agreement, signed by the parties and their lawyers.

alimony: Money paid to a former spouse for his or her support; same as maintenance or spousal maintenance.

allegation: A statement by one of the parties as to what he or she believes—and intends to prove—is true.

ante-nuptial agreement: An agreement made by a couple before they marry about how their assets will be divided if their marriage ends by divorce or death.

appeal: A challenge to a court decision by taking the case to another, higher court.

appeals court: See *appellate court*.

appearance: Accepting the court's jurisdiction, either by actually appearing at a hearing or by submitting pleadings with the court.

appellant: The person who initiates an appeal.

appellate court: Also called appeals court. Most states have two levels of appellate courts. The first hears appeals from trial courts; the second hears appeals from the first appellate courts.

arbitration: A form of dispute resolution in which parties submit issues to a third party who decides how they should be resolved; can be binding or nonbinding.

bifurcation: Hearing a case in two parts. In divorces that usually means a hearing on the divorce itself, then another hearing on all the other issues.

brief: A written argument of facts and law, with references to other relevant decisions, submitted by a lawyer at trial or on appeal.

chambers: A judge's office.

change of venue: Moving a case from one location to another. This usually is done to hear a case where children live or where most of the property is located. One of the parties must live in the place of venue, at least when the case begins.

child support: Money paid for the support of children.

collaborative law: A form of alternate dispute resolution in which the lawyers agree that they will put their energies into settling the case. If they are unsuccessful, they will withdraw and other lawyers will take the case to trial.

community property: The name given to the property acquired during a marriage in so-called community property states, which refers to the property as belonging to the married couple.

complaint: See *petition*.

contempt: Disobeying a court order.

counterclaim: A response to claims made in the complaint, or petition, or the claims made in a motion.

court reporter: A person trained to use a stenograph, who takes down what is said at a trial, a motion, or a deposition. The court reporter will provide a transcript of the matter upon request. The person who requests the transcript pays for it.

cross-examination: Questions put to a witness by the other side's attorney.

custody: The care and upbringing of the children of divorce.

custody evaluation: A study done by trained professionals—social workers, psychologists, or child development experts—to make recommendations to the court about a custody arrangement that is in the children's best interests.

decision: The judge's conclusions in a case; includes the judge's reasoning and how the judge saw the facts.

default: A hearing at which only one side appears, either because an agreement has been reached before the hearing or because one side does not show up despite having notice of the hearing.

defendant: One who defends against a lawsuit brought against him or her by the plaintiff. (See *respondent*.)

deposition: The testimony of a potential witness to a trial taken out of court and under oath. The deposition is ordinarily transcribed into a written document for later use.

direct examination: Testimony produced when a lawyer questions the witnesses on his or her side.

discovery: Gathering information needed for settling or trying the divorce case.

discretion of the court: The latitude given a trial court by statute to decide issues.

dissolution: The current word for divorce.

domestic violence: When one member of a household causes harm, makes threats of harm, or acts in a way to create fear of harm against another household member.

emancipation: When parents are no longer legally responsible for the children. Parents are legally responsible for their children until the kids reach a certain age (eighteen or twenty-one in most states), marry, join the military, or choose to live independently.

equitable: Reasonable under the circumstances. Usually refers to property division.

evidence: The information provided to the court at trial, or the information used by the parties and their lawyers to reach agreement.

ex parte: When one side goes to a judge for relief, usually in an emergency. Most states require the party seeking relief to notify the other, who may choose whether to appear in response.

expert: A person with specialized knowledge about issues within the divorce.

forensic: Done for purposes of providing testimony in court. For instance, a forensic psychologist is one who does studies, then testifies to explain them to the court.

foundation: The factual background that tells the court the witness has the necessary knowledge and information to testify about something.

garnishment: Collection of money—child support and alimony—from a paycheck by a governmental agency that then forwards payments according to existing court orders.

gladiator: A litigator lawyer who takes everything to court and fights to the death.

grounds: The legal basis for claiming that the marriage is over. This may be marital misconduct, incompatibility, or irretrievable breakdown. Some states require the parties to have lived apart for a specific period of time, ranging from ninety days to two years.

guardian ad litem: Also called law guardian. A lawyer appointed by the court—and usually paid for by the parties—to provide information about what custodial arrangement would be in the children's best interests.

hearing: An appearance before the court at which evidence is produced and arguments are made.

hold harmless: One of the parties agrees to be responsible for a debt and protects the other from any expenses or losses related to the debt collection.

homestead: The real estate that was the parties' residence during the marriage.

impeachment: Using a statement made at another

time—like a deposition—that is different from current testimony to show a witness is lying.

indemnification: To promise to reimburse another person if he or she suffers harm or loss; same as to hold harmless.

independent neutral expert: An expert selected by both sides to provide information the parties can then use to resolve issues.

interim order: Same as *temporary order.*

interlocutory decree: A judgment of the court that is not final until a specified time has elapsed. During this period the parties are not free to marry again.

interrogatories: Written questions submitted by one side to the other to be answered under oath within thirty days.

joint custody: When divorcing parents share responsibility for child rearing.

joint legal custody: When the parties make major decisions about their children's education, medical care, and religious upbringing together.

joint petition: When people getting divorced are in agreement from the outset, they may prepare a joint petition for dissolution that sets out the facts and a stipulation that sets out their agreements. Both parties sign this document. They do not need a summons, and papers do not need to be served.

joint physical custody: When parents share physical care of their children. While the time division need not be fifty-fifty, it is usually close to that.

judgment: A court order, based on the parties' agreement or following a trial on the issues.

judgment and decree: The document that says the parties are divorced and contains the court's decisions on issues before it.

jurisdiction: The authority of the court over persons and things, usually based on where the people live and where the property is located.

law guardian: See *guardian ad litem.*

legal custody: Parental decision-making about the child's education, medical care, and religious upbringing.

legal separation: Also called separate maintenance. Some people don't want a divorce (often for religious reasons) but need a court order setting rules for their behavior. They may seek a decree of legal separation that addresses custody and support but usually cannot divide real estate. The decree does not dissolve a marriage.

litigation: Bringing issues to court and presenting them in the form required by the rules.

litigator: An attorney who specializes in trial work.

maintenance: See *alimony.*

marital property: The property acquired by the parties during the marriage not by gift or inheritance. This property is subject to division in a divorce.

marital termination agreement: A written document lawyers prepare that sets out the settlement reached by the parties. The parties and their attorneys sign it and submit it to the court for approval.

mediation: A form of dispute resolution in which the parties meet with a third person, a mediator, to resolve their differences. Most mediators want the parties to be represented by lawyers who can advise them of the implications of their agreements because the mediator cannot give legal advice.

modification: To change to an existing court order, usually because of a change in circumstances.

motion: The legal document used to bring issues to the court.

negotiations: The communications among the parties and their lawyers as they work to resolve the issues.

no-fault divorce: The rule in most states today. It is only necessary to prove an irretrievable breakdown of the marriage has occurred, not that one of the parties is "at fault."

noncustodial parent: The parent with whom the children do not live.

nonmarital property: Property acquired before the marriage or by inheritance or gift. The court can only award nonmarital property to the other party if it is necessary to avoid "substantial hardship."

notice to remove: The one free shot at getting rid of a judge assigned to hear your case.

order: A written court decision directing behavior. An order can be based on an agreement of the parties or a court decision after a contested hearing.

order for protection: An order issued in a domestic violence matter that directs one party to stay away from the other and not to harm that person. Violating an order for protection is a basis for arrest and criminal charges.

order to show cause: An order directing a person to come to court and show cause why he or she should not be found in contempt for disobeying a previous court order. A judge signs this order. Failure to come to court as ordered can result in issuance of a warrant for the person's arrest. If the judge finds a person in contempt, the judge may send the person to jail.

parenting consultant: A person designated by the court to make parenting decisions when the parties are unable to do so. These decisions have the effect of a court order.

parenting plan: The actual practical arrangement worked out by the parties that says when each will provide care and take responsibility for the children.

paternity: Fatherhood. In court, this means verifying a man is the father of a child. Today sophisticated testing makes this determination close to 100 percent accurate.

perjury: Lying under oath.

petition: Also called complaint. This document, together with a summons, begins a divorce. It sets out the facts required by state statutes and asks the court to grant certain things.

petitioner: The party who initiates the divorce; also called the plaintiff.

physical custody: The actual hands-on care of the children.

plaintiff: See *petitioner*.

post-decree: After a divorce has been granted by judgment and decree, the parties may bring issues back to court. To do this, they make post-decree motions.

precedent: A previous decision of the appellate court that tells the judge hearing your case how to decide that same issue if it arises.

pretrial: A hearing shortly before the trial to narrow issues, set a final timetable, and try to persuade the parties to settle.

privilege: Information shared between lawyer and client or doctor and patient that cannot be released without consent of the client or patient.

pro per or **pro se**: Acting as your own lawyer.

record: The written version of a deposition, a hearing, or a trial, together with all the exhibits that were made a part of them.

referee: A judicial officer hired by the court to help handle the caseload; also called a magistrate, commissioner, or hearing officer.

removal: When a custodial parent wants to move a significant distance away from the noncustodial parent and asks for court permission to do so; also called relocation.

removal for cause: Shows actual prejudice on the part of the judge. If you've used your free shot to remove a judge (notice to remove), and you get another judge you don't want, you must show cause for removing this new one.

request for admissions: A document sent by one side to the other with a list of statements and a provision that if there is no response within thirty days, these statements will be deemed admitted as true. (Example: The other side submits to you the statement, "I have a secret bank account in Switzerland.")

request for production of documents: A document sent by one side to the other asking for documents believed to be in its possession or that it has the ability to obtain. These also are to be produced in thirty days.

respondent: The person who responds to divorce papers served by the petitioner. If the initiator is called the plaintiff, then the responder is called the defendant.

retainer: Money paid to a lawyer to obtain the lawyer's services.

retainer agreement: The written contract between lawyer and client governing fees and, perhaps, behavior. (For instance, the lawyer writes, "I will return telephone calls within twenty-four hours.")

rules of civil procedure: The legal rules governing how lawsuits are run (the lawsuit cookbook).

rules of evidence: The legal rules governing what information can come before a court.

separate maintenance: See *legal separation*.

settlement: An agreement reached by negotiation.

settlement conference: A meeting of parties and lawyers to discuss settlement. This conference can be convened voluntarily, or a court can order one.

sole custody: One parent is responsible for the children.

sole legal custody: One parent makes all the decisions about education, medical care, and religious upbringing

sole physical custody: One parent provides most of the actual child care.

special magistrate or **special master:** A person hired by the parties and their lawyers to act as judge in their case. In counties that have long waits to get before a judge, parties may prefer to hire their own judge. They then give this person the same authority as a judge to decide their contested issues. Appeal of a special magistrate's decision goes to the first-level appellate court.

spousal maintenance: See *alimony*.

stock options: The right to purchase shares of stock in the company at a specific price after a specific holding period. Often part of an executive's bonus package. If one chooses to buy the stock, it is called exercising the stock option.

subpoena: A legal document requiring a person to appear before a court to testify

subpoena duces tecum: A legal document requiring a person to appear before a court to testify and to bring certain documents listed.

summons: The initiating document of a divorce that requires a response in thirty days and usually contains restraining orders governing behavior and assets.

temporary order: Also called an interim order. An order issued during a divorce to set rules until a divorce is final. A temporary order is usually not subject to appeal.

testimony: Oral evidence given under oath at a deposition or a trial.

transcript: The written record of a deposition, motion, or trial provided by a court reporter who recorded all the testimony.

trial: A contested hearing before a judge.

vacate: To undo something.

visitation: The time spent by a noncustodial parent with children.

vocational assessment: An evaluation to determine a person's employability and job interests.

with prejudice: If a motion is denied with prejudice, this means you will have to prove the decision was wrong if you want to overturn it.

without prejudice: If a motion is denied without prejudice, this means you can bring the motion again at another time without having to show the first decision was wrong.

Appendix B
Worksheets

Monthly Expenses Sheet	
EXPENSE	PETITIONER/RESPONDENT
Residence	$
Rent or mortgage payment	$
Contract for deed payment	$
Real estate taxes	$
Insurance	$
Utilities	$
Heating fuel	$
Water, sewer	$
Electricity	$
Gas	$
Telephone	$
Waste disposal	$
Home maintenance	$
Housecleaning	$
Household repairs	$
Yard and landscaping	$
Snow removal	$
Laundry and dry cleaning	$
Food and other grocery store household items	$
Automobile	$
Gas and oil	$
Repairs and maintenance	$
Licenses	$
Insurance	$

Monthly Expenses Sheet

EXPENSE	PETITIONER/RESPONDENT
Installment payments	$
Clothing	$
Grooming, cosmetics	$
Medical	$
Insurance	$
Unreimbursed doctor and hospital	$
Unreimbursed drugs	$
Unreimbursed dental and orthodontics	$
Counseling or therapy	$
Life insurance	$
Personal property insurance	$
Miscellaneous personal	$
Newspapers, magazines, books	$
Club or association dues	$
Vacations	$
Gifts	$
Education	$
Tuition	$
Room and board	$
Transportation	$

Monthly Expenses Sheet

EXPENSE	PETITIONER/RESPONDENT
Books and supplies	$
Activities	$
Charitable contributions	$
Debt payments (list each separately with monthly payment)	$
Child care	$
Animal care	$
IRA contributions	$
Savings	$
Other (list each item)	$
Children's Expenses	$
Clothing	$
Grooming	$
Formula/diapers	$
Tuition	$
School lunches	$
Athletics/other activities	$
Allowances	$
Medical	$
Dental or orthodontics	$
Total expenses	$

Asset Summary Sheet			
ASSET	WIFE'S VALUES	HUSBAND'S VALUES	VALUES STIPULATED FOR SETTLEMENT ONLY
Personal property	$	$	$
Furniture	$	$	$
Furnishings (pots, towels, etc.)	$	$	$
China, silver, crystal	$	$	$
Jewelry and furs	$	$	$
Homestead (purchase date)	$	$	$
Market value	$	$	$
Mortgage	$	$	$
Second mortgage	$	$	$
Net equity	$	$	$
Other real estate (purchase date)	$	$	$
Market value	$	$	$
Mortgage	$	$	$
Net equity	$	$	$
Boats and vehicles	$	$	$
Automobile	$	$	$
Market value	$	$	$
Encumbrance	$	$	$
Net value	$	$	$
Second automobile	$	$	$
Market value	$	$	$

Asset Summary Sheet

Asset	Wife's values	Husband's values	Values stipulated for settlement only
Encumbrance	$	$	$
Net value	$	$	$
Other vehicles	$	$	$
Market value	$	$	$
Encumbrance	$	$	$
Net value	$	$	$
Securities	$	$	$
Stock (purchase date)	$	$	$
Bank accounts	$	$	$
Savings (account number)	$	$	$
Checking (account number)	$	$	$
Life insurance	$	$	$
Company/policy number	$	$	$
Face amount	$	$	$
Cash surrender value	$	$	$
Loan	$	$	$
Retirement accounts	$	$	$
Deferred comp./account number	$	$	$
Plan name	$	$	$
Owned by	$	$	$
Profit sharing	$	$	$
Pensions	$	$	$

Asset Summary Sheet

ASSET	WIFE'S VALUES	HUSBAND'S VALUES	VALUES STIPULATED FOR SETTLEMENT ONLY
Keoghs	$	$	$
IRAs	$	$	$
Business interests	$	$	$
Name	$	$	$
Type	$	$	$
Ownership interest	$	$	$
Debts	$	$	$
Credit card name	$	$	$
Loans	$	$	$
Total	$	$	$

Proposed Division of Assets

Asset	Wife	Husband
Homestead	$	$
Other real estate (list separately)	$	$
Furniture	$	$
China, silver, etc.	$	$
Jewelry and furs	$	$
Automobiles	$	$
Boats	$	$
Other vehicles	$	$
Stock	$	$
Deferred comp.	$	$
Life insurance cash value	$	$
Other retirement assets	$	$
Debt	$	$
Business	$	$
Grand total	$	$

Appendix C
Resources

Books for Children

Brown, Marc, and Laurene Krasny. *Dinosaurs Divorce*. Boston, New York, London: Little, Brown and Co., 1986.

Lansky, Vicki. *It's Not Your Fault, Koko Bear*. Minnetonka, Minnesota: Book Peddlers, 1998.

Thomas, Pat. *My Family's Changing*. Hauppauge, New York: Barrons' Educational Series, Inc., 1998.

Books about Children and Parenting

Condrell, Kenneth N., and Linda Lee Small. *Be a Great Divorce Dad*. New York: St. Martin's Griffin, 1998.

Erickson, Beth. *Longing for Dad, Father Loss and Its Impact*. Deerfield, Florida: Health Communications, Inc., 1998.

Lansky, Vicki. *Divorce Book for Parents*. Minnetonka, Minnesota: Book Peddlers, 2000.

Ricci, Isolina. *Mom's House, Dad's House*. New York: Simon & Schuster, 1997.

Thomas, Shirley. *Parents Are Forever*. Longmont, Colorado: Springboard Publications, 1995.

Wallerstein, Judith S., and Joan B. Kelly. *Surviving the Breakup*. Boston, New York: Houghton, Mifflin Co., 1979.

Books about Domestic Violence

Deaton, Wendy Susan, and Michael Hertica. *Growing Free, A Manual for Survivors of Domestic Violence*. Binghamton, New York: The Haworth Maltreatment and Trauma Press, 2001.

Evans, Patricia. *The Verbally Abusive Relationship: How to Recognize It and How to Respond*. Avon, Massachusetts: Adams Media Corporation, 1992 and 1996.

Nelson, Noelle. *Dangerous Relationships*. Cambridge, Massachusetts: Perseus Publishing, 1997.

Switzer, M'liss, and Katherine Hale. *Called to Account*. Seattle: Seal Press, 1987.

Books about Alternative Dispute Resolution

Doyle, Stephen Patrick, and Roger Silva Haydock. *Without the Punches: Resolving Disputes Without Litigation*. Minneapolis: Equilaw, Inc., 1991.

Tesler, Pauline H. *Collaborative Law, Achieving Effective Resolution in Divorce Without Litigation*. Chicago: American Bar Association, 2001.

Books with General Information on Divorce

Ahrons, Constance R. *The Good Divorce*. New York: HarperCollins, 1994.

Cohen, Harriet Newman, and Ralph Gardner Jr. *The Divorce Book for Men and Women*. New York: Avon Books, 1994.

Friedman, James T. *The Divorce Handbook*. New York: Random House, rev. 1998.

Gold, Lois. *Between Love and Hate, A Guide to Civilized Divorce*. New York: Plume, 1996.

Margulies, Sam. *Getting Divorced Without Ruining Your Life*. New York: Simon & Schuster, 1992.

Talia, M. Sue. *How to Avoid the Divorce from Hell*. Danville, California: Nexus Publishing Co., 1997.

Other Resources

American Academy of Matrimonial Lawyers

150 N. Michigan Ave., Suite 2040
Chicago, IL 60601
Phone: 312-263-6477; fax: 312-263-7682
Web site: *www.aaml.org*

The academy is a resource for finding the top divorce lawyers around the country. It also has several outstanding publications available for purchase, and articles of interest on its Web site.

American Bar Association, Family Law Section

Web site: *www.abanet.org/family/advocate*

Publishes *The Family Advocate*, a quarterly magazine that often has useful information for the divorce client. Copies can be ordered from ABA Publications Orders, P.O. Box 10892, Chicago, IL 60610, or call 800-285-2221.

Association for Conflict Resolution

1527 New Hampshire Ave. N.W., Third Floor
Washington, DC 20036
Phone: ✆ 202-667-9700; fax: 202-265-1968
Web site: ✎ *www.acresolution.org*

This organization was formed by the merger of
the Academy of Family Mediators, the Conflict
Resolution Education Network, and the Society
of Professionals in Dispute Resolution. The
association publishes the *Conflict Resolution
Quarterly* directed primarily to the professionals.
It also is a source of referrals if you're looking
for a mediator.

Association of Family and Conciliation Courts

6515 Grand Teton Plaza, Suite 210
Madison, WI 53719-1048
Phone: ✆ 608-664-3750; fax: 608-664-3751
Web site: ✎ *www.afccnet.org*

Association members are lawyers, judges, and
mental health professionals from all over the
world. The organization has excellent
pamphlets, books, and audio and videocassettes
available for purchase.

National Domestic Violence Hotline

Phone: ✆ 800-799-SAFE (7233)
Web site:
✎ *www.divorcesource.com/info/childsupport*

This site has all kinds of useful information on
all aspects of divorce.

Index

A

addiction treatment, 7
admissions, request for, 99
advocates, domestic abuse
    and, 121
affidavits, 108, 131–132
    sample, 162–164
agreements, *see*
    stipulations/agreements
alimony, *see* spousal
    maintenance
alternative dispute resolution,
    52, 77–90
    arbitration, 78, 87–89
    mediation, 78, 84–87
    negotiation, 78, 79–80
    negotiation with lawyers, 78,
        80–84
    special master, 90
American Academy of
    Matrimonial Lawyers, 46
anger
    controlling, 124
    discussion of divorce and,
        14
    effect on children, 242
    expressing appropriately, 18
appeal, of final order, 234–236
    possible outcomes, 236
    preparation for, 235
arbitration, 78, 87–89
    -mediation hybrid, 88–89
assets, 185–202
    bankruptcy and, 194, 202
    debt and, 194–195
    division of, 196–200
    inventory of, 189–190

marital versus premarital,
    186–189, 201
multiple marriages and,
    200–201
protection of, 200–201
retirement benefits, 198–200
summary of, 190–195
summary worksheet,
    275–277
see also valuation
attire, *see* clothing
attorney, *see* lawyer(s)

B, C

bankruptcy, 7, 194, 202
Bar Association, lawyer
    referrals from, 45
budgets, 182–183, 207. *See
    also* financial issues
case law, 42, 71–72
Case Management, 104. *See
    also* Divorce with Dignity
checks, canceled, 219
children
    best interest of, 232
    care of, 18–19, 30, 32
    counseling/therapy for, 19,
        157–158
    court system and, 68–70
    emotional abuse of parent
        and, 119
    emotions of, 28–29, 32–40
    experts and, 150–153
    how to refer to at trial, 226
    impact of divorce on, 9
    interviewed by judge,
        168–169

involving in new interests,
    260
keeping out of court, 138,
    221
marital stress and, 3
moving with, 169–170, 243,
    245
need for contact with
    fathers, 160
parent's legal right to
    information about,
    156–157
parent's new relationships
    and, 261–262
parental anger and, 242
preferences of, 168
talking to after divorce, 254
telling about divorce
    decision, 15–16, 28–30
tips about, 39
see also child support;
    custody; parenting
child support, 171–178, 183,
    238
    enforcement of, 177–178
    health care costs, 178
    imputed income, 175–176
    income, 173–174
    joint custody and, 176–177
    legal guidelines/approaches
        to, 172–173, 176
    modifications of, 181–182
    not dischargeable in
        bankruptcy, 202
    requesting changes in, 100
    Social Security, 174–175
clothing, appropriate for
    court, 137, 211, 221

THE EVERYTHING BUDGETING BOOK

By Tere Drenth

Filled with practical tips and advice you can use immediately, *The Everything® Budgeting Book* can be used time and time again as your life—and financial picture—changes. Whether you need to restructure debt, save for retirement, or are just looking for ways to trim costs on everyday expenses, this book will help you get in the black fast. Featuring seventy worksheets that you can copy and use over and over again, this user-friendly guide will help keep you financially healthy for years to come.

Trade paperback,
$14.95 ($22.95 CAN)
1-58062-786-2, 304 pages

OTHER *EVERYTHING*® BOOKS BY ADAMS MEDIA CORPORATION

BUSINESS

Everything® **Business Planning Book**
Everything® **Coaching & Mentoring Book**
Everything® **Home-Based Business Book**
Everything® **Leadership Book**
Everything® **Managing People Book**
Everything® **Network Marketing Book**
Everything® **Online Business Book**
Everything® **Project Management Book**
Everything® **Selling Book**
Everything® **Start Your Own Business Book**
Everything® **Time Management Book**

COMPUTERS

Everything® **Build Your Own Home Page Book**
Everything® **Computer Book**

Everything® **Internet Book**
Everything® **Microsoft® Word 2000 Book**

COOKING

Everything® **Bartender's Book, $9.95**
Everything® **Barbecue Cookbook**
Everything® **Chocolate Cookbook**
Everything® **Cookbook**
Everything® **Dessert Cookbook**
Everything® **Diabetes Cookbook**
Everything® **Low-Carb Cookbook**
Everything® **Low-Fat High-Flavor Cookbook**
Everything® **Mediterranean Cookbook**
Everything® **One-Pot Cookbook**
Everything® **Pasta Book**
Everything® **Quick Meals Cookbook**
Everything® **Slow Cooker Cookbook**

Everything® **Soup Cookbook**
Everything® **Thai Cookbook**
Everything® **Vegetarian Cookbook**
Everything® **Wine Book**

HEALTH

Everything® **Anti-Aging Book**
Everything® **Dieting Book**
Everything® **Herbal Remedies Book**
Everything® **Hypnosis Book**
Everything® **Menopause Book**
Everything® **Stress Management Book**
Everything® **Vitamins, Minerals, and Nutritional Supplements Book**
Everything® **Nutrition Book**

HISTORY

Everything® **American History Book**

All Everything® books are priced at $12.95 or $14.95, unless otherwise stated. Prices subject to change without notice.
Canadian prices range from $11.95–$22.95 and are subject to change without notice.

Everything® **Civil War Book**
Everything® **World War II Book**

HOBBIES

Everything® **Bridge Book**
Everything® **Candlemaking Book**
Everything® **Casino Gambling Book**
Everything® **Chess Basics Book**
Everything® **Collectibles Book**
Everything® **Crossword and Puzzle Book**
Everything® **Digital Photography Book**
Everything® **Drums Book (with CD),**
    $19.95, ($31.95 CAN)
Everything® **Family Tree Book**
Everything® **Games Book**
Everything® **Guitar Book**
Everything® **Knitting Book**
Everything® **Magic Book**
Everything® **Motorcycle Book**
Everything® **Online Genealogy Book**
Everything® **Playing Piano and**
    Keyboards Book
Everything® **Rock & Blues Guitar**
    Book (with CD), $19.95,
    ($31.95 CAN)
Everything® **Scrapbooking Book**

HOME IMPROVEMENT

Everything® **Feng Shui Book**
Everything® **Gardening Book**
Everything® **Home Decorating Book**
Everything® **Landscaping Book**
Everything® **Lawn Care Book**
Everything® **Organize Your Home Book**

KIDS' STORY BOOKS

Everything® **Bedtime Story Book**
Everything® **Bible Stories Book**
Everything® **Fairy Tales Book**
Everything® **Mother Goose Book**

NEW AGE

Everything® **Astrology Book**

Everything® **Divining the Future Book**
Everything® **Dreams Book**
Everything® **Ghost Book**
Everything® **Meditation Book**
Everything® **Numerology Book**
Everything® **Palmistry Book**
Everything® **Spells and Charms Book**
Everything® **Tarot Book**
Everything® **Wicca and Witchcraft Book**

PARENTING

Everything® **Baby Names Book**
Everything® **Baby Shower Book**
Everything® **Baby's First Food Book**
Everything® **Baby's First Year Book**
Everything® **Breastfeeding Book**
Everything® **Get Ready for Baby Book**
Everything® **Homeschooling Book**
Everything® **Potty Training Book,**
    $9.95, ($15.95 CAN)
Everything® **Pregnancy Book**
Everything® **Pregnancy Organizer,**
    $15.00, ($22.95 CAN)
Everything® **Toddler Book**
Everything® **Tween Book**

PERSONAL FINANCE

Everything® **Budgeting Book**
Everything® **Get Out of Debt Book**
Everything® **Get Rich Book**
Everything® **Investing Book**
Everything® **Homebuying Book, 2nd Ed.**
Everything® **Homeselling Book**
Everything® **Money Book**
Everything® **Mutual Funds Book**
Everything® **Online Investing Book**
Everything® **Personal Finance Book**

PETS

Everything® **Cat Book**
Everything® **Dog Book**
Everything® **Dog Training and Tricks**
Everything® **Horse Book**
Everything® **Puppy Book**
Everything® **Tropical Fish Book**

REFERENCE

Everything® **Astronomy Book**
Everything® **Car Care Book**
Everything® **Christmas Book, $15.00,**
    ($21.95 CAN)
Everything® **Classical Mythology Book**
Everything® **Divorce Book**
Everything® **Etiquette Book**
Everything® **Great Thinkers Book**
Everything® **Learning French Book**
Everything® **Learning German Book**
Everything® **Learning Italian Book**
Everything® **Learning Latin Book**
Everything® **Learning Spanish Book**
Everything® **Mafia Book**
Everything® **Philosophy Book**
Everything® **Shakespeare Book**
Everything® **Tall Tales, Legends, &**
    Other Outrageous Lies Book
Everything® **Toasts Book**
Everything® **Trivia Book**
Everything® **Weather Book**
Everything® **Wills & Estate Planning**
    Book

RELIGION

Everything® **Angels Book**
Everything® **Buddhism Book**
Everything® **Catholicism Book**
Everything® **Judaism Book**
Everything® **Saints Book**
Everything® **World's Religions Book**
Everything® **Understanding Islam Book**

SCHOOL & CAREERS

Everything® **After College Book**
Everything® **College Survival Book**
Everything® **Cover Letter Book**
Everything® **Get-a-Job Book**
Everything® **Hot Careers Book**
Everything® **Job Interview Book**
Everything® **Online Job Search Book**
Everything® **Resume Book, 2nd Ed.**
Everything® **Study Book**

All Everything® books are priced at $12.95 or $14.95, unless otherwise stated. Prices subject to change without notice.
Canadian prices range from $11.95–$22.95 and are subject to change without notice.

WE HAVE EVERYTHING . . . .

SPORTS/FITNESS

Everything® **Bicycle Book**
Everything® **Fishing Book**
Everything® **Fly-Fishing Book**
Everything® **Golf Book**
Everything® **Golf Instruction Book**
Everything® **Pilates Book**
Everything® **Running Book**
Everything® **Sailing Book, 2nd Ed.**
Everything® **T'ai Chi and QiGong Book**
Everything® **Total Fitness Book**
Everything® **Weight Training Book**
Everything® **Yoga Book**

TRAVEL

Everything® **Guide to Las Vegas**
Everything® **Guide to New England**
Everything® **Guide to New York City**
Everything® **Guide to Washington D.C.**

Everything® **Travel Guide to The Disneyland Resort®, California Adventure®, Universal Studios®, and the Anaheim Area**
Everything® **Travel Guide to the Walt Disney World® Resort, Universal Studios®, and Greater Orlando, 3rd Ed.**

WEDDINGS & ROMANCE

Everything® **Creative Wedding Ideas Book**
Everything® **Dating Book**
Everything® **Jewish Wedding Book**
Everything® **Romance Book**
Everything® **Wedding Book, 2nd Ed.**
Everything® **Wedding Organizer, $15.00 ($22.95 CAN)**

Everything® **Wedding Checklist, $7.95 ($11.95 CAN)**
Everything® **Wedding Etiquette Book, $7.95 ($11.95 CAN)**
Everything® **Wedding Shower Book, $7.95 ($12.95 CAN)**
Everything® **Wedding Vows Book, $7.95 ($11.95 CAN)**
Everything® **Weddings on a Budget Book, $9.95 ($15.95 CAN)**

WRITING

Everything® **Creative Writing Book**
Everything® **Get Published Book**
Everything® **Grammar and Style Book**
Everything® **Grant Writing Book**
Everything® **Guide to Writing Children's Books**
Everything® **Writing Well Book**

ALSO AVAILABLE:
THE EVERYTHING® KIDS' SERIES!

Each book is 8" x 9¼", 144 pages, and two-color throughout.

Everything® **Kids' Baseball Book, 2nd Edition, $6.95** ($11.95 CAN)
Everything® **Kids' Bugs Book, $6.95** ($10.95 CAN)
Everything® **Kids' Cookbook, $6.95** ($10.95 CAN)
Everything® **Kids' Joke Book, $6.95** ($10.95 CAN)
Everything® **Kids' Math Puzzles Book, $6.95** ($10.95 CAN)
Everything® **Kids' Mazes Book, $6.95** ($10.95 CAN)
Everything® **Kids' Money Book, $6.95** ($11.95 CAN)

Everything® **Kids' Monsters Book, $6.95** ($10.95 CAN)
Everything® **Kids' Nature Book, $6.95** ($11.95 CAN)
Everything® **Kids' Puzzle Book $6.95,** ($10.95 CAN)
Everything® **Kids' Science Experiments Book, $6.95** ($10.95 CAN)
Everything® **Kids' Soccer Book, $6.95** ($11.95 CAN)
Everything® **Kids' Travel Activity Book, $6.95** ($10.95 CAN)

Available wherever books are sold!
To order, call 800-872-5627, or visit us at everything.com

Everything® is a registered trademark of Adams Media Corporation.